Chen Yi

WOMEN COMPOSERS

The short, readable books in the Women Composers series introduce significant women composers to students and general readers and provide a convenient reference for performers and scholars.

Series books treat the broadest range of women composers, combining concise biographical information with a comprehensive survey of works.

A list of books in the series appears at the end of this book.

Chen Yi

LETA E. MILLER
AND
J. MICHELE EDWARDS

Urbana, Chicago, and Springfield

Publication of this book was supported by grants from the Donna Cardamone Jackson Endowment of the American Musicological Society, funded in part by the National Endowment for the Humanities and the Andrew W. Mellon Foundation; the University of California, Santa Cruz, Committee on Research and Arts Research Institute; and the Henry and Edna Binkele Classical Music Fund.

© 2020 by the Board of Trustees
of the University of Illinois
All rights reserved
1 2 3 4 5 C P 5 4 3 2 1
∞ This book is printed on acid-free paper.

Library of Congress Control Number: 2020946722
ISBN 978-0-252-04354-3 (hardcover)
ISBN 978-0-252-08544-4 (paperback)
ISBN 978-0-252-05242-2 (e-book)

Contents

CHAPTER 1. Introduction 1
CHAPTER 2. Biography and Framework 6
CHAPTER 3. Compositional Processes 45
CHAPTER 4. Solo and Chamber Music Works 76
CHAPTER 5. Works for Large Instrumental Ensembles 102
CHAPTER 6. Choral and Solo Vocal Works 124
CHAPTER 7. Issues 159

Glossary 179
List of Works 183
Notes 207
References 223
Index 237

Chen Yi

CHAPTER 1

Introduction

THE WOMEN COMPOSERS SERIES by University of Illinois Press aims to be "international in scope," drawing on "the great range of regional, social, ethnic, and other communities" that have shaped the sonic expressions of women's creativity, and describing the music women have created, why they created it, and with what results.[1] The present study of the music of Chen Yi addresses all of these issues, highlighting the musical expression of a composer whose rich fusion of divergent cultures has marked her both as a renowned composer in general and as a woman composer in particular. Chen Yi was the first woman to earn a master's degree in composition at the Central Conservatory of Music in Beijing (CCOM). She also stands out as the most prominent woman among the group of high-achieving, headline-grabbing mainland Chinese composers who came to the United States in the late 1980s—a group that included Chen's husband Zhou Long as well as Tan Dun, Bright Sheng, Ge Gan-ru, and others. Furthermore, Chen was composer-in-residence for three years with the Women's Philharmonic in San Francisco, and she has advocated widely for women composers throughout the world. Her rise to prominence in the United States was linked closely to another woman pioneer, conductor JoAnn Falletta. Yet despite all of these "female" credentials, Chen, like many other women, expects her works to be judged on their merits rather than on her gender; she claims that her sensitivity to gender discrimination was relatively recent, only awakened after she arrived in the United States (1986) and began working with the

Women's Philharmonic (1993). So the inclusion of this book in UIP's Women Composers series carries with it a certain amount of dialectical tension, an issue we discuss—among others—in Chapter 7.

Grappling with Chen's impressive musical output has also compelled us to confront a number of other pressing issues that transcend the evaluation of a single compositional voice and to interpret her musical works through diverse lenses, including not only gender but also ethnicity, transnationalism, border crossing, diaspora, exoticism, and cultural fusion. This last area has formed a consistent idée fixe in published reviews of her music and in the numerous dissertations that she or her compositions have inspired. We purposefully avoid employing the overused, and now rather outdated, term *multiculturalism*, and we even question the value of *hybrid*, which, as Tim Taylor reminds us, is becoming "another kind of authenticity."[2] Yet Chen's music consistently fuses her Chinese cultural background with her Western training. Her early musical education in China was almost completely Eurocentric through intensive study of piano and violin and listening to her father's large collection of classical music recordings. Her awareness of Chinese musical styles developed later (and gradually), after her displacement to a re-education program in the countryside during the Cultural Revolution. This awakening of interest in her homeland culture continued through her eight years as the leader of the orchestra in a Beijing opera company and subsequent studies at CCOM. At Columbia University in the late 1980s, composer Chou Wen-chung, who consistently maintained that the "true *role* of the Chinese composer" is "to contribute to the *confluence* of musical cultures,"[3] and who was instrumental in bringing Chen and other new wave composers to the United States, urged her to link this cultural heritage to avant-garde compositional techniques.

In the years since her doctoral work at Columbia, Chen has devoted herself to merging elements from both cultures, using markers of Chinese music such as pentatonic scales and sliding tones embedded in a thoroughly contemporary musical language. To Western listeners, these traits may evoke the exotic; to Chen, they reference her homeland. As Jonathan Bellman cautions, in reference to the "exotic" in Western music: "For all the unmistakable musical codes . . . much depends on who is doing the composing and who the listening."[4]

When we asked Chen Yi whether she considers herself a Chinese or an American composer, she responded, as she has to many other interviewers, that Chinese is her native language—both linguistically and musically. At the same time, she notes that her move to the United States in 1986 intensified her appreciation of her heritage. Only through rigorous study of Western music, she says, did she truly come to appreciate the richness of Chinese music. Learning an adopted culture made her treasure more deeply her inherited one.

Chen's studies at CCOM and Columbia also led her to recognize both the musical diversity and the artistic commonalities among various peoples. She has often expressed a desire to unite those who speak different languages through the medium of musical sound. To this end, Chen references very specific traits drawn both from Western music history and from the distinct musical styles of China's numerous ethnicities and subcultures, which she sometimes combines within a single composition. Thus Chen at once heralds the potential of music to cross cultural boundaries while identifying strongly with specific musical markers that link directly to her national heritage. Throughout this book, we highlight this positive tension in her philosophy by demonstrating her creative interweaving of elements drawn from diverse sources.

Chen is part of the third wave of Chinese immigrants to the United States, a group of young intellectuals who came to the West after the death of Mao in 1976, taking advantage of the new open political climate in China and the complementary embrace of cultural exchange. These émigrés were able to connect almost immediately with a supportive diasporic community who were part of the earlier second wave—involuntary immigrants who found themselves stranded in the United States after the Communist takeover in 1949.[5] On the practical side, the Chinese community in New York proved vital for Chen in securing performances and commissions. On the conceptual side, the question of whether she identified as a US composer or a Chinese composer became more complicated by her strong allegiance to the expatriate Chinese community—first in New York and later in San Francisco. Chen constantly crosses borders—both geographical and musical—but never seeks to eradicate them.

Although these themes intermingle throughout our discussion of Chen's life and works, a full appreciation of them emerges through familiarity with the consistent elements in Chen Yi's musical language. Therefore, after a detailed examination of her compositional processes and an exploration of representative works, we return to consider these pressing issues more deeply in Chapter 7. We treat the analytical parts of this book in two ways: first by dissecting her musical style to highlight specific compositional strategies that make her music distinctive (Chapter 3) and then by illustrating and illuminating these strategies through an examination of a variety of pieces in the areas of chamber music, large ensemble works, and choral/vocal compositions (Chapters 4–6).

We deal with individual works in terms of genre rather than chronology for two reasons. First and most important, we have not identified distinct stylistic periods in Chen's work, despite some notable changes that have taken place in her approach to compositional practice during her highly productive career. Twelve-tone rows, for instance, appear quite frequently in Chen's earlier works, but assume diminishing importance beginning in the 1990s. In later works, she also seems to have dispensed with some recurrent melodic figurations that she may have felt were too pervasive. Nevertheless, our analysis of numerous works suggests that stylistic consistencies are far more prevalent than changes. We have come to view Chen Yi's compositional journey not as a series of compartmentalized periods exploring differing approaches to creation, but rather as an evolving process of growth, refinement, and sophistication. As we characterize and define this growth, we have found that Chen Yi exhibits a unique voice that links her earliest works with the most recent ones. We detail these consistencies in Chapter 3 (Compositional Processes) and then show their manifestation in specific works in the following chapters.

The second reason for our approach by instrumentation is to provide a user-friendly resource to the reader who wishes to program Chen's music. In a book of this length, we have had to be highly selective. Chen Yi has written more than 150 works ranging from solos for Western or Chinese instruments, to chamber works, to choral pieces, to nearly three dozen compositions scored for chamber or full orchestra. The only major genre in which she has not composed is opera. Over the years, she has declined several opera commissions, fearing that such a sweeping project would derail her attention from her other creative work and her teaching. From this massive body of material, we have selected pieces in a variety of genres, focusing on those we find most compelling and most illustrative of Chen's musical language at different times in her life. Our selections reflect our own tastes; we unabashedly admit to choosing the pieces that most powerfully moved us. A complete works list at the end of the book provides information on all of Chen's compositions up to the time of our writing, and we urge readers to explore compositions listed there that we have not had the space to analyze.

Our text is based not only on our own research and analysis, but also on extensive interviews we conducted with Chen Yi at her home in 2015 and 2016. Quotes attributed to her without notes come from these interviews, as does much of the biographical and analytical information. Chen Yi has kindly read our text and corrected any errors, but she has never attempted to control the content of the book. She spoke to us with great candor, even in conversations about painful events such as the Cultural Revolution, and she has responded to our many questions with patience and understanding. We thank her for her eagerness to work with us and hope that this book may stimulate in others the joy we have found in listening to, and analyzing, her dynamic compositions. We also thank others who kindly spoke to us at length about Chen Yi's life and works: Zhou Long, Susan Cheng, Wu Man, and Honggang Li.

Throughout the text we use Pinyin spellings (with rare exceptions for names of people), and for Chinese personal names we either retain the Chinese practice of placing family name first or adopt Western placement of given name first according to individual preference or usage. At the end we include a glossary of terms that includes the Chinese characters. We are indebted to Yunxiang Gao, who meticulously translated many articles for us and aided in tracking down Chinese citations, and to Jessica Loranger, who typeset the musical examples. We are also grateful to members of the editorial, design, and production staff and especially to UIP director and music editor Laurie Matheson, who supported and encouraged us throughout the entire process from early formulation of our ideas to finished production, and to Yayoi Uno Everett and an anonymous reader, who offered numerous valuable suggestions.

CHAPTER 2

Biography and Framework

Beginnings

ON APRIL 4, 1953, DR. DU DIANQIN (1919–2012), an award-winning pediatrician at the No. 3 People's Hospital in Guangzhou, gave birth to her second daughter, the future composer Chen Yi. Although Du was born in Guangdong Province, her family moved to Hong Kong in 1922, when she was only three years old. Her sister went to Thailand to live with family friends and four younger children were born after the family's relocation. Du's family was Baptist; in fact, her brother and his son became Mùshī (preachers). In the mid-1930s Du returned to Guangzhou for secondary school, and in 1938 she began her study in the medical school program at Lingnan University, where she met her husband, Chen Ernan. She was the only female member of her graduating class.

Chen Ernan (1919–90) came from a large family with ten children. After the 1937 Japanese invasion, his family dispersed to Hong Kong, Australia, and elsewhere, but he and one younger sister remained on the mainland. Upon completing his medical training, Chen became an internist, serving the population in Guangdong. He had no idea that his decision not to emigrate with the rest of his family would subject him, his wife, and their children to a series of traumatic experiences in the years to come.

By the end of World War II, Chen Ernan had founded two medical facilities in Guangzhou serving thousands of patients: the Huaying Hospital and the

PHOTO 1. The Chen family in 1957. The three Chen children, left to right: Chen Yun, Chen Yi, and Chen Min, with their parents, mother Du Dianqin (pediatrician and pianist/accordionist) and father Chen Ernan (internist and amateur violinist). Photo courtesy of Chen Yi.

Shameen (later Shamian) Clinic, located on Shamian Island—a beautiful area within the city inhabited by many intellectuals and foreign service officers. In the 1950s the clinic merged with several other local institutions to form the No. 3 People's Hospital. Chen Ernan became part of the hospital's leadership team.

Both Chen Ernan and Du Dianqin were fluent in English and they translated numerous medical articles for Chinese journals. They were also nonprofessional musicians and provided their three children with practical training on Western instruments as well as extensive exposure to Western music in concerts and on recordings. Du was an accomplished pianist and an accordionist. Chen began to study violin after medical school, encouraged by a classmate, Huang Feili. Huang also kindled in Chen a passion for acquiring classical records, which Chen would play, during family meals, on a sophisticated turntable sent to him by his expatriate siblings. He assembled much of his record collection from discs left at the American consulate after diplomats exited mainland China following the 1949 Communist takeover.

Biography and Framework

Chen Yi and her two siblings (sister Chen Min and brother Chen Yun) all became professional musicians, and they married musicians as well. The eldest, Chen Min (b. 1951), is a renowned pianist in Beijing. When she was six years old, Liu Shaoqi, who was, at the time, the vice chairman of the Communist Party, visited Guangzhou in the company of the premier of Poland.[1] Chen Min performed for them. A photo taken on the occasion—which would later haunt the family[2] after Liu's fall from grace in 1966—shows her sitting on the vice chairman's lap. (Originally groomed as Mao's successor, Liu was discredited during the Cultural Revolution. He was tortured and died in prison in 1969.) Chen Min's husband, Liang Yulin, is a cellist and their daughter, Liang Xiaomin, holds degrees in piano from Juilliard and Northwestern.

Chen Yi's younger brother Chen Yun (b. 1955) is a professional violinist who graduated from Beijing's Central Conservatory of Music (CCOM) in 1982. He led the China Youth String Quartet, was acting concertmaster of the Singapore Symphony, and established an orchestra in Macao. At present Chen Yun is concertmaster and assistant to the music director of the China Philharmonic, as well as professor of violin and chair of the chamber music division at CCOM. His wife Yang Jie is a mezzo-soprano.

Chen Yi (b. 1953) began piano lessons at age three with Li Suxin, a professor at the Guangzhou Academy of Music (now called the Xinghai Conservatory). But her real talent lay in the violin, which she started studying the following year. Twice a week, on Tuesdays and Fridays, she had lessons with Zheng Rihua or his brother Zheng Zhong—the two most respected violin teachers in the city. Zheng Zhong was also a composer and laced his pedagogy with instruction in music theory and history.

Chen Yi's parents took her to symphony concerts and ballet performances presented by artists from the Soviet Union, England, and France, and her father introduced her to Romanian, African, and Japanese folk dance. Chen Ernan particularly inspired in Chen Yi an admiration for "the sincerity and simplicity of Mozart," she recalls, "in which the weeping tear hid behind a smiling face."[3]

The children's exposure to Chinese traditional music was far more limited, coming primarily from Huang Li, one of the family's maids. Huang was the widow of a Kuomintang government official who had committed suicide after the Communist revolution. Although Huang was highly educated, her husband's Nationalist affiliation relegated her to menial work in post-1949 China. She loved to listen to Cantonese opera on the radio. The three Chen children enjoyed the stories and the musical style but learned nothing at this time about the music's structure or compositional processes.

PHOTO 2. Chen Yi at the start of her piano study in 1956. Photo courtesy of Chen Yi.

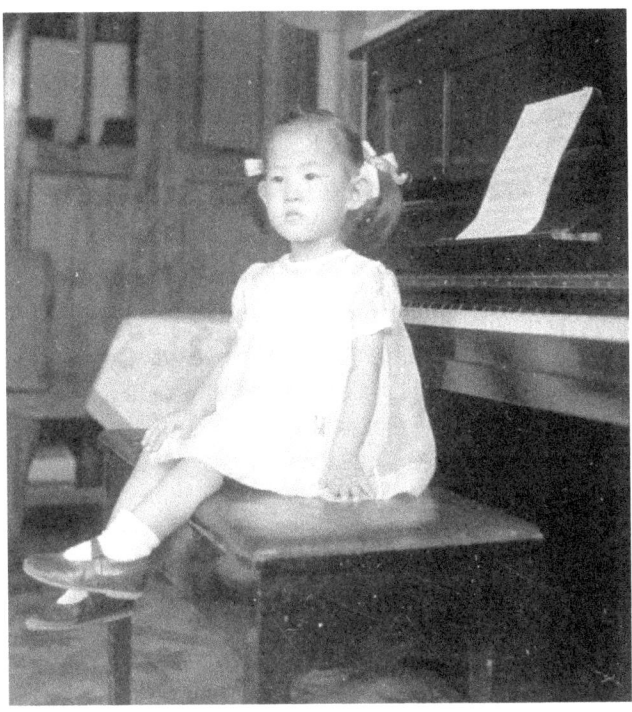

PHOTO 3. Chen Yi's main instrument is the violin. This photo dates from 1961. Photo courtesy of Chen Yi.

The early to mid-1950s brought to China a welcome respite from the strife engendered first by the Sino-Japanese War (1937–45) and then by the civil war that resulted in the Communist Party takeover (1946–49). Chen Yi's early years in Guangzhou were comfortable, culminating in the optimistic Hundred Flowers period in 1956–57, when citizens were encouraged to express frank opinions about political, social, and economic conditions, albeit within the broader confines of meeting the "needs of the workers, peasants and soldiers."[4] Mao Zedong, however, was taken aback by the "alarming explosion of criticism from intellectuals"[5] that followed. The government responded with an Anti-Rightist Campaign beginning in 1957 that sent a cold wind of repression throughout the country. Because Chen Yi's parents spoke fluent English, had friends and patients in the foreign consulates, and had accepted medical supplies from the British Red Cross, authorities entered a secret notation in their files, branding them as "suspected international spies." The damaging accusation was removed years later only after Mao's death in 1976.

During the Anti-Rightist Campaign of 1957–59, Chen Ernan lost his leadership position at the hospital. He and Du Dianqin continued to practice medicine, but government officials reduced their salaries and searched their home repeatedly, confiscating jewelry and other valuables. Chen Yi recalls her fright when the police shone a flashlight in her eyes in the middle of the night to ascertain whether "the face" of the five-year-old child "matched the file."[6] These raids turned out to be harbingers of trouble for a family that had too many connections with the West.

Despite this political crackdown, Chen Yi continued to thrive. From 1960 to 1965 she attended an advanced primary school on Shamian Island in which six years of education were compressed into five. Families were closely drawn into the students' education. Each night the parents annotated a school diary: "When did you finish your homework? Did you help out in your neighborhood? Did you help the elderly? Have you done housework to help your parents? Did you read books outside of your class work?"[7]

In 1962 eleven-year-old Chen Min moved to Beijing, 1,500 miles from home, to enter the primary school linked to the CCOM. Two years later Chen Yi applied to the same program, but the conservatory chose not to open the primary school section that year. In the interim the political climate had changed dramatically: school admissions were increasingly based less on achievement than on social class and political affiliations.[8] In 1965 Chen Yi applied to the secondary school associated with the South China Normal University, but her outstanding primary school academic record was insufficient to overcome her tainted background. Children from "bad" classes—*di fu fan huai you* (landlords, the wealthy, counterrevolutionaries, those of bad character, and rightists—which included most intellectuals) had lowest priority. Chen enrolled instead in her second choice, the No. 29 Middle School in Guangzhou.

The Early Years of the Cultural Revolution (1966–70)

Although the No. 29 Middle School was founded by European Christians as the Guangzhou West District Pui Ying Secondary School, the education was in no way religious. Chen Yi blossomed there, musically and otherwise: she led the student choir and performed on the violin during celebration concerts.

In the same year as Chen Yi began at No. 29, Mao issued Order 626, which was designed to upgrade medical services in rural areas by transferring experienced urban physicians to rural villages to train collectives of "barefoot doctors." The directive relegated Chen Ernan to the countryside, although he returned to Guangzhou every weekend to visit his wife and children. Chen Ernan worked at the Shiling Commune Clinic (Huaxian County) and soon rose to a leadership position as associate director of the Huaxian County Hospital, where he gained the trust and admiration of the populace. "When he later passed away in Guangzhou," recalls Chen Yi, "people came from the countryside and waited in a long line to pay their last respects to him." In retrospect, Chen Yi views her father's forced dislocation as fortunate: had he remained in Guangzhou, he might have been killed in the anti-intellectual violence that erupted in the late 1960s.

Chen Yi's success at the No. 29 Middle School came to an abrupt end after only one year. On August 8, 1966, Mao's Sixteen Articles formally launched what would become known as the Great Proletarian Cultural Revolution. Empowering students throughout the country to combat the Four Olds (old ideas, old culture, old customs, old habits) and to physically attack members of the "exploiting class" that embodied them, Mao welcomed to Beijing the newly organized radical youth, known as the Red Guards. Ten days after the Sixteen Articles, the Guards gathered en masse in Tiananmen Square. Lin Biao, vice premier of the People's Republic, denounced enemies of the revolution; Mao donned a Red Guard armband. Emboldening this youthful anti-intellectual, anti-Western, and anticapitalist radicalism led to severe brutality that was, in many cases, ignored (or even condoned) by police. Teachers, intellectuals, and representatives of the "old ways" were beaten, humiliated, and made to endure public criticism sessions. In August–September 1966 alone, 1,722 people were murdered in Beijing. Shanghai witnessed 704 suicides in a single month. In the Chinese music conservatories, the Guards attacked or humiliated teachers of Western music. By the end of the Cultural Revolution in 1976, seventeen Shanghai Conservatory professors or their spouses had committed suicide.[9] Others died in prison or in forced labor camps. The Guards defaced or destroyed historical and cultural sites, reducing valuable artistic relics to rubble. Books were burned, historical texts destroyed. Revolutionary committees replaced provincial governments.

In Guangzhou two of Chen Ernan's close colleagues killed themselves. In this southern city, as elsewhere in the country, the violence caused closure of the schools, as students from worker and farmer families—the new political elite—subjected the teaching staff to humiliating public condemnation. A mentor of Chen Yi—a high school student assigned to her class to coach younger students in mathematics—was shot through the heart. She survived but was permanently disabled.

The Red Guards came to the Chen home in 1966, but neighbors prevented violence by telling them about the life-saving medical work of Chen Ernan and Du Dianqin. The Guards did not seize any property, but they did seal the furniture and the cupboards full of food. A month later, when there was no sign that they would return, the Chens surreptitiously removed the seals.

In late summer 1966 Chen Yi and her fellow students went to the countryside to help with the harvest. She returned with a serious kidney infection that required her to be hospitalized for a month and remain home for the next three.

Unleashing the power of the proletariat, the Communist government authorized free travel throughout the country from September 5 to December 21, 1966, for Red Guards who wished to spread the new gospel or visit the capital to pay respects to Chairman Mao. Three million people descended on Beijing. Trains became moving prisons; housing became choked; diseases became endemic. With students moving freely throughout the country, schools were nonfunctional.

When Chen's period of quarantine from her kidney infection ended, it was too dangerous to return to the No. 29 Middle School. Red Guards toting guns blocked the entries, admitting only those from "good" classes. Chen Yi, her brother, and her mother huddled in their home, listening apprehensively to gunshots in the street. "The students had grabbed these arms from the army and police," Chen Yi recalls. "They drove tanks on the street and shot guns. Then people would grab someone from the street and hang them on a tree."

Du Dianqin taught her children at home, borrowing books from colleagues with older children and engaging a former schoolmate to help educate Chen Yi and Chen Yun. Chen Yi received some English lessons from a slightly older student and gave some instruction in other subjects to her younger brother's friends. Using the precious old family typewriter, Chen Yi assiduously copied textbooks, not only learning their subject matter but also improving her English. When she had time, Du Dianqin taught Chen Yi Japanese.

Under the new political structure, life for the Chens continued in a drastically altered and highly restricted manner. Du continued practicing as a pediatrician, but revolts erupted against her at the hospital. For many years she had been in a position of authority, distributing bonuses designed to encourage hard work. Chen Yi spotted big-character posters condemning her mother, hung by workers who felt they had not been properly rewarded. Afraid of being overheard practicing Western compositions, but unwilling to give up their musical activities, Du and her children threaded a blanket between the hammers and strings of their upright Zimmermann piano and the youngsters attached mutes to their violins. With shades drawn, they continued to indulge their love of Western classical music.

In September 1968, however, when a new round of attacks erupted, their situation deteriorated dramatically. Chen Yi and Chen Yun were home alone when intruders from the Revolutionary Committee entered the house (not members of the Red Guards, as stated in many other sources about Chen Yi; the Guards were defunct by this time).[10] The raiders turned everything upside down, scattering medical supplies and thousands of pictures on the floor. They moved the piano and tore up the floorboards searching for valuables but found nothing; everything of value had already been taken during the Anti-Rightist Campaign in the late 1950s. Chen Yi seated herself on the piano bench and remained resolutely planted. The intruders had no idea that the bench opened, much less that Western classical scores lurked inside.

Meanwhile a political team at the hospital had taken Du prisoner. Branded as an enemy of the people, she was not allowed to return home. Chen Yi, 15, and Chen Yun, 13, waited anxiously for her, standing on the balcony outside their kitchen, a vantage point that gave them a clear view of the street. They had expected her home by 7 p.m. She arrived four hours later, in the custody of the hospital's political team. Chen Yi recalls that

> the whole team came with a huge car ... to carry things taken from our home. In the first round of the Cultural Revolution [that is, the Red Guards' raids in 1966], people burned things. In this second round, they took things to make an exhibition ... to show everything in the hospital. "See, this family is capitalist. That is what they own." They took everything away in their car. The piano was too heavy, though they tried to remove it.

On a high shelf in the tallest wardrobe closet was Chen Yi's violin. Du was not permitted to speak to her children, but as her captors were about to seize the instrument, she exclaimed, "That doesn't belong to me. It's a child's toy." They left the violin in the house but seized other instruments to add to the public display of "capitalist possessions." Eventually the family recovered some belongings, but their phonograph records were so scratched that they no longer functioned.

For ten months the hospital workers held Du prisoner. She was no longer allowed to practice medicine but instead worked in the kitchen, cleaned floors, carried coal, and was subjected to demoralizing public self-criticism sessions. Chen Yi could deliver clothes to her mother but not see her.

The month after the raid, all students were recalled to their schools and assigned to deportation groups to fulfill Mao's "down-to-the-countryside" mandate, which ultimately displaced about seventeen million young people. Students from intellectual families went to farms and factories to be reeducated in the work of the peasant class. Had Chen Yi been one year older, she might have gone to Hainan Island, which offered more physical comfort and intellectual development. "You would have enough food there because it was a state-run farm," she says. For example, violinist Xiao Tiqin, also from Guangzhou, spent four years on Hainan as part of a cultural work team that included a thirty-piece orchestra, singers, dancers, and technical assistants, most of whom were children of intellectuals and capitalists.[11] But because she was not yet sixteen, Chen Yi was sent to the small village of Shimen. Thirteen-year-old Chen Yun remained in Guangzhou, left alone to fend for himself. His situation was hardly unique. Anne Thurston, who interviewed numerous victims of the Cultural Revolution in the early 1980s, documented the plight of thousands of children, some as young as eight, who were abandoned when their parents were imprisoned or shipped off to reeducation camps.[12] Chen Yun, however, was among the more fortunate: his violin teacher, Zheng Rihua (today a professor at the Hong Kong Performing Arts Academy), took him in, leaving the Chen house vacant.

In the countryside Chen Yi labored in the rice and vegetable fields ("I didn't wear shoes for many months," she recalls) and attended the No. 64 Middle School in Xincun village in the Shimen district. The school's rudimentary curriculum supplemented the students' "reeducation" through manual labor by offering courses in political doctrine and elementary science.

Chen Yi lived in a dormitory with eight students to a room. In the evenings, she would play revolutionary tunes on her violin for the farmers. Folk music, a remnant of a pre-Communist "feudalistic" culture, was forbidden; in fact, the love songs of the "folk" were considered close to pornographic. Some of the new revolutionary tunes were adapted from folk material, however, giv-

PHOTO 4. Chen Yi (left) and her brother Chen Yun (right) with their violin teacher Zheng Rihua in 1972. Zheng took Chen Yun into his home during the Cultural Revolution. Photo courtesy of Chen Yi.

ing Chen Yi her first taste of the songs of the rural population. Chen Yi would embellish the simple tunes with ornamentation—thereby creating her first compositions—and she would deftly insert virtuosic Paganini-style cadenzas between the stanzas.

Also taboo was the Western "capitalistic" classical repertoire. During mealtimes, when no one could hear her, Chen would occasionally find the time and solitude to play forbidden classical works. Many others throughout the country similarly indulged in this solitary, clandestine practice.[13]

In spring 1969, territorial disputes between China and the USSR sparked anxiety about a new war, a fear that gained justification from a border clash on Zhenbao Island in March and a Russian attack in the Xinjiang region in August. The country went on high alert and citizens began to dig tunnels and build air raid shelters. In Beijing alone, an underground city of eighty-five square kilometers arose, containing restaurants, clinics, schools, theaters, and factories. By the end of 1970, China's seventy-five largest cities had built shelters to hold 60 percent of their residents.[14] The students of No. 64 school involuntarily contributed to this frenetic defense activity. The army transported Chen Yi and

Biography and Framework

her schoolmates to Conghua, at the time a county near Guangzhou and now a district in the northern part of the city. The army forced the young people to haul wet concrete up a mountain to construct a watch tower and underground rooms large enough to house vehicles and serve as a military safe haven. The students arose at 4 a.m. to start work before the heat of the day. Tiny Chen Yi, who weighed about ninety pounds, carried a double basket equal to her body weight across her shoulders. With this load she struggled up the mountain in a line of workers that kept moving steadily, preventing her from stopping to rest. By the time she reached the top, Chen's legs were so weak that she could barely stand. "I had to use my hands to grab the earth and straw in order to walk down for another load," she recalled years later.[15] The students labored up to sixteen hours a day for three weeks.

In addition to this back-breaking work, the interminable hours of farming, the restrictions on musical repertoire, the inferior schooling, and the bare feet, Chen Yi was lonely. Moreover, she could see no escape from her bleak existence—no end to her physical toil, no opportunities for artistic or intellectual fulfillment. In retrospect, however, she looks back on the Shimen period as providing an opening to a new cultural world:

> Frankly, it was not until then that I found my roots, my motherland, and really appreciated the simple people on the earth and the importance of education and civilization. I learned to overcome hardship, to bear anger, fear and humiliation under the political pressure, to get close to uneducated farmers on a personal and spiritual level, and to share my feelings and thinking with them, to learn to hope, to forgive, to survive, and to live optimistically, strongly and independently, and to work hard in order to benefit more human beings in society.[16]

Then suddenly, without warning, Chen Yi's life changed; and it was her violin that came to her rescue.

Eight Years Playing Beijing Opera (1970–78)

One day in January 1970, two men in a jeep arrived in Shimen. One was Chang Xuyou, the army supervisor in an administrative team controlling the Guangzhou Beijing Opera Troupe. The other was Fu Hongjiu, an oboist from the troupe's orchestra, which was a mixed ensemble that skillfully blended the timbres and tuning systems of Chinese and Western instruments.[17] The opera troupe faced a trial that very evening. An army review board would evaluate their performance of one of eight model (political) operas that had been created by teams of composers under the Communist regime. If the ensemble passed the test, it would be permitted to perform the opera in town and on tour; but the group needed a good violinist to lead the orchestra—one who could learn the part immediately. Most of the musicians with violin training had been sent to the countryside for reeducation, but Fu Hongjiu remembered Chen Yi's skills on the instrument from the time when they had attended the same primary school. A check with the Shamian Primary School sent them to the No. 29 Middle School and then to Shimen, where they found Chen Yi in the rice fields. "We hear you are a good violinist," they told her. "Please bring your violin, without any luggage, and go back to the city with us immediately." Chen Yi recalls: "Because I was a student, I was considered not so bad as [older] intellectuals."

Chang Xuyou and Fu Hongjiu took Chen Yi back to Guangzhou and tested her skills. First she played Sarasate's *Zigeunerweisen*. Then she sight-read two excerpts from the model opera scheduled for presentation, *Taking Tiger Mountain by Strategy*.[18] "It was simple," she recalls. They found her more than qualified.

That evening, the main trio—which in Beijing opera consists of two bowed chordophones (a *jinghu* and a *jing erhu*) and a round-bodied "moon lute" (*yueqin*)—sat in the front row of the orchestra, located on the side of the stage. (The jinghu, the leading melodic instrument of Beijing opera, is the smallest member of the *huqin* family—two-stringed bowed fiddles without fingerboards; the hair of the bow passes between the strings. The jinghu is piercingly high-pitched. The jing erhu plays an octave lower.) Directly behind the trio sat Chen Yi, the orchestra's new principal violinist. Although fenced in by a screen, she and the trio were visible to the audience. The other instrumentalists were hidden, giving center stage to the singers and actors.

The Guangzhou Beijing Opera Troupe passed the audition and for the next eight years Chen Yi led its orchestra in performances throughout the region.[19] She lived with the other musicians, sharing a room with Zhu Lei, who played the *pipa*—a large, full-bodied Chinese lute with an articulated fingerboard. Chen not only learned the intricacies of the instrument from Zhu, but also helped her translate pipa parts from Western notation into cipher notation. Through her wholesale immersion in the Beijing opera genre, Chen Yi learned its stylistic features, which would later resurface in many of her compositions. On a personal level, she also reunited with her brother, whom the orchestra hired a month after Chen joined the group.

Taking Tiger Mountain by Strategy and the other model operas were the brainchildren of Mao's fourth wife, Jiang Qing. Mao firmly believed in the power of culture to effect revolutionary change. Jiang, a former actress from

PHOTO 5. Chen Yi leads the orchestra of the Guangzhou Beijing Opera Company in 1973. Behind her and to her right (left side of the photo) is her brother Chen Yun. Photo courtesy of Chen Yi.

Shanghai, enthusiastically supported this philosophy and assumed the leadership role in creating new works that became the staple of the Chinese population for nearly a decade.

Opera reform had begun soon after the Communist takeover in 1949. The government encouraged revision of traditional works and the creation of new operas on revolutionary themes. Traditional Beijing opera, a beloved genre to the Chinese people, is a composite art involving singing, reciting, acrobatics, dance, instrumental music, lively percussion, and colorful costumes. Traditionally the orchestra is small (perhaps only six to ten instruments) and sits in a corner of the stage. The jinghu leads the melodic instruments, following the vocal contours in heterophonic fashion. The percussionists, in contrast, play from a repertory of complex rhythmic patterns that signal various types of action. Chinese opera's vocal style prioritizes a nasal tone quality unlike Western operatic singing, and many male roles call for falsetto. Traditional role types are stylized and singers (traditionally all men) adopt the personas of the stock characters. The new works that the government encouraged after the Communist revolution maintained many of these musical characteristics but featured updated revolutionary plots and dispensed with the traditional role types.

To acclimate the populace to the new works, performances during the Hundred Flowers movement of 1956–57 often juxtaposed these new creations with old favorites.[20] Eventually, however, the traditional works, denounced by Mao and Jiang as "feudalistic, superstitious and vulgar,"[21] were suppressed in favor of the model operas (*yangbanxi*) created under Jiang's direction.

This movement to create modern operas culminated in summer 1964 with a grandiose National Festival of Peking Operas on Contemporary Themes. Two hundred performances of thirty-five operas featuring two thousand performers from twenty-nine opera companies took place in Beijing over a period of five weeks. Among the operas presented were preliminary versions of four of the first five yangbanxi.[22]

By 1967 creative teams under the watchful eye of Jiang Qing had completed five yangbanxi: *Shajiabang*, *The Red Lantern*, *Taking Tiger Mountain by Strategy*, *On the Docks*, and *Raid on the White Tiger Regiment*, as well as two ballets (*The White-Haired Girl* and *The Red Detachment of Women*) and a symphonic suite based on *Shajiabang*. These eight works were performed throughout the country: their arias were adapted with piano accompaniment, they were made into films, and they were broadcast repeatedly on the radio. "Eight works for eighty million people" became the (hyperbolic) slogan of the era. Traditional operas were banned. To combat the cultural sparseness, Jiang Qing's teams created seven more works in the early 1970s and as the stringencies of the Cultural Revolution relaxed, local troupes were eventually permitted to develop their own works. Pang Laikwan makes the important point that the rise of the yangbanxi was coterminous with the demise of the Red Guards. The government shifted its emphasis from live exemplars (brutal heroes extolled as models for emulation) to imaginary ones. "The regime found fiction more reliable than reality," she asserts.[23]

Why was there such an emphasis on this artistic genre? Beijing opera was a highly popular dramatic entertainment, but its subject matter was anathema to the Communist authorities. The traditional opera plots reflected the old culture based on aristocratic privilege, and the stereotyped roles were inconsistent with modern political dogma. Mao and Jiang Qing recognized that opera was the most conservatively entrenched of the art forms. If it could be reformed, then the other arts would follow.[24] Radical elements in the government also recognized that opera could serve as a widespread platform for populist reform. Indeed, opera had figured decisively in the genesis of the Cultural Revolution. Nine months before Mao's Sixteen Articles formally launched the campaign, Yao Wenyuan (an accomplice of Jiang Qing) published a scathing criticism of the opera *Hai Rui Dismissed from Office*, created by the respected historian Wu Han (1909–69). Yao's review is often cited as the "opening salvo" in the Cultural Revolution.[25]

The new model operas drew on the traits of Beijing opera but with plots modernized and character development substituting for the old static fixed roles. Like the socialist realism in Stalin's Soviet Union, these art works aimed for "revolutionary realism and revolutionary romanticism."[26] Political dramas featuring heroes who were triumphant by virtue of their ideological purity replaced now-banned love stories. Plots heralded a brave new world celebrating the uprising of the people.

The orchestral forces in the yangbanxi were far larger than in the old traditional operas and included both Chinese and Western instruments. Although it may seem odd that Western instruments were welcomed into the model opera orchestras, Mao saw no irony in this embrace of a foreign culture. In fact, he advocated adopting Western elements if they served the goals of the Communist state. Richard Kraus succinctly encapsulates Jiang Qing's principles in creating the new operas:[27] independence from Western bourgeois styles without elevating native "feudalistic" folk culture; maintenance of traditional Chinese vocal styles to prioritize the clarity of the text; modernization of Chinese instruments but preservation of their distinctive timbres; and inclusion of European instruments to expand the orchestra's range and timbral scope.

Although Jiang and Mao readily embraced mixed ensembles, some of the model operas relied primarily on Chinese instruments. Thirty-six of the forty-seven instruments in *Shajiabang*, for example, are Chinese. Although Western strings and winds take part in this piece, they play a subsidiary role.[28] In these cases, Chen Yi learned to play Chinese instruments, particularly the *ruan* (a four-stringed lute with a round body, bridge, and fretted neck).

One manifestation of the modernization of the old operas was the act of composition itself. In the traditional style, musicians improvised using a conventional menu of tunes and percussion motives. The new operas, on the other hand, were composed throughout. Perhaps the most important contributor was Yu Huiyong, who eventually became Minister of Culture and acted from 1971 as the country's de facto arts administrator. Yu had been admitted to the

Shanghai Conservatory largely on his "politically reliable family background and activist credentials."[29] In April 1968, at the height of the Cultural Revolution, Yu presided over a brutal televised struggle session against the conservatory's deposed president, He Luting.[30] Yu became Jiang Qing's "viceroy for musical revolution"; under the pen name Chu Lan, a group of writers under his supervision[31] produced 165 articles touting the political role of art. After Mao's death in 1976 and the downfall of the notorious Gang of Four, Yu was imprisoned. He killed himself by drinking a bottle of sulfuric acid.[32]

The meticulous composition and widespread dissemination of the model operas, which underwent repeated revisions,[33] set high standards for the quality of performance, requiring skilled professionals such as Chen Yi and her brother. Politics may have figured in the move to involve virtuosi on Western instruments as well. According to Richard Kraus, Yu and his team aimed "to keep China's violinists busy on works such as *The Red Detachment of Women*, rather than having them show their resistance by playing Mozart."[34]

Staging was also modernized with the addition of not only a curtain but also sophisticated scenery and set changes. When performances were given in formal theaters in the city, stage sets and lighting could be changed rapidly while the orchestra played the opera's interludes. For performances in the countryside, with no professionally built stages, scene changes took more time, providing Chen Yi with her first serious compositional experience: she wrote music for the violin ensemble of the orchestra to perform in front of the closed curtain while the stage hands worked. For some of the music performed between scenes, Chen orchestrated revolutionary tunes and even folk songs, which were creeping back into the culture as the political atmosphere relaxed.

The model operas eventually became highly popular, creating a sense of community and enhancing efforts at social leveling. Peasants participated in performances by singing familiar tunes. Factories formed their own troupes. People learned to play instruments. In short, the operas became, in the words of Nancy Rao, "an outlet for youthful energy, creativity, and leisure activities."[35]

At the same time, however, the paucity of artistic repertoire led to a relaxation of the stranglehold on creative production. The yangbanxi had permitted no improvisation—"We were not allowed to change a single note," says Chen Yi—although authorities allowed adaptations to accommodate variants in dialect and the tonal and rhythmic demands of regional speech. (Bell Yung, for example, describes authorized changes in *Shajiabang* to accommodate the Cantonese declamation spoken in Guangzhou.[36]) Official yangbanxi companies had toured the country demonstrating proper performance, and regional leaders would travel to Beijing or Shanghai to participate in tutorials.[37] Nevertheless, the noose gradually loosened and local companies gained permission to create their own operas. These new works required approval by a chain of supervising bodies, a process that could take years.

The Guangzhou Beijing Opera Troupe managed to create two or three new works, and Chen Yi contributed to their musical composition. She wrote overtures, incidental music, and orchestral interludes; and she orchestrated the accompaniments for arias. She also provided music for concert performances by members of the ensemble.

The conductor of the opera orchestra, cellist Ge Wu, recommended that Chen take formal lessons in music theory. So she turned to Zheng Zhong, the brother of her old violin teacher. He not only taught her harmony but also inspired her for the first time to compose music in her own voice. His instruction and her compositional experience with the opera troupe would prove invaluable when Chen Yi applied for admission to Beijing's Central Conservatory after the Cultural Revolution ended in 1976.

At the Central Conservatory of Music in Beijing (1978–86)

On September 9, 1976, Mao Zedong died, and with him the last gasp of the Cultural Revolution. One month later, Jiang Qing and her colleagues in the notorious Gang of Four were arrested and imprisoned. When Jiang was finally brought to trial in 1980, charges centered on the persecution of artists. Her death sentence was commuted to life imprisonment in 1982. Nine years later, after her release to a hospital, Madame Mao hanged herself in a bathroom.

For the Chen family, the end of the Cultural Revolution brought about Chen Ernan's return to the No. 3 People's Hospital in Guangzhou, where he assumed the position of head of the internal medicine department. He actually "came back unwillingly," says Chen Yi, "because he loved the countryside. He loved the people there." Among his other activities, he began to train a cohort of young Chinese doctors to instruct visiting Americans in scientifically verified Chinese medical practices.

Throughout the country, schools reopened (they had effectively been closed for ten years), and education-thirsty youth from intellectual families scrambled to make up for lost time. In 1977 the Central Conservatory of Music—founded in 1950 in Tianjin, relocated to Beijing in 1958, and renowned for a curriculum that included both traditional Chinese music and European Classic and Romantic period styles[38]—called for applicants to its first class since the late 1960s. About seventeen thousand people applied for admission to twenty-eight majors; CCOM accepted less than two percent.[39]

Chen Yi took the three-day entrance exam in October 1977. As samples of her works, she submitted scores from her Beijing opera years. In the theory section of the test, she discovered an error: one question had no correct answer.[40] The mistake was one of notation rather than substance: the octave specification for what should have been the correct choice was wrong.[41] Chen Yi bravely pointed out the error; the exam administrators huddled and then reported that she was correct. This event brought her to the attention of Wu Zuqiang (b. 1927), who would become her composition teacher. The exam was highly demanding with focused testing in the areas of composition, musicianship, and performance. Chen easily passed the ear training component due in part to having perfect pitch; then she played a piano reduction of an orchestral score and a piano work from the Western repertoire; she sang a Beijing opera aria, and on the violin she played the first movement of the Tchaikovsky concerto and Paganini's Caprice No. 13. In addition, she wrote a brief article on a given subject and composed an art song for female voice and piano using a provided text.

CCOM accepted Chen Yi to both the violin performance and the composition departments, but she could accept admission to only one area. She decided that she was too old to develop a successful performance career and thus, in the spring of 1978, she entered the conservatory as one of thirty-two composition students. The semester from April to September was an unofficial introduction to the conservatory. By the time the program officially began in fall 1978, three men had moved into a newly established conducting major and two others had left the country. Therefore, the class was reduced to twenty-seven, but even these were not all composers: six were in the ear training program.[42] Among the group of twenty-one composers were five women, including Liu Sola (experimental composer, author, producer, and one of China's first rock stars) and Jin Yueling, known at the time for her song "I Love Tiananmen Square in Beijing." The Guangzhou Beijing Opera Troupe would not release Chen until spring 1978 but thereafter supported her financially throughout her undergraduate years. Chen's brother also entered the conservatory—in his case in violin performance.

Facilities were woefully inadequate. For three months, women students slept on chairs in the recital hall. Then the conservatory housed them in practice rooms—two students in a space of less than a hundred square feet.[43] Pianos were in short supply. "I often had to stay on my bed to memorize the singing assignments of Chinese folk songs in various dialects, and the fingerings of Bach's pieces from the Well-Tempered Clavier," Chen says. The upside was that she learned to hear the music in her head without relying on any instrument.

The composition students were divided into A (advanced) and B (less advanced) groups for the purpose of ear training. Chen was not only a member of the A group, but also the student head of both her ear training and counterpoint classes. The "student head" was the teacher's assistant, usually the strongest student in the class, "whose homework would be introduced to the other students as sample work," she explains. Among her classmates in the A group was a quiet man from the north, Zhou Long, who would later become her husband.

Zhou had grown up in an artistic family in Beijing. His mother, He Gaoyong, was a vocal teacher at CCOM and his father, Zhou Zutai, was a painter on the faculty of the Stage Art Department at Beijing's Central Academy of Drama. At the beginning of the Cultural Revolution, the Red Guards invaded the Zhou home and burned his father's paintings in the courtyard. Zhou Long and his younger sister Zhou Feng (now recently retired from her position as a costume designer for the Central Ballet in Beijing) were sent to work in factories while the parents were deported to farming camps run by the military, leaving the two children, ages 14 and 10, alone in the house for three years. Zhou worked in a steel factory, handling heavy equipment that flattened metal into thin sheets. In 1969 he was sent, in a group of about fifty, to a remote region in the province of Heilongjiang, near the Soviet border. The youngsters traveled for seventeen hours, first by train, then by army truck, and finally by small carts pulled by a tractor to a desolate state farm at Hegang—a thousand miles from home. When they arrived, they lived in simple tents, a curtain separating men and women. The cold was nearly unbearable. Zhou helped relieve the gloom by playing revolutionary tunes on his accordion and leading the group in singing songs set to Mao's words. Eventually the young people built their own houses.

For five years Zhou drove a tractor and served as the group's cook. (He still loves to cook for Chen Yi and their many guests.) "We had no hope," he recalls. "We thought we'd spend our whole life there."[44] Surreptitiously at night under the cover of a blanket, Zhou and his friends would tune in to Soviet radio, where they heard forbidden Chinese folk songs and traditional Beijing opera.

After carrying two hundred pounds of material to storage facilities every day, Zhou injured his back. In 1973 his father managed to arrange for a transfer to Zhangjiakou, three hundred miles northwest of Beijing. There, Zhou joined the Zhangjiakou City Art Troupe, a midsized company consisting of a thirty-piece orchestra (Western instruments and a small group of Chinese instruments), a twenty-four-member choir, and a similar-sized dance group. Occasionally he traveled to Beijing by train to take private lessons in theory, orchestration, and composition with some of his mother's former colleagues at the conservatory. For the troupe, Zhou not only played accordion but also created orchestrations for Western and Chinese instruments by arranging dance scores and writing small orchestral pieces and a cantata.

PHOTO 6. Zhou Long in 1970 on a farm in Hegang during the Cultural Revolution. Photo courtesy of Zhou Long.

In 1977 the troupe sent Zhou and others to Inner Mongolia for field work. He spent two weeks on the Hulunbuir Prairie listening to folk songs sung by Oroqen (Elunchen) nomads,[45] who "lived in camps and had no [running] water, no electricity. But their folk songs were beautiful," Zhou recalls.[46] As he returned to Zhangjiakou, Zhou heard an announcement on the radio that the universities were about to reopen. He rushed to take the entrance exam.

Chen Yi and Zhou Long soon developed a romantic relationship ("he stayed in my practice room all day long," Chen recalls),[47] but they were not allowed to marry until they were thirty. On July 20, 1983, they took out a marriage certificate in Beijing and a few days later had a small ceremony in an elegant hotel in Guangzhou.[48]

At the conservatory, Chen Yi took her first formal lessons in composition from Wu Zuqiang, who accepted only three students. Wu had been educated in Nanjing and Moscow, and in 1982 he became head of the entire conservatory. During the Cultural Revolution he headed a composition team at the Central Philharmonic, one of several institutions that worked under the guidance of Jiang Qing and her colleagues to compose the model operas.[49] He published

Biography and Framework

PHOTO 7. Chen Yi and Zhou Long, photo taken by the marriage office, 1983. Photo courtesy of Chen Yi.

a number of theoretical works, including a book on form and analysis, *Qushi yu zuopin fenxi* (1962).[50] As Chen's main composition teacher, Wu provided a solid foundation, demanded a rigorous work regimen, and encouraged her to seek a personal language.

Chen Yi recalls that the composition department included more than forty instructors, who taught not only composition but also harmony, counterpoint, analysis, orchestration, and ear training. Chen studied counterpoint with Yu Suxian; took courses in harmony, analysis, and orchestration; had extensive training in musicianship; took violin lessons with Lin Yaoji and piano lessons with Li Juhong; and studied folk music.

The revalidation of folk music after the Cultural Revolution stimulated a revival of performance, research, and pedagogy.[51] Traditional groups reemerged, often embracing enlarged instrumental resources; folk tunes found their way back into popular culture; and, most important for Chen Yi, scholars engaged in active fieldwork and analysis. In 1979 the Ministry of Culture began a massive Anthology of Chinese Folk Music aimed at documenting folk song, op-

PHOTO 8. Chen Yi with Prof. Wu Zuqiang of the Central Conservatory of Music in Beijing, taken in Kansas City in 2005. Photo by Zhou Long; used by permission.

era, narrative singing, instrumental music, and dance. CCOM was one of the institutions at the forefront of this research. Its new folk music classes restored (and enhanced) educational offerings that had been a staple of its curriculum before the Cultural Revolution.

The folk music courses Chen Yi took at the conservatory have influenced her compositional language up to the present day. She has written numerous choral settings of folk tunes and often uses folk song themes in her instrumental works. Her conservatory training in traditional Chinese music was both extensive and systematic—a full three years of study. The first two semesters, under Mr. Geng Shenglian and Mr. Zhao Songguang, covered folk songs spanning all provinces and nearly all minority groups. Students memorized four songs per week, analyzing various styles and techniques and then singing them in weekly quizzes. By the end of the year Chen and her colleagues had each learned nearly a hundred songs. At the final exam, they drew cards containing the names of four of them. After one minute of preparation they had to perform them from memory with precise pitch, diction, and style.

Biography and Framework

In the third semester students studied *quyi*, or musical storytelling, with Ms. Zhang Hongyi. Chen Yi describes this popular teahouse genre as "half singing, half talking," with a single performer simultaneously recounting a tale and playing an accompanying instrument. Exams included "drop the needle" tests in which students identified, from one-minute examples, the schools of a given classic type of quyi. The CCOM students not only wrote articles about the genre but also composed their own works to given lyrics. Chen has used this experience as inspiration in her own compositions, for example in her *Chinese Rap* for violin and orchestra (2012).

In the fourth semester Ms. Luo Yinghui taught musical theater (Chinese opera from various regions sung in dialect), including analysis of form and structure, recitation styles, accompaniment styles, and staging. The final year, led by Ms. Yuan Jingfang, focused on instrumental music—first the solo tradition and then ensemble music. Students learned the technique of the various instruments and the theory of folk ensemble music in order to compose idiomatically.

The conservatory supplemented the academic study of folk music with trips to rural villages for about two weeks during vacation periods. The most influential trip for Chen was to Guangxi Province in January 1981. The villagers treated the Beijing students as honored guests. "We ate tail of mouse . . . served in bamboo with salt," Chen recalls. The villagers dressed in costume and performed for the visitors. Drawing on this experience Chen later wrote a piano work, *Duo Ye* (1984), which won first prize in China's fourth composition contest (see Chapter 4). Subsequently she created a solo version of the piece for pipa and also orchestrated it for chamber orchestra; then she enlarged the instrumentation and expanded the work into a version for full orchestra.

The Beijing conservatory's training program in folk music inspired Chen to introduce Chinese traditional melodies into her compositions, a hallmark of her style ever since. "I want to compose in my own language," she told her father. Realizing that he had instructed her almost exclusively in European music, Chen Ernan began sending Chen Yi books on Chinese philosophy and aesthetics.

A special opportunity arose for Chen Yi when Alexander Goehr (b. 1932) visited China at the invitation of Wu Zuqiang for a three-week residency from May 19 to June 12, 1980. Chen was one of four students from Beijing and two from Shanghai selected to take private lessons (three per week) with the Cambridge University professor. In addition to teaching the six students (an assignment he had requested), Goehr presented a general course on modern European and American music, consisting of ten two-hour lectures. About two hundred musicians attended, including teachers and students from conserva-

PHOTO 9. Some members of the composition class of 1978, the first class to enter the Beijing Central Conservatory after the Cultural Revolution, on a trip to Guangxi Province in 1981. Chen Yi is in the front row, with one hand on the strap of a cross-body bag. Zhou Long is on the far right. Photo courtesy of Chen Yi.

tories throughout the country.[52] The lectures were recorded and transcribed, then sent to conservatories throughout China.[53] With the private students, Goehr explored rhythmic concepts and modality and had them write a string trio as well as short songs on a text by Li Po (aka Li Bai, 701–62). Although Wu had emphasized the importance of Bartók, Goehr's visit marked Chen's first exposure to contemporary procedures such as twelve-tone serialism. Chen was intrigued and tried her hand at using a tone row in the middle section of *Duo Ye*; but she never used strict serialist procedures, even during her study of them in her doctoral courses at Columbia University, which began in 1986. Indeed, by the time he came to China, Goehr himself had moved away from the Schoenbergian principles he had explored in the 1960s toward a far more flexible approach that embraced an "element of chance" and exploited the contrast with tonal and modal elements.[54]

Chen Yi was highly productive at the conservatory. In 1982 her string quartet won an internal prize and was performed in Yugoslavia, and her set of variations on the Uighur folk song "Awariguli," was performed in Italy and Scandinavia.[55] She in turn acted as a kind of spokesperson for the school: as a representative of arts universities to the Beijing City People's Congress, she introduced proposals to improve facilities.

After Chen completed her undergraduate work in 1983, she continued at the conservatory for its three-year master's program while Zhou went to the China National Broadcasting Symphony as a resident composer. In this capacity he became the first Chinese classical composer to release (on the China Record Company label) an entire album of chamber works for Chinese traditional instruments. Chen received a prestigious Shen Xingong fellowship and in 1986 became the first woman awarded a master's degree in composition from the conservatory.

During their years at CCOM, Chen and Zhou also earned some money writing commercial music for radio and record companies. Chen's Hong Kong uncle bought her a synthesizer, which her brother brought back to China when he finished his year of study at the Wollongong Conservatorium of Music in Australia. Chen learned to use MIDI and create synthesized orchestrations.

Chen's conservatory work culminated in a concert by the Central Philharmonic Orchestra held at the Beijing Concert Hall on May 31, 1986, conducted by En Shao and Lan Shui (conductor of the Singapore Symphony, 1997–2019). Sponsored by the conservatory along with the Chinese Musicians Association, Radio Beijing, CCTV, and *People's Music* magazine, the full evening's program included *Two Sets of Wind and Percussion Instruments*, *Duo Ye* (in its version for chamber orchestra), *Sprout* (for string orchestra), *Xian Shi* (the first Chinese viola concerto), and Symphony No. 1. China Record Company released a disc of this music in the same year.

In 1985 CCOM hosted a visit by Columbia University Professor Chou Wen-chung, who had traveled to mainland China several times beginning in 1972, presented lectures at various institutions there, and established a Center for US-China Arts Exchange in New York.[56] During their undergraduate years, Chen and Zhou had attended some of Chou's lectures. While he was in China in 1985, Chou met with Li Ling, vice president of the Chinese Musicians Association, to explore bringing promising Chinese composers to Columbia. Li recommended Zhou, who submitted scores. Impressed, Chou invited Zhou to enter Columbia's doctoral program. Thus, in August 1985 Zhou set off for New York, leaving Chen Yi to complete her master's degree. The following year, Chen, too, was accepted for the Columbia program and joined her husband in the United States.

Doctoral Studies at Columbia (1986–93)

Chou Wen-chung's arts exchange program, founded in 1978, sponsored a variety of activities: conferences, professional exchanges, field work, children's education, and artistic productions (concerts, films, ballets), in addition to facilitating doctoral education for a group of third-wave Chinese émigré composers.[57] In addition to Zhou Long and Chen Yi, Columbia's composition program also supported their CCOM classmate Tan Dun and Shanghai Conservatory students, Bright Sheng and Ge Gan-ru.

Chou strongly urged Chinese composers to delve deeply into their cultural history and put its legacies into practice.[58] He advocated a revival of the spirit of the *wenren*—ancient philosopher-artists who held "a unified theory for all artistic media." But, Chou lamented in 2007, some of his students failed to "stir the cultural interaction" and thus missed the opportunity to "play a genuine role in shaping the future of music."[59] Not so Chen Yi. She took Chou's views very seriously and, in the wenren spirit, assiduously studied a wide range of topics, often staying at the Columbia library until nearly midnight. Chou later told reporter Yu Yiqing that Chen Yi was "one of the most hard working in my class. She likes to challenge herself by choosing the most difficult courses. She has an open mind."[60]

It was not only Chinese culture that absorbed Chen Yi's attention. At Chou's suggestion she took extremely demanding courses with Patricia Carpenter in medieval and Renaissance European music. Chen struggled with this unfamiliar material; the courses seemed a bit like carrying intellectual concrete up an academic mountainside. Ultimately, however, the study gave her "the ability to consider not new music versus historical music, not East versus West, but . . . human thought. I began to see similarities in musical styles, aesthetics, customs, feelings, principles."[61]

Chen also enjoyed the contemporary popular music cultures around her in cosmopolitan New York, attending jazz concerts and delighting in ad hoc performances in subway stations. She particularly recalls her first exposure to steel drums. "I forgot to go home. I just stood there." She and Zhou went to dance clubs on Wednesday and Thursday nights, when admission was free. "We never drank; just danced."

At Columbia Chen also worked with Mario Davidovsky, who provided training in contemporary compositional processes and taught Chen Yi how "to arrange major materials logically."[62] "I began to take my inspiration even from scientific principles," she notes.[63] Chou retired shortly before Chen completed

PHOTO 10. Chen Yi with Chou Wen-chung in 2001. Photo by Zhou Long; used by permission.

her degree; Davidovsky guided her dissertation, a piano concerto commissioned by conductor Dennis Russell Davies and the Brooklyn Philharmonic, in which she combined Davidovsky's instruction in timing and sonic design with Chou's inspiration to employ Chinese source materials (we discuss this piece in Chapter 3). Chen especially credits Davidovsky with providing invaluable instruction in orchestration, particularly in exploring variations in texture and tone color.

Although Chen taught musicianship to Columbia undergraduates, gave private violin and piano lessons, performed at birthday parties, and even played violin duets on the street with her Beijing classmates Tan Dun and Hu Yongyan, she and Zhou Long struggled financially. Shortly after she arrived in New York, she became Chou's assistant at the Center for US-China Arts Exchange. "I translated documents between Chinese and English and wrote many letters, signing them for him." In 1988 Chou hosted a conference bringing together ten composers from Taiwan and ten from mainland China. Chen, one of those representing the mainland, was the only woman in the group.

In her first year at Columbia, Chen wrote a woodwind quintet that drew on her new studies and built on her work with Goehr a few years earlier. She based the opening section on a twelve-tone row, but her application of serialist ideas is personal and distinctive. She does not use numerous row forms, for example, nor does she explore retrograde and inversional forms. Furthermore, she sometimes omits one or more tones of the row and regularly alternates full statements of the row with partial ones (see discussion and examples in Chapter 4). In the middle section, Chen departs from the row entirely, instead using the inspiration of a Chinese melody. Chen submitted the quintet to Davidovsky's Composers' Conference at Wellesley and was chosen as a fellow.

In Fall 1987 the Central Philharmonic from Beijing toured the United States, playing a program of Western classical and Chinese contemporary music in ten cities. Included was Chen Yi's *Duo Ye No. 2* (a full orchestra version of *Duo Ye*), which garnered strong reviews. As "a celebration of timbre," wrote Bernard Holland in the *New York Times*, the piece sent a "vivid message" with its "cricket-like percussion effects, swirling wind choirs, frenetic brass episodes with intervening pools of quiet." David Buendler in the Pasadena *Star-News* called the work "an episodic study in tension and turbulent emotion."[64]

Earlier that year, JoAnn Falletta, conductor at the time of the Denver Chamber Orchestra, had issued a call for scores for a "Celebrate China" concert. Chen Yi submitted the chamber orchestra version of *Duo Ye*, which Falletta selected. Chen flew to Denver but had no time to introduce herself to the conductor before arriving during the dress rehearsal. She seated herself quietly in the audience. At the close of the rehearsal, Falletta addressed the orchestra: "The composer is supposed to be here, but I guess he has not arrived yet." Chen Yi jumped up exclaiming, "I'm here! I'm here!" Falletta's embarrassment over the gender assumption was short-lived: the two artists became fast friends and continue today to laugh at this encounter in what would become one of the most productive collaborations in both of their careers.[65]

The Chinese community in New York provided a welcome grounding for the new immigrants. Particularly important to Chen and Zhou was Music From China (MFC), a quintet founded in 1984 as a breakaway from a much larger Chinese Music Ensemble.[66] Whereas the large group played only traditional works, the new quintet welcomed contemporary compositions as well. MFC founders included Herman Wong on *dizi* (transverse bamboo flute); a husband-wife team, Tienjou and Aiyan Wang on erhu and pipa; Huokui Chen on dulcimer, saxophone, and *guan* (a double reed instrument); and George Lee, percussion. After Chen Yi joined the group, she performed on various Chinese instruments, including erhu, *sheng* (a free-reed mouth organ), *liuqin* (a four-stringed mandolin with a pear-shaped body), and percussion. The energetic administrator was Susan Cheng, an amateur musician from Hong Kong who worked at the time in a biology lab at Rockefeller University.

MFC first commissioned a piece from Zhou Long. After Chen came to New York, the group asked her for compositions as well, and she became one of their most active collaborators. The quintet performed in schools, conducted residencies at universities, and presented concerts at Weill Recital Hall and Merkin Hall for an eclectic audience consisting of members of the Chinese community interested in their traditional fare and highly trained composers intrigued by the cultural fusion of the new works. Among the projects Chen Yi spearheaded was a composer competition and an eponymously named quarterly bilingual newsletter published for nine years and circulated both in the United States and China. The competition offered particularly valuable opportunities for young Chinese composers who had limited opportunities to have their works performed. In the early years there were as many as thirty submissions, vetted by Chen, Zhou, and the performers. Each year, beginning in 1992, MFC presented the winning composition in a Premiere Works Concert along with pieces by others.[67] Despite their limited resources, Cheng and Chen invested their own funds in MFC projects: Cheng paid for the awards in the composition contest; Chen contributed her time voluntarily, and she occasionally used her own funds for the newsletter.

In 1989 Chen and Zhou visited Taiwan—the first mainland Chinese composers to do so. The following year Chou Wen-chung organized a Pacific Music Festival Composers Conference in Sapporo, Japan. He had envisioned it for mainland China, but the Tiananmen revolt in 1989 forced relocation. Chen thus traveled to Asia twice, but without visiting her parents. The Japan festival was particularly influential for her. She attended concerts conducted by Leonard Bernstein, Michael Tilson Thomas, and Marin Alsop, and met composers José Maceda, Isang Yun, Joji Yuasa, and many others.

Unfortunately in 1990 Chen Ernan died after a heart attack. Chen Yi had spoken to her father often by phone from New York (at $7 for the first minute!) but had not seen him since she left China four years earlier. In great pain, she rushed home for his funeral. A melody of grief came to her mind, which she later wove into her Symphony No. 2 (1993). Meanwhile, in 1989 Chen traveled to Poland as one of twenty composers featured in a series of films sponsored by the International Society for Contemporary Music. Each film paired an emerging composer with an established one. Chen Yi's partner was Luciano Berio. The film features interviews, evaluations of her work, and performances by members of Muzyka Centrum, Krakow, including excerpts from her woodwind quintet, *As in a Dream* (violin, cello, and voice), and the sextet *Near Distance*. Chen Yi joined the Polish musicians, playing the violin in *Near Distance* and singing the vocal part in *As in a Dream*, which draws on her Beijing opera experiences. Berio, reflecting on her singing her own music, called her a "Chinese troubadour."[68]

The Women's Philharmonic, San Francisco (1993–96)

After JoAnn Falletta performed Chen's *Duo Ye* with the Denver Chamber Orchestra, she conducted the full-orchestra version (*Duo Ye No. 2*) four more times in the next few years: with the Women's Philharmonic in 1990 and 1992, the Cabrillo Music Festival in 1991, and the Long Beach Symphony in 1993.[69] Although the Women's Philharmonic was based in San Francisco, its January 1992 performance took place at the Kennedy Center in Washington, DC, to celebrate the twenty-fifth anniversary of the National Organization for Women.[70]

That same year the Philharmonic, which Falletta conducted from 1986 to 1996,[71] successfully applied to the Meet The Composer New Residencies Program to support a resident composer. The orchestra's management first offered the position to Augusta Reed Thomas, but she declined after accepting a job at Eastman. The Philharmonic then turned to Chen Yi, who had, in the meantime, completed her doctorate and obtained her green card (under the sponsorship of the Music From China ensemble).

The Meet The Composer grant provided $30,000/year for three years, assuming a 75 percent appointment. To fulfill program requirements of bringing classical music to an extended community, the Women's Philharmonic teamed up with two other organizations: the Aptos Creative Arts Program (led by Joan Murray), which provided artistic enhancements for middle school children, and the male vocal ensemble Chanticleer (founded by Louis Botto and directed by Joseph Jennings). Chen Yi sent Chanticleer a recording of *Three Poems from the Song Dynasty* (1985) and a lasting partnership was born.

Chen's contract mandated that she compose one new work for each ensemble during her three-year appointment; but she wrote far more. The Women's Philharmonic had already commissioned her Symphony No. 2 through a Ford Foundation program for women composers. Chen also wrote *Ge Xu* (*Antiphony*) for the orchestra, which premiered it in 1995. For Chanticleer's Singing in the Schools program, Chen arranged a group of ten Chinese folk songs. And

Biography and Framework

to culminate the residency, she composed the thirty-six-minute *Chinese Myths Cantata* (discussed at length in Chapter 6), which included both groups as well as several Chinese instruments: erhu, pipa, zheng (a twenty-one-string zither), and yangqin (a dulcimer). The cantata's premiere took place during a three-day festival (June 14–16, 1996) in a multimedia production that included the Lily Cai Chinese Dance Company. This extravaganza also featured performances of *Duo Ye No. 2*, *Ge Xu*, the folk song settings written for Chanticleer, a four-movement a cappella work entitled *Tang Poems*, and Symphony No 2.

For Murray's school program, Chen taught composition and Chinese folk songs. She brought the entire school choir to the Chinese Cultural Center for a public concert, and a string quintet from the Women's Philharmonic to Chanticleer's Singing in the Schools program. "It is hard to tell whether Chen Yi is the den mother or composer-in-residence," wrote Mamie Huey in June 1996. "She gives boxes of candy and tea to her peers, helps with costumes, and coaches musicians." Murray compared Chen to the Pied Piper. "When immigrant Chinese parents did not allow their children to go to early morning orchestra practice, Chen Yi was on the phone convincing them."[72] She spoke to the parents of San Francisco's large Chinese American community in Cantonese and Mandarin. By teaching the children her arrangements of Chinese folk songs, she linked generations together and bolstered legitimacy for the Chinese diasporic culture.

The Philharmonic also ran a Women Composers Resource Center, which collected and evaluated scores and made recommendations to orchestras. When funding for the center's director dried up, Chen voluntarily assumed the administrative tasks. She says that this center first made her cognizant of discrimination against female composers.

In 1995 Chen returned to mainland China for a tour by the Stanford University Orchestra under the leadership of J. Karla Lemon.[73] Chen was welcomed as a hero who had made her mark on the US musical landscape. She gave lectures at CCOM, and Beijing Radio interviewed her and Lemon for a two-hour broadcast introducing orchestral music by women composers from around the world.

Facing the end of her San Francisco residency, Chen applied for, and received, a Guggenheim Fellowship. It was one of many honors she had begun to accrue since completing her degree. In 1994, for example, she won an NEA Composer Fellowship, the Lili Boulanger Award from the Women Composers Resource Center, and awards or commissions from Meet The Composer, the Rockefeller Foundation, and the Aaron Copland Fund for Music. In 1995 she was a guest composer with Chorus America in Seattle, and grants from the Rockefeller Foundation, the San Francisco Art Commission, and the NEA helped fund the *Chinese Myths Cantata*. In the same year, a Lilly Foundation Grant provided Bradley University with funds for a residency and a commission for *Tang Poems Cantata* (an orchestration of the a cappella work she had written for Chanticleer). The aim of Bradley University's program was to enhance the campus climate for ethnic minorities. Administrators of the grant chose Chen because of her reputation for combining "Chinese and American traditions."[74] Two weeks before the cantata's premiere by the student orchestra and chorus on April 27, 1995, the local Peoria Symphony also programmed *Duo Ye No. 2*; more than two thousand people attended. The university's performance attracted a standing-room-only crowd in the five-hundred-seat theater.

At the Peabody Conservatory (1996–98)

Just as she was reveling in the Guggenheim award, Chen Yi received another pleasant piece of news: an appointment to the faculty of the Peabody Conservatory. The orchestra conductor, Hajime Teri Murai, knew Chen's work from her Columbia years. He had brought her as a guest in 1992 when he programmed *Duo Ye*. At first Chen thought she would need to decline the fellowship, but she soon discovered that the Guggenheim Foundation would allow her to divide the award into two years and work at it irregularly.

During her two years at Peabody, Chen continued to amass honors. In 1996 the Center for Women in Music at NYU's School of Education awarded her the Elizabeth and Michel Sorel medal, a $5,000 prize "for excellence in composition." Judges included composers Robert Beaser and John Corigliano.[75] In the same year, Chen won a Goddard Lieberson Fellowship from American Academy of Arts and Letters and contributed a work to a Lincoln Center concert honoring Yehudi Menuhin on his eightieth birthday. In 1997 she received a $50,000 Herb Alpert award from the California Institute of the Arts (CalArts); was offered commissions from the Stuttgart Chamber Orchestra, the New Heritage Music Foundation, and the Singapore Symphony; and served as a visiting composer, along with Harvey Sollberger, Richard Festinger, and Olly Wilson, at a ten-day summer composition conference at California State University, Long Beach. The conference included professional performers and twelve invited advanced student composers. That fall Chen (and other outstanding artists and scientists) dined at the State Department with Vice President Al Gore and China's President Jiang Zemin, who visited the United States from October 27 to November 3. On the heels of this visit, Hu Yongyan, conductor of the

PHOTO 11. Chen Yi with US Vice President Al Gore and Chinese President Jiang Zemin, 1997. Photo by Zhou Long; used by permission.

Duluth-Superior Symphony, presented a concert entitled "Mao to Mozart," taking its title from the 1979 film about Isaac Stern's residency in China after Mao's death. The concert featured works by Chinese musicians "who emerged in the wake of the Cultural Revolution." Hu drew on compositions by three of his CCOM classmates: Tan Dun, Qu Xiaosong, and Chen Yi. Chen's new flute concerto, *The Golden Flute* garnered enthusiastic reviews.[76]

Although the State Department luncheon was perhaps the most prestigious of these honors, the Alpert Award from CalArts had the greatest impact on Chen's career. Each year, beginning in 1994, the Alpert Foundation has granted the college five awards of $50,000 given to early- to mid-career professionals in dance, film/video, music, theater, and the visual arts. The intensive selection process begins with fifty anonymous nominators (ten in each of the five categories). Nominees then submit work samples and written materials that are evaluated by fifteen panelists. The five recipients may use the award in any way they wish. Their only obligation is to participate in a residency at the college. Steven D. Lavine, president of CalArts, wrote that Herb and Lani Alpert wanted to pass on their own good fortune by supporting artists at a stage when it would be most beneficial.... As individuals with deep social commitments themselves, Herb and Lani also hoped to find a way to identify artists who were sensitive to the artist's potential contribution to society.[77]

Chen Yi was incredibly productive during her Peabody years. In addition to the flute concerto cited earlier, she composed three chamber works (*Qi* for flute, cello, percussion, and piano; *Sound of the Five* for cello and string quartet; and *Feng* for woodwind quintet); one choral work ("Spring Dreams"); and no fewer than five orchestral works. The last group includes her *Fiddle Suite* for huqin accompanied by string quartet, string orchestra, or Chinese orchestra (funded by the Fromm Music Foundation); the Percussion Concerto (written for Evelyn Glennie and the Singapore Symphony); *Momentum* (dedicated to the Peabody Symphony Orchestra); *Eleanor's Gift* for cello and orchestra (honoring Eleanor Roosevelt's efforts on behalf of the United Nations' Universal Declaration of Human Rights, 1948); and *Romance and Dance* for string orchestra and two violins.

As satisfying as Peabody's artistic quality was, the institution did not grant faculty members tenure, but rather made appointments year-by-year. Thus, when Chen was offered a tenured endowed professorship at the University of Missouri, she moved to Kansas City.

To the Present

In 1998 the University of Missouri–Kansas City (UMKC) Conservatory of Music and Dance appointed Chen Yi as the Lorena Searcy Cravens/Millsap/Missouri Endowed Distinguished Professor of Composition, a position she retains to the present day. Under Dean Terry Applebaum the conservatory obtained funding for five endowed professorships: in cello, piano, choral conducting, jazz, and composition. James Mobberley, professor of composition, who had met Chen through the Meet The Composer New Residencies Program, invited her to apply. She told us modestly that she was not the university's first choice: several others apparently declined. The arrangement, however, has worked excellently both for Chen and for UMKC. With the hard work of Chen and her colleagues, the composition program has mushroomed, at present boasting fifty to sixty students from undergraduates through the doctoral level.

Chen's life after her move to Kansas City has become increasingly busy and filled with honors, awards, commissions, and performances. To detail them all would take up most of the rest of this short book. We therefore offer just a brief list of the most important events.

1999	Chen receives Eddie Medora King Composition Prize from the University of Texas at Austin with a residency there.
1999	Chen and Zhou become US citizens.
2000, December	Chen receives the Charles Ives Living award from the American Academy of Arts and Letters, which provided $75,000/year for three years. Ezra Laderman, chair of the selection committee (which included Gunther Schuller, Francis Thorne, Joan Tower, and Olly Wilson), commented at the award ceremony: "Chen Yi's music has passion, control, color, originality, and elasticity. She interweaves East and West cultures into a seamless fabric of constant tension. The music is all-embracing, moving effortlessly from a taut chromatic language to a gentle pentatonic modality, to a vibrant, exuberant use of non-pitched and pitched percussion."[78] The conditions of the award mandated that Chen resign all salaried employment for three years. She therefore took a leave from UMKC from July 2001 to June 2004. Zhou Long replaced her and continues to teach there today alongside her.
2001, March	The China National Symphony and Chorus in Beijing present an entire evening of Chen's works, including the *Chinese Myths Cantata*, *KC Capriccio*, *The Golden Flute*, and Symphony No. 2.[79]
2001, May	Premiere of Chen's trio *Ning* for violin, cello, and pipa, by Young-Nam Kim, Yo-Yo Ma, and Wu Man. The Chamber Music Society of Minnesota brought together composers from China, Japan, Korea, and the United States in the spirit of political reconciliation. *Ning* (discussed in Chapter 4), commemorates the 1937 Nanjing massacre by Japanese forces—sometimes called the Asian Holocaust.
2002	Chen wins the Stoeger Prize from the Chamber Music Society of Lincoln Center. The $25,000 award honors a composer who has made significant contributions to the chamber music literature over the previous two years.

2003, August	Percussionist Evelyn Glennie appears at the renowned BBC Proms in Royal Albert Hall, London, to play the European premiere of Chen's Percussion Concerto.
2004, March	Premiere of Chen's *Ballad, Dance, and Fantasy* for cello and orchestra with Yo-Yo Ma and the Pacific Symphony, followed in the same month by the premiere of her Symphony No. 3 by the Seattle Symphony, which commissioned the work. One reviewer called the symphony simply "a dazzler."[80]
2004	Chen is the featured composer at Carnegie Hall's Making Music program in a concert of her chamber works.
2004	Chen receives the Roche Commission to compose the symphonic work, *Si Ji*, premiered in 2005 by the Cleveland Orchestra at the Lucerne Festival and then repeated at Severance Hall in Cleveland and Carnegie Hall in New York.[81] (Percussion Concerto, *Ballad, Dance, and Fantasy*, Symphony No. 3, and *Si Ji* are all discussed in Chapter 5.)
2005	Chen is elected to membership in the American Academy of Arts and Sciences.
2005, October	Premiere of Chen's *Spring in Dresden* for violin and orchestra by Mira Wang and Staatskapelle Dresden, commissioned by Friends of Dresden Music Foundation as an American commemoration of the reconstruction of the Dresden Frauenkirche.
2006	Chen receives the prestigious Cheung Kong Scholar Visiting Professorship at CCOM in Beijing. The award, named after a Hong Kong donor, provides funding from the China Education Ministry for universities to hire visiting faculty. Chen's residency, involving her for two months per year for three years, was the first award in the humanities; a superb review led to an extension for two additional years. As part of the CCOM program, Chen helped to establish the Beijing International Composition Workshop, an ongoing activity in which composers write for both Chinese and Western instruments, and she helped Ye Xiaogang in enriching the Beijing Modern Music Festival.

2006	*Si Ji*, the Roche Commissions work, is selected as a finalist for the Pulitzer Prize.
2007	Chen is honored as the Special Guest Composer at the 28th New Music & Art Festival, hosted by the MidAmerican Center for Contemporary Music at Bowling Green State University, OH.
2008	The China National Symphony Orchestra presents a full evening of Chen's orchestral works as a featured event for the 2008 Beijing Olympics.
2008	The BBC commissions the orchestral work *Olympic Fire* (later renamed *Rhyme of Fire*), which the Royal Philharmonic premiered at the BBC Proms on the opening day of the Beijing Olympics, conducted by Leonard Slatkin.
2009	Chen fulfills a residency with the St. Paul Chamber Orchestra, sponsored by Music Alive (and administered by the League of American Orchestras). As part of this residency, she composed *Prelude and Fugue*.
2009	*From the Path of Beauty*, Chen's seven-movement suite for string quartet and SATB chorus (written for Chanticleer and the Shanghai Quartet and discussed in Chapter 6), is performed in tours throughout the United States and also presented in Shanghai and Beijing. Chen composed the piece to fulfill nearly simultaneous requests from the two ensembles. The work was part of the American Masterpieces in Chamber Music initiative of the National Endowment for the Arts.
2009	Chen Yi's chamber music album, *Sound of the Five* (Third Angle New Music Ensemble, New World Records) is named one of the top ten CDs of NPR's Best Classical Recordings of 2009.
2010	Chen is Keynote Speaker at the 29th International Society of Music Education World Conference in Beijing.
2011	Zhou Long wins the Pulitzer Prize for his opera *Madame White Snake*.
2011	Chen is honored as the Roger D. Moore Distinguished Visitor in Composition at the University of Toronto, with eighteen works performed in six concerts.

2012	Chen's mother Du Dianqin dies.
2012	*Symphony Humen 1839* by Chen and Zhou, commissioned and premiered by Guangzhou Symphony wins the first prize at the China National Composition Competition.
2012	Chen and Zhou are appointed Distinguished Visiting Professors at the Tianjin Conservatory. Originally a three-year commitment, the appointment was extended until July 2017.
2013	Chen is Co-Conference Director of the China National Composition and Composition Education Symposium, Tianjin Conservatory of Music.
2014	Chen and Zhou Symphonic Works Concert performed by the Shanghai Philharmonic Orchestra at the Shanghai Spring International Music Festival.
2015	Chen is featured guest composer at the Eighth Shanghai Conservatory Contemporary Music Week.
2015	Chen is Guest Composer at the Composition Symposium "From China to America: A Musical Journey" at the New York Historical Society with WQXR broadcast.
2017	Chen Yi Portrait Concert performed by Curtis 20/21 Contemporary Music Ensemble presented by Columbia University at the Miller Concert Hall in New York and at the Curtis Institute of Music in Philadelphia.
2018	Chen and Zhou are named Honorary Members of the Society for American Music.
2018	Chen and Zhou become members of the Advisory Committee at the Chou Wen-chung Music Research Center at the Xinghai Conservatory of Music in Guangzhou, China.
2019	Two concerts entitled Legacy from the East: The Choral Music of Chen Yi and Zhou Long performed by UMKC Choirs, Wind Symphony, String Quartet, soloists, and Conservatory Dancers at the ACDA National Conference in Kansas City.
2019	Chen is elected to membership in the American Academy of Arts and Letters.

This list gives only a hint of Chen's frenetic schedule. To get a bit of insight into the activities of this always-on-the-go artist, we conclude with a recounting of her activities in the summer of 2015, when we asked her to find time for our first interviews. She wrote that she was flying to China May 19 for the Tianjin Conservatory residency, then to Guangxi for China-ASEAN New Music Week, followed in mid-June by a lecture and master class at the South China Technology University School of the Arts in Guangzhou and a lecture at the China National Research Institute of the Arts in Beijing. Next came a residency with the Qingdao Symphony the last week in June followed by the Bowdoin Music Festival in Maine the second week of July. Then she flew to Hong Kong to participate in a dissertation defense and judge the Hong Kong International Youth Choral Competition before teaching at CCOM's Composition Workshop. After that came a visit to Singapore in early August to judge an international composition contest. The end of August was "peaceful," she wrote, but then she was heading back to China for the Shanghai Contemporary Music Week where she was the featured composer. In October and November, she returned again to Asia to judge composition contests at the Sichuan Conservatory and for the Singapore International Chinese Orchestra. She squeezed us in during that "peaceful" interlude in late August and seemed neither tired nor jet-lagged!

CHAPTER 3

Compositional Processes

Chen Yi's Bicultural Affinities

Chen Yi's overriding compositional philosophy can be summarized as the balance of head and heart. "I always consider feelings," she says. "If I lose my passion and emotion, the music dies"; but "if the music only has passion [and not enough structure] to be analyzed, it is music you only want to hear once."[1] Emotion and logic, sentiment and intellect, inspiration and deliberation: Chen seeks an equilibrium. She carries out this philosophy in her compositional process, which begins with a general concept, often inspired by poetry, painting, calligraphy, or narrative. She frequently writes down a set of adjectives based on these broad impressions and then "grabs the image musically"[2] and jots down a messy page or two of musical ideas. At that point the brain overtakes the heart and serious planning controls the next stage of the process: dividing the work's overall length (determined by the specifications of the commission) into logical sections with tempo and texture changes. Chen generally maps out the number of measures in the first few sections, and, after composing the material for them, borrows from earlier parts of the piece to create a coherent and logical overall framework. The initial planning stage can be time consuming, but once she begins the detailed compositional process, she works quickly: two weeks for her first symphony, a month for the second, a month-and-a-half for the orchestral piece, *Momentum*, to cite a few examples. She engages in most of the process away from a piano, singing the instrumental lines and hearing the music in her head. Her skill in this process stems from her early years at CCOM, not only because pianos were in short supply but also because Professor Su Xia, chair of the Composition Department, prohibited their use during exams in order to teach young composers to hear the music silently.

Despite Chen's early training exclusively on Western instruments, almost all of her music draws to some degree on her Chinese heritage. "That is my native tongue," she reminds her audiences. Folk music, Beijing opera, Chinese speech patterns, and the sounds of Chinese instruments provide some stimulus in nearly all of her works, even those exclusively for Western instrumental ensembles. Chen only rarely combines instruments from China and the West—although there are notable pieces that do, such as *Song in Winter*; *Chinese Fables*; *Ning*; Septet; and the *Chinese Myths Cantata* (see the Works List for instrumentation). Most of Chen's music calls exclusively for standard Western instruments; yet almost all of these works reflect the inspiration of Chinese musical culture. Among the most obvious manifestations of this influence are pentatonic modes; sliding tones; and single, double, and triple grace notes (which mimic vocal and instrumental inflections in Chinese speech and Beijing opera). These traits appear in almost every score. At the same time, focusing on such obvious surface features, which have long typecast Chinese music, carries a serious risk: that of perpetuating a reductionist exoticism by situating Chen's "Chineseness" in formulaic well-worn clichés. In fact, for Chen, Chinese compositional practices function not only on the surface, but also on a deeper level, allowing her to forge a unique identity that transcends the most obvious aural manifestations of hybridity. As we will show in this chapter, influences from Chinese music have guided both the background and the surface of Chen's music and frequently function as guides for large-scale structural planning, providing a scaffolding upon which she can unfold melodic and textural details.

At the same time, Chen's training in Euro-American compositional practices also figures strongly in her compositional language. In some sense, Chen can't help fusing Western and Chinese influences: musically, she was raised biculturally, and the blending of traditions is the essence of her artistic language. In this chapter we attempt to tease apart the distinctive strands forming the cultural connectivity characteristic of Chen's works by identifying pervasive compositional processes, both Chinese and Western, in her music. The interconnectivity is so ubiquitous—and embedded in her aesthetic principles—that untwining the rope into distinctive strands is difficult; yet doing so reveals her sources and methods.

For Chen, cultural blending fulfills both artistic and ethical goals: she sees her role as a composer to reach out to audiences from divergent cultures through the nonverbal medium of sound and to forge international connections by highlighting the beauties in disparate traditions. This objective draws on long-held principles from Chinese philosophy regarding the function of art in society. Traditionally the Chinese composer transcended aural constraints: "You are a calligrapher," Chen says, "you are a painter, you are a musician, you are a poet..., you dance." As Chen's Columbia mentor Chou Wen-chung emphasized, by citing the model of the wenren, the traditional Chinese artist connected the senses, allowed sounds to suggest parallels in nature, and felt an obligation to use his/her talents to pay back the debt owed to society. "I don't think one should live for oneself," says Chen. "I got [an] education, I got the love of the word from the society. Now I must give it back."

In this sense, the Chinese historically did not recognize abstract music—a concept antithetical to a vision of music that embraces influences outside of sound. Chinese instrumental works traditionally bear expressive titles. In fact, during the Cultural Revolution, a major thrust of anti-Western musical propaganda was a vigorous campaign against "music without titles."[3] Chen upholds this philosophy both in her search for extra-musical stimuli at the start of her compositional process and in her overarching use of descriptive titles for instrumental compositions. Rarely do her works bear generic labels such as String Quartet No. 1. Her use of titles, however, does not imply that Chen's music is programmatic. The titles simply suggest her inspiration, much as a poem might evoke sound images. Listeners are welcome to envision other, equally valid, metaphors.

Variation Techniques, Pentatonicism, Tone Rows, and Ostinati

Chen's indebtedness to Chinese compositional practices also manifests itself in other concrete ways, for instance in her devotion to **variation techniques**. As we have seen, her first forays into composing involved creating variations on revolutionary tunes during her years in Shimen: the farmers loved her violin renditions of these melodies, to which she added ornaments and inserted virtuosic interludes between stanzas, particularly referencing Paganini's Capriccio No. 24 in A Minor.

Thereafter, variation became an essential device in Chen's compositional toolbox. She identifies two procedures that appear frequently in her works, both derived from traditional Chinese music: "flowery variation" (*jiahua*)—

EXAMPLE 3.1. Illustration of "flowery variation" in *The Golden Flute* concerto (1997)

A. The opening phrase of the tune *Baban*, shown at the pitch level in which it appears at the start of the concerto. (Chen learned the tune from an article by Du Yaxiong, where it appeared in cipher notation and therefore not on a fixed pitch.) See Example 3.14 for the entire tune.

B. Solo flute part, mm. 9–10: first quotation of the Baban theme (A–D–G–F), with "flowery" ornamentation by Chen. She uses this four-note motive systematically throughout the concerto, occasionally adding the next three pitches (C–D–F).

transforming a tune through improvised techniques; and "form variation"—expanding the source material to create large-scale structures. We explore form variation later in this chapter in our discussion of the Piano Concerto (1992), for which the folk tune Baban provided a delimiting scaffold. A striking example of flowery variation is *The Golden Flute* (1997), in which the opening notes of this same tune—manipulated by transposition, imitation, rhythmic augmentation, contrapuntal contrasts, and melodic decoration—saturate the entire eighteen-minute concerto. Example 3.1 shows flowery variation of the tune's opening four pitches (A–D–G–F). Occasionally Chen interpolates an extra pitch within the motive or expands her quotation to include the tune's next three pitches (C–D–F). The entire flute concerto constitutes a tour de force in the exploration of this single germinal cell drawn from an ancient Chinese source. Chen traces the inspiration for this type of flowery variation process to her studies of folk music at CCOM but emphasizes that in traditional practice variations typically engage the entire melody, whereas she uses small fragments so that the melody will not stand out as "too obvious."[4]

Another approach appears in the third movement of the *Fiddle Suite*, where Chen quotes the famous *qupai* (fixed tune) "Ye Shen Chen" ("The Night Deepens"), the Sword Dance from the traditional Beijing opera *Ba wang bie ji* (*Farewell, My Concubine*). After introducing the eight-measure melody intact, Chen divides it into four submotives, each of which she treats independently, subjecting it to augmentation, contrapuntal treatment, fragmentation, and ornamentation.

FIGURE 3.1. Chinese modes

gong 1 2 3 5 6

shang 2 3 5 6 1

jue 3 5 6 1 2

zhi 5 6 1 2 3

yu 6 1 2 3 5

A. Basic modal forms

mode	pitches in *Chinese Poems*						interval pattern				
gong	D	E	F♯	A	B	(D)	M2	M2	m3	M2	m3
shang	D	E	G	A	C	(D)	M2	m3	M2	m3	M2
jue	D	F	G	B♭	C	(D)	m3	M2	m3	M2	M2
zhi	D	E	G	A	B	(D)	M2	m3	M2	M2	m3
yu	D	F	G	A	C	(D)	m3	M2	M2	m3	M2

B. Modes assuming a fixed starting pitch of D (as in Chen Yi's *Chinese Poems*)

Pentatonicism, an integral feature of Chinese music, characterizes much of the motivic material in Chen Yi's works. Chinese modal theory postulates five modes—gong, shang, jue, zhi, and yu—all anhemitonic (without semitones), distinguished by different arrangements of major seconds and minor thirds (Figure 3.1a). (Other modal structures, including non-pentatonic modes, appear in some regional folk musics, as we will see.) Figure 3.1b shows the same modes starting on a fixed pitch, along with their characteristic interval patterns. The first movement of the choral work *Chinese Poems* (1999) features all five modes exposed in a continuous linear fashion, prompted by the text, which describes climbing a tower (Example 3.2).[5] This scalar presentation of the modes recurs twice more in the movement separated by contrasting sections, thus defining a type of rondo form.

Chen Yi also tends to introduce modal shifts that create complex interactions of pentatonic scales, thereby enhancing the harmonic richness of her compositions. A new accidental or a new pitch can effect a change in mode,

Compositional Processes

EXAMPLE 3.2. *Chinese Poems* for treble chorus (1999), mvt. 1 ("Up the Crane Tower"), showing the use of all five traditional pentatonic modes starting on D

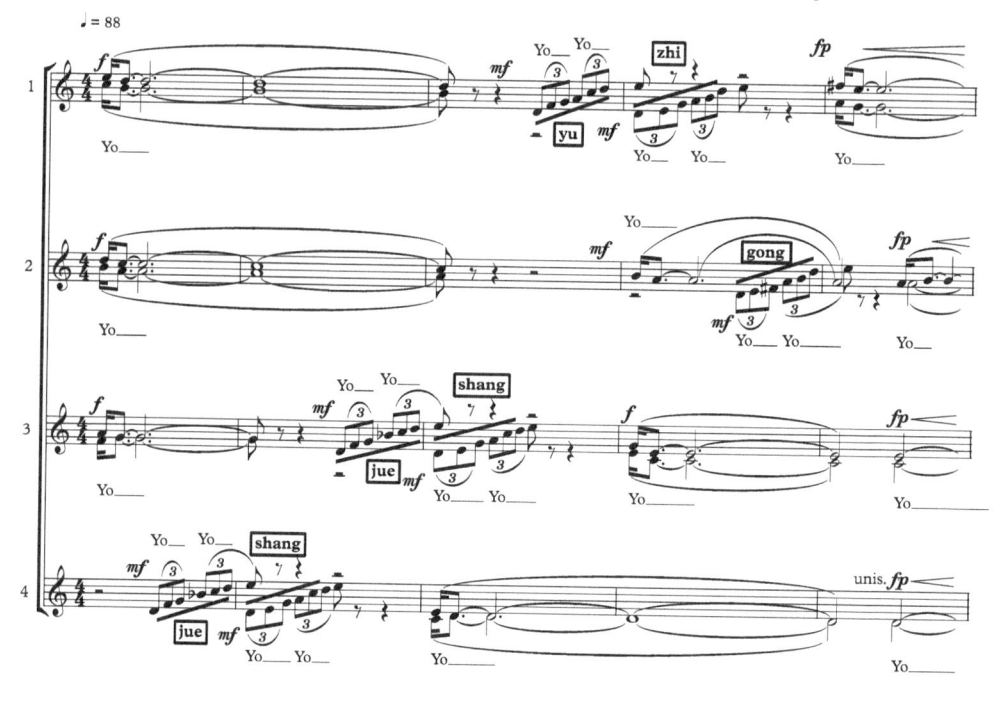

with the transition smoothed through common tones, as shown in the choral work *Landscape* (Example 3.3).

Another pervasive Chinese influence involves **ostinato** accompanimental figurations, which Chen first used in *Variations on Awariguli*, a piano piece composed during her initial year at CCOM. She not only found the technique effective and beautiful but was also struck by its connection to Beijing opera, where ostinato patterns sometimes appear as part of the background music accompanying dialogue or movement sections on the stage.[6] Chen at times employs ostinati to create juxtapositions of Euro-American and Chinese compositional practices—a musical syncretism that appears as early as *Duo Ye*, the award-winning piano work she composed in 1984. The middle section of the piece contains an ostinato in the left hand that includes all twelve chromatic pitches, against which Chen set a theme referencing Chinese mountain songs (Example 3.4).

Chen's early works often feature **twelve-tone rows** used as ostinati: for example in the Woodwind Quintet (1987), Symphony No. 2 (1993), and the

EXAMPLE 3.3. *Landscape* (chorus, 2003), mm. 14–17, soprano part, demonstrating modal shifting. (Text—vocables—not shown.) Note: the printed score contains an error: the eleventh note in m. 15 is printed as E rather than F.

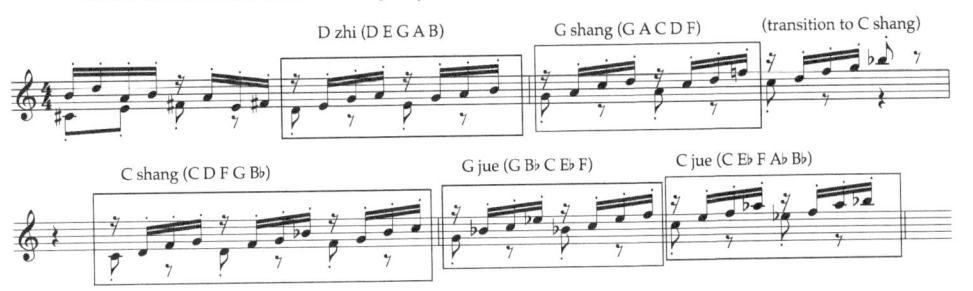

EXAMPLE 3.4. *Duo Ye* (original piano version, 1984), mm. 74–77. The ostinato in the left hand includes all twelve chromatic pitches. The right hand plays a theme in the style of a Chinese mountain song.

Percussion Concerto (1998).[7] Other pieces written during the late 1980s and 1990s contain tone rows that are *not* used as ostinati: for instance *Near Distance* (1988), *Sparkle* (1992), the Piano Concerto (1992), *Song in Winter* (1993), and *Ba Ban* (1999).

In later pieces Chen tended to use **ostinati** containing fewer than twelve pitches, but she continued to be attracted to systematic precompositional processes for manipulating them, and she often employed them in cross-cultural mixtures. The quartet *Qi* (flute, cello, piano, and percussion, 1997), includes an ostinato that makes use of a telescoping rhythmic pattern characteristic of

Compositional Processes

the music played by Chinese *shifan luogu* ensembles (a type of folk percussion band, sometimes including wind instruments as well). This ostinato (beginning in m. 25) consists of a quintuplet group repeated thirteen times; then eleven times; then nine, seven, five, three times; and finally only once. Chen marks the end of each repetition pattern by inserting a *septuplet* that disrupts the established rhythm. These septuplet interruptions represent Chen's personal interpretation of a folk practice in which the ending notes of an ostinato pattern are marked by tutti interjections.[8] Furthermore, by transposing each quintuplet group to a different pitch level, Chen references the Baban tune shown earlier in Example 3.1a, but a fourth lower (E–A–D–C–G–A–C). *Qi*'s ostinato pattern begins with a dyad whose upper notes are consecutively E (thirteen times)—A (eleven times)—D (nine times)—C (seven times)—and G (five times). Then it continues with Baban's fifth and sixth notes sounding as the *lower* dyad note: on G (three times) and A (one time). The last note of Baban's first phrase (C) appears in the cello, and ushers in a repeat of the 13–11–9–7–5–3–1 pattern. Example 3.5a shows the end of the first ostinato section, illustrating the repetitions of the quintuplet figure starting on G and A, the interrupting septuplets, and the final arrival on C. Note as well the polyrhythms (5 against 6, 7 against 6), which characterize much of Chen's music.

The second movement of the woodwind quintet *Feng* (1999) includes a rhythmically migrating ostinato, another technique Chen enjoys. As Example 3.5b shows, the movement begins with a nine-note melodic line (B–F–C♯–D–F♯–G♯–G–D–E) divided between bassoon and horn. This figure repeats eight times, each time creeping forward by an eighth note. The A♯, added at the beginning of the pattern in the bassoon starting in measure 2, facilitates ensemble coordination, a "trick" Chen first used in the "Wild Grass" movement of *Tang Poems* (1995).[9] After rising an octave at the fifth repetition, *Feng*'s ostinato recurs three more times, still migrating forward by eighth notes, but now transposed up a fourth and moving from the lowest instruments to the highest. Meanwhile the other instruments interject exclamatory melodic lines. The ostinato figure defines the movement's A B A' B' A" form. It disintegrates in the contrasting lyrical B section but recurs whenever the A material returns.

Chen's interest in ostinati comprises a constant in her compositional language, appearing even in her most recent works. Example 3.6a shows a sophisticated passage with three layered ostinati that she used in *Dragon Rhyme* (wind ensemble, 2010) and *Blue, Blue Sky* (orchestra, 2012). The glockenspiel plays a nine-note figure in groups of sextuplets (crossing the beat); but in four of those repetitions, one note is replaced by a rest. Simultaneously the harp plays a polyrhythm of four against six comprising two simpler ostinati, one of six notes and

EXAMPLE 3.5. Ostinato usage

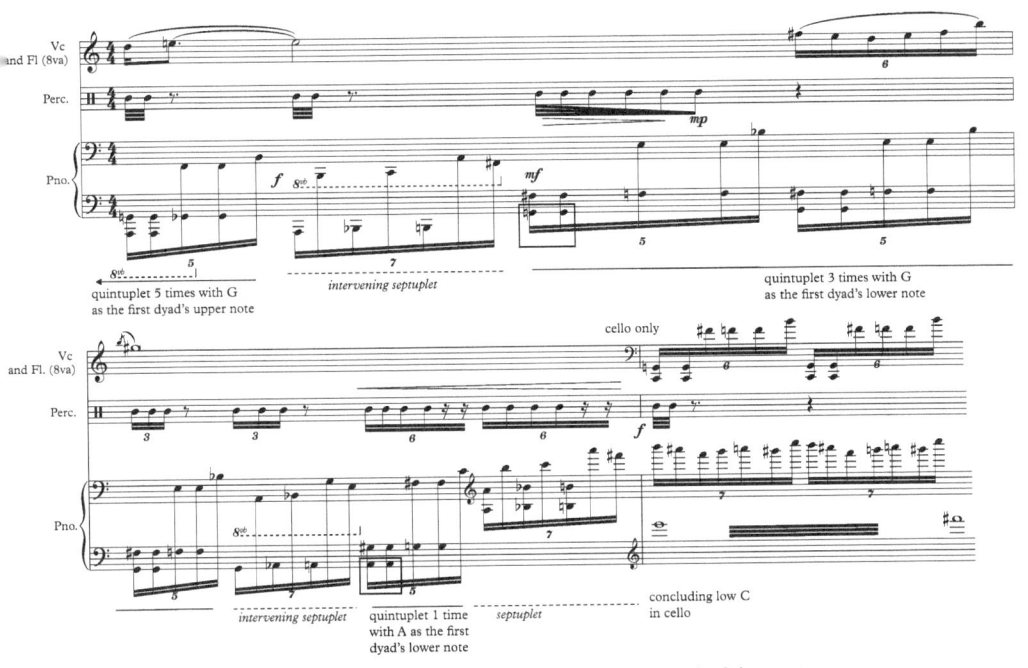

A. *Qi* (flute, cello, piano, percussion, 1997), mm. 37–39 (end of the ostinato section)

B. *Feng* (woodwind quintet, 1999), mvt. 2, beginning, bassoon and horn. A nine-note ostinato migrates forward by an eighth note. The A♯ beginning in m. 2 is added to facilitate ensemble coordination. Pattern transposed up an octave at the fifth repetition.

EXAMPLE 3.6. Layered ostinati in *Blue, Blue Sky* (orchestra, 2012)

A. Mm. 18–20, showing a triple ostinato figuration (also used in *Dragon Rhyme* for wind ensemble, 2010). A nine-note ostinato in the glockenspiel, with rests intermittently substituting for pitches, appears simultaneously with six- and two-note ostinati in the harp.

B. Mm. 25–28, showing a pentatonic motive from a xiongling folk tune, which occurs simultaneously with the ostinato. The mode bears resemblance to jue, but with the fourth pitch raised, resulting in a mode with a semitone.

the other of two. After eight repetitions of the glockenspiel motive and twelve repetitions of the six-note harp motive, the ends of the two patterns coincide (8x9 = 12x6). This entire pattern repeats five times, accompanying a flurry of ornamental figures in the woodwinds and a slow descending scalar motive in the trombone, referencing a *xiongling* folk tune (Example 3.6b; a xiongling is a Tibetan wooden fipple flute). Though pentatonic, the brass motive does not reflect one of the five modes described earlier. It is similar to the jue intervallic pattern but with the fourth note raised a half step to create a hemitonic mode. Reading from the lowest pitch upward: m3 M2 M3 m2 M2.

The Influence of Beijing Opera

Naturally Chen's musical encounters figure heavily in her compositional language. None is more vivid for her than her eight years leading the Guangzhou Beijing Opera troupe's orchestra, which inspired her to use specific opera tunes in both vocal and instrumental works and to mimic many of the genre's distinctive gestures. In a general sense, this experience taught Chen Yi the art of combining Western and Chinese instruments. The emphasis on unified instrumental forces in the model operas presented a compositional challenge: not only are the timbres of the instruments dissimilar, but even more importantly, the tuning systems are based on different principles. Chen's experiences in matching the pitches on her violin to those of the Chinese traditional instruments, and her early compositional experiences in creating overtures and interludes for the troupe's performances provided hands-on training that served her well in future years.[10]

More specifically, Chen learned the essence of the opera's recitation and aria styles. In the model operas, arias became fixed through the use of notation, but singers learned the recitation parts by rote. Nevertheless, Chen notated these recitation phrases with precise pitches for use in her own works—a practice, she says, that became one of her "major methods of composing melodies." Chen frequently references opera aria and recitation styles in both vocal and instrumental compositions. Examples 3.7a and b show typical examples: the recitation style in a cello passage from the quintet *Happy Rain on a Spring Night* (2004) and the aria style in the orchestral work *Momentum* (1998). For the second movement of the Percussion Concerto (1998) Chen calls on the soloist to declaim in operatic style a text by the eleventh-century poet Su Shi ("Prelude to Water Tune") while simultaneously playing the marimba, Japanese wood block, and a Beijing opera gong (Example 3.7c).[11]

EXAMPLE 3.7. Beijing opera influences in instrumental works

A. *Happy Rain on a Spring Night* (flute, clarinet, violin, cello, piano, 2004), mm. 65–70. Cello imitates the opera's recitation style.

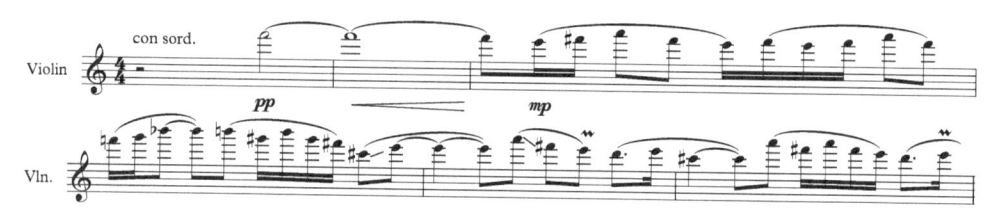

B. *Momentum* (orchestra, 1998), mm. 156–61. Violin imitates the opera's aria style.

C. *Percussion Concerto* (1998), mvt. 2, mm. 10–18. The percussionist declaims a poem by Su Shi (1037–1101) in operatic style, while also playing.

Another influence from Beijing opera is Chen's frequent use of the interval of a rising seventh (major or minor). The small, high-pitched jinghu, which plays a leading role in the opera's instrumental ensemble by following the vocalists in unison or heterophony, often performs a gesture of a rising *minor* seventh, which made a particularly strong impression on Chen Yi during her years with the Guangzhou opera troupe.[12] She generalized this gesture to upward leaping, simultaneous, or overlapping minor/major sevenths, as in the ostinato figure from *Qi* shown above in Example 3.5a. Similarly, the combination of a fast instrumental accompaniment and slow flexible singing typifies much of the operatic genre. An adaptation of that texture to a purely instrumental context can be seen in Example 3.6a and b from *Blue, Blue Sky*.

Chen's use of an opening section in free meter followed by a more rhythmically structured main section also reflects practices typical of Beijing opera. One example is the *Dunhuang Fantasy* for organ and wind ensemble (1999), which begins with a minute-long organ introduction featuring fantasia-like passages of thirty-second notes that create a sense of metrical freedom, along with clusters that evoke the sheng (a mouth-blown free-reed organ; Example 3.8a).[13] The section that follows (Example 3.8b) introduces repeated note percussion figures that reference Beijing opera—a characteristic of the genre that Chen frequently evokes in her works—and then a motive of intertwined major and minor seconds in the high woodwinds that conjures the sliding tones of the opera's vocal style.

The major-minor second interweave at the end of this example—which suggests the visual image of a tightly wound rope—is a favorite device of Chen. She calls the figure, which she first used in the 1980s as connective tissue between phrases, a "wandering chromatic." "I thought that I should find some way to avoid using straight chromatic or diatonic" lines to connect phrases with different textures, she says. "I wanted a transition figure with a narrow range" but one that would "avoid the pure chromatic lines that identify Romantic music." Chen became so fond of the wandering chromatic that she began using it not simply as connection but also as a predominant theme in its own right. In fact, it has become a marker of her style and appears even in her most recent works, such as the guitar duo, *Nian Hua* (2016–17). For another instance, see Example 3.7c, m. 18.

A defining characteristic of Beijing opera is its complex percussion patterns, coordinated with specific types of actions on the stage. Indeed, percussionists typically master more than a hundred such patterns. Beginners learn them by rote using phonetic syllables called *luogu jing*, which convey not only rhythm, but also timbre and instrumentation.[14] In the second movement of the *Chinese*

EXAMPLE 3.8. *Dunhuang Fantasy* (organ and wind ensemble, 1999)

A. Beginning (rhythmically free organ solo introduction)

B. Measures 16–19, flute, contrabassoon, percussion, and organ parts only, showing the influence of opera percussion and Chen's "wandering chromatic" motive in the flute

Folk Dance Suite for violin and orchestra (2001), entitled "Yangko," Chen has all the players chant during the opening section on vocables that imitate luogu jing syllables (see Example 3.9).

Folk Music Influences

Folk song forms a defining characteristic of Chen Yi's musical output, drawing on her intensive study at CCOM and the trips she took to outlying villages. Many individual tunes, or imitations of the style of such tunes, have found their way into her works in all genres. She classifies her music into three categories: arrangements of actual songs, pieces that make use of folk song style, and more abstract compositions inspired by folk music principles. In this tripartite division, she says, she follows the model of Bartók.[15]

EXAMPLE 3.9. *Chinese Folk Dance Suite* (violin and orchestra, 2001), mvt. 2, "Yangko," mm. 10–12. The chanting on vocables references luogu jing.

For the second of the three categories—pieces using folk music style—Chen often draws inspiration from regional singing characteristics, coupled at times with quotations from specific tunes. One example is *Ballad, Dance, and Fantasy* for cello and orchestra, composed for Yo-Yo Ma in 2003. According to Chen, the first movement "is drawn from the folk music in Shaanxi Province, the birthplace of the Silk Road," an ancient network of trade routes winding from East Asia to the Arabian Peninsula and southern Europe. Example 3.10 shows the cello soloist evoking this regional singing style, complemented by chanting on vocables in the woodwinds and brass, and microtonal intervals in the second violins. In this case, the folk reference is particularly apt, honoring Yo-Yo Ma's Silk Road Project, which he established in 1998 to enhance intercultural artistic exchange.[16] Some recent scholarship has countered the present-day idealization of the ancient Silk Road as a syncretic interaction of diverse cultures, noting that it "has become fashionable nostalgia, expressing longing for a perceived time when universalism was a norm." These critiques emphasize the risk of using an idealized Silk Road image to construct Orientalism.[17] Such claims aside, the Silk Road, as "a metaphor of cultural rapprochement and mutual exchange,"[18] strongly influenced Chen Yi, as it resonated with her overriding philosophy that music in general, and her music in particular, should serve as a cultural bridge. This philosophy is manifest in her attempts to unite Chinese and Western musical instruments, tuning systems, and compositional processes. The Silk Road plays a role not only in *Ballad, Dance, and Fantasy*, but also, even more prominently, in her Symphony No. 3 (see Chapters 5 and 7).

Symphony No. 2 opens with an imitation of the low-pitched singing by a tribal elder that Chen heard on a village visit to the Yao minority people in Guangxi Province during her CCOM years (Example 3.11a.) Three years later she would use the same inspiration for the opening of her *Chinese Myths Cantata* (discussed in Chapter 6). Although the symphony is one of Chen's few

Compositional Processes

EXAMPLE 3.10. *Ballad, Dance, and Fantasy* (cello and orchestra, 2003), mvt. 1, mm. 1–10. The cello evokes Shaanxi folk singing style; the orchestral winds chant; second violins play microtones.

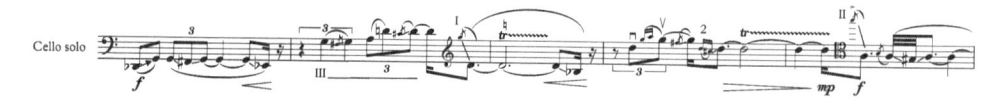

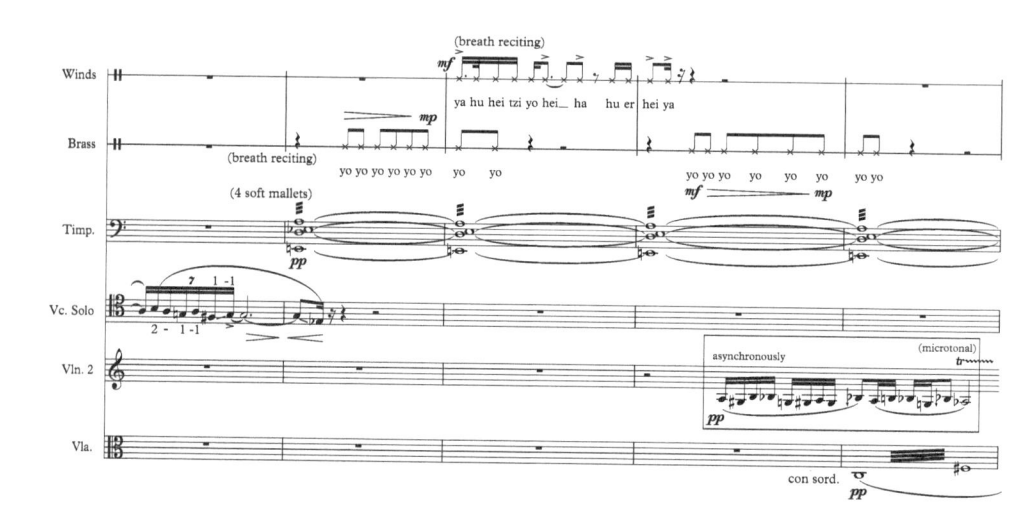

works without a descriptive title, its inspiration was nonmusical: it is an elegy to her father, who died three years before its completion. The low rumbles in the double bass, timpani, tuba, and contrabassoon that open the symphony, though inspired by singing in this Chinese village, also create a more sweeping emotional impression—what Nancy Rao calls a "gesture of agony" reflecting Chen's sorrow.[19] As in other works, Chen combined Chinese influences with non-Asian inspirations, including a twelve-tone line (basses, mm. 12–14, imitated by the tuba) and a special "Chen Yi motive" that came to her "unconsciously" in 1990 when she learned that her father had suffered the heart attack that led to his death (Example 3.11b).[20] As the symphony's premiere approached, she wrote in a report to the Knight Foundation:

> I hear the tragic motif of my symphony again and again, and I can't stop a tear from running down my cheek. That motif has been haunting me since I first learned my dear father had a heart attack.... He led me into the realm

EXAMPLE 3.11. Symphony No. 2 (1993)

A. Beginning. The low rumble, inspired by Chen's visit to the Yao community in Guangxi Province in 1980, is followed by a twelve-tone line in the basses, imitated by the tuba.

B. Trumpet, m. 94: The "Chen Yi motive"

C. Flute, mm. 61–63: The Buddhist praying tune

of music when I was only three and helped me understand the sincerity and simplicity of Mozart.[21]

The same twelve-tone line—which Chen had previously used in her Piano Concerto and the octet *Sparkle*—features prominent tritones and semitones, historical markers of grief in Western music. Chen also inserted a Buddhist praying tune in the piece (Example 3.11c), which reappears near the end of the symphony in a *forte* climax as "the brass section cries out in clusters FATHER or BABA."[22]

Inspired by her father's devotion "to the people of his motherland," Chen imbued the symphony with "a voice of yearning for civilization." The dark colors of her sorrow, however, ultimately lead to hope for humankind. She writes: "The ending part, presented by the soft lingering gestures on percussion and sliding harmonics on strings, carries a mysterious dream toward the future."[23]

The use of **vocables** (discussed in more detail in Chapter 6), which Chen Yi draws from diverse regional dialects and mixes at will, represents another persistent folk music influence. As we have already seen in *Ballad, Dance, and Fantasy* and the *Chinese Folk Dance Suite* (Examples 3.9 and 3.10), Chen calls upon instrumentalists as well as vocalists to chant. The movement shown in Example 3.9 ("Yangko") takes its name from a country dance form in which people "play rhythmic patterns on drums hung around their waists while singing and dancing."[24] The chanting by orchestra members on ostinato patterns imitates drumming.

Stylistic blending is a guiding principle for Chen. Just as she draws vocables from various regions of China, she also mixes unrelated folk song styles and references folk traditions from disparate parts of the country. The opening movement of the *Chinese Folk Dance Suite* (2001), "Lion Dance," draws on Cantonese and Chaozhou melodies and imitates the loud double-reed *suona*, while the work's finale, "Muqam," takes inspiration from Uighur music and dance (Example 3.12). The Uighurs, one of fifty-five ethnic groups in China, are of Turkish lineage and live primarily in Xinjiang Province. The modal characteristics of this movement are strikingly different from those of the first two movements (and indeed from most of Chen's other music), featuring a Middle Eastern mode with half steps and augmented seconds. The lively 7/8 meter (also quite unusual for Chen) captures the rhythmic vivacity of the Uighur dance tradition.

Another example that draws specifically from diverse regional folk traditions is the *Three Bagatelles* of 2006, originally for flute and piano, but also available in versions for two flutes; piano and clarinet; two clarinets; piano and con-

EXAMPLE 3.12. *Chinese Folk Dance Suite* (violin and orchestra, 2001), mvt. 3, "Muqam," beginning. The inspiration is Uighur music.

trabass; flute and clarinet; flute and guitar; and sheng and guan (a cylindrical double reed instrument). The first bagatelle, "Shan Ge," was inspired by the solo piece "Shange Diao" and musical patterns of the *kouxian*, a jaw harp of the Jingpo people. "Nai Guo Hou," the second bagatelle, evokes the *bawu*, a side-blown free reed pipe with finger holes, and uses pitch material of the folk song "Ashima" of the Yi people. The finale, "Dou Duo," captures the sound effect of the *lusheng* ensemble of the Miao culture. In this work, discussed in greater detail in Chapter 4, Chen at times quotes the folk material exactly, but at other times only hints at the song's melody. In the second movement, she combines two tunes simultaneously but allows them to remain rhythmically uncoordinated, a technique she has used on occasion to enhance contrapuntal independence. In the finale, the piano imitates a Hmong instrument with multiple bamboo pipes.

Like Beijing opera, most Chinese folk music includes extensive use of percussion. Chen often imitates characteristic patterns using both pitched and nonpitched instruments. A striking example, in which she adapts an instrumental folk music genre from southern China to a work for Western instruments, is the third movement of *Ba Yin* for saxophone quartet and string orchestra (2001). The movement, entitled "Shifan Gong-and-Drum," replicates a common rhythmic structure found in the shifan luogu repertory that Chen had studied in her instrumental folk music course at CCOM.[25] The metric pattern she mimics consists of a decreasing number of percussive strikes in the order 10–8–6–4–2. In traditional performances, the ten-strike pattern is divided 3+7, the eight-strike 1+7, the six-strike 1+5, the four-strike 1+3, and the two-strike 1+1. These strikes, however, are of unequal length. In the three-, five-, and seven-note patterns, folk musicians typically subdivide all beats except for the last one. Thus the seven-strike pattern actually encompasses four beats, the five-strike pattern three beats, and the three-strike pattern two beats:[26]

7-strike: *xx xx xx* x (= 4 beats)
5-strike: *xx xx* x (= 3 beats)
3-strike: *xx* x (= 2 beats)

Compositional Processes

In Chen Yi's adaptation of the pattern (Example 3.13), the strikes are translated into eighth notes; but she also subdivides some of the intermediary ones (creating two sixteenths) and she adds an additional subdivision to the last beat of each pattern, thus in effect creating an extra strike. Nevertheless, with the exception of the opening three strikes, which encompass three beats rather than two, Chen retains the distinctive number of beats in the folk tradition: four beats for the seven-strike pattern, three for the five-strike pattern, and two for the three-strike pattern. As Example 3.13 shows, each pattern is sounded twice 10–10–8–8–6–6–4–4–2–2, which is also characteristic of the folk practice. Chen's extra strike on the last eighth note of each pattern keeps the forward momentum energized. Her objective in rendering the opening three strikes as three beats, rather than two, reinforces the opening interval (a m9), which represents the leading instrument, the cymbals.[27] In fact, the various intervals in this section literally represent different instruments: m9 (A–B♭) cymbals; m2 (D♯–E) a small gong; m6 (G–E♭) a drum; and m3 (F♯–A) a medium gong. The large gong is represented by the simultaneous sounding of all four intervals. (In the vocal piece "Riding on a Mule," discussed in Chapter 6, Chen Yi uses different vocal phonemes, rather than specific intervals, to represent various percussion instruments, but the principle is the same.) At the end of this passage the saxophone quartet (which has been silent since m. 44) reenters with Chen Yi's distinctive wandering chromatic motive. The passage shown in Example 3.13 recurs in varied form three more times in the movement. The rhythmic patterns are identical each time, but the intervals representing the instruments are rearranged in sequence, indicating that a new "leading instrument" is established as in a traditional shifan luogu performance. Chen Yi liked this exciting movement so much that she reworked it into five other pieces (discussed in Chapter 4).

Chen's choral settings of Chinese folk songs—such as those she composed during her San Francisco years—are as much attempts to preserve Chinese cultural artifacts as are recordings of folk musicians or earlier ethnomusicological transcriptions of indigenous populations. Her incorporation of folk influences into more abstract instrumental works serves a similar function, preserving and extolling her musical heritage, while embedding these references in a language that speaks to a Western-educated audience.

Around the turn of the century, Chen consciously made a decision to revisit many of the folk songs she had studied at the Central Conservatory. She also read Stephen Jones's *Folk Music of China*, which further encouraged her to incorporate the folk traditions of her native land into her compositions. The works we have cited here represent only a small proportion of the compositions

EXAMPLE 3.13. *Ba Yin* (saxophone quartet and strings, 2001), mvt. 3, mm. 44–55. In this section, intervals represent percussion instruments: minor 9th = cymbals; minor 2nd = small gong; minor 6th = drum; minor 3rd = medium gong; all intervals = large gong.

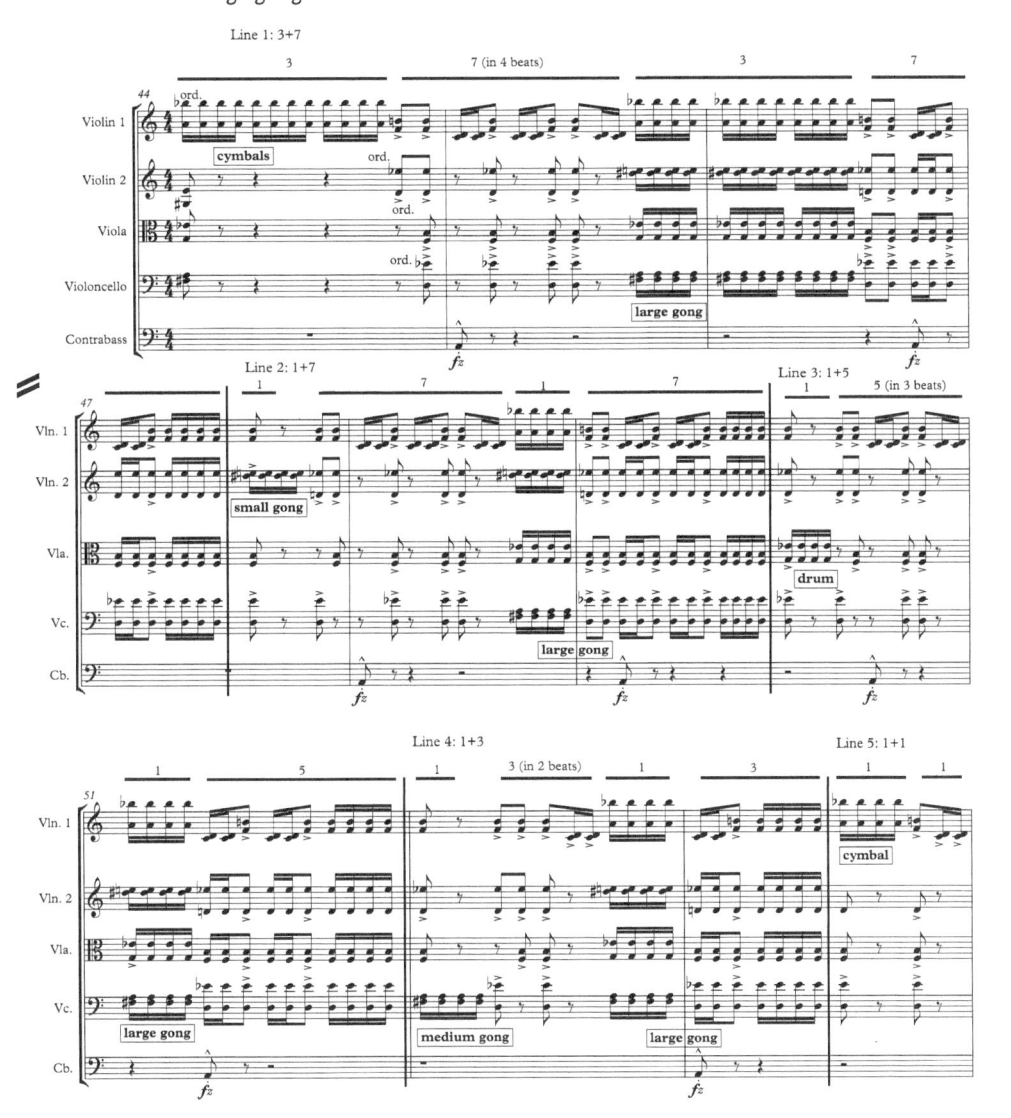

EXAMPLE 3.13. Continued.

in which she subsequently used folk song material. One tune, however, had influenced Chen prior to her systematic revisitation of folk materials, functioning as the guiding principle of her 1992 Piano Concerto; it has continued to wield a strong influence on her until the present time, making its appearance in more than twenty of her compositions. This tune is the ancient qupai Baban.

Baban: A Model for Melodic, Rhythmic, and Structural Shaping

Shortly before Chen Yi left for the United States, she read a 1984 article by Du Yaxiong, professor of ethnomusicology at the China Conservatory of Music, Beijing, an institution specializing in traditional music.[28] In this article Du described the ancient folk tune "Baban," whose lineage, though sketchy, might date back as far as the Song Dynasty (960–1279). Du analyzed the tune, as transmitted from a source published in 1814, and highlighted its symbolism in relation to the Fibonacci sequence, the Golden Section, the mystical number 8, and the I Ching. The Golden Section is a proportional relationship in which the ratio between large and small segments (a:b) equals the ratio of the whole (a + b) to the larger part (a). The ratio yields a proportion close to, but not exactly 3:2. In planning the structural proportions of her works, Chen often relates adjacent sections in approximately 3:2 proportions (or 2:3, which she calls the "Reverse Golden Section")[29] and she frequently inserts the climactic moment of a work about two-thirds of the way through the piece.

Baban is often classified as a type of *qupai*, a term used to identify a variety of "named" melodies, generally associated with opera, that have served as models for instrumental repertoire. Although Baban is a folk tune rather than an opera tune, it is often classified as a qupai because it is fixed and has been used for a great many variations over the centuries. Chen Yi wrote in her dissertation that Baban formed the basis for more than a thousand later pieces. Alan Thrasher, a noted specialist on the Sizhu instrumental music of south China, calls Baban "the most widespread of all instrumental structures in China."[30] Example 3.14 presents the form of the melody as Chen first used it, in her Piano Concerto of 1992; Du presented the tune in cipher notation and therefore not on a fixed pitch.

Baban consists of sixty-eight beats divided into eight lines. Each line (except the fifth) contains eight beats, sometimes in groups of 3–2–3, sometimes 4–4, and once 5–3. Indeed, the word *Baban* is usually translated as "eight beats." In her article "Tradition and Creation," Chen Yi highlights the centrality of the number eight in Chinese tradition, where it denotes the "most famous mountains, the directions of the compass, the divisions of the agricultural seasons ..., the sounds of musical instruments as classified by their physical sound-producing materials, the standard [number of] strokes of the character 'yong' in calligraphy, the Eight Diagrams in Taoism."[31] The tune also contains irregular repetition of several short motives, indicated in Example 3.14 by similarly shaped brackets. In addition, the second pattern in line 1 (D–E–G) recurs not only in line 2, but also in lines 4 and 5. Such motivic repetition supports Baban's classification as a qupai, which, as Thrasher notes, typically contains regular or irregular repetition of small phrases.[32] The fifth line of Baban stands as an exception; it is extended by four beats and the Golden Section of the entire tune (that is, approximately two-thirds of the way through) occurs in the middle of those extra beats. (Thrasher's version of Baban presents line 5 with only eight beats; he adds the extra four beats at the end of line 8 instead of line 5.)[33]

Compositional Processes

EXAMPLE 3.14. Baban tune as used by Chen Yi in more than twenty works. The tune is not tied to a specific pitch. The version given here, starting on B♭, is that used for the Piano Concerto (1992), the first work in which Chen used Baban. Brackets with similar shapes highlight repeated subphrases.

At Columbia, Chou Wen-chung urged Chen Yi to integrate her Chinese heritage into her compositions. She fulfilled this directive by basing her 1992 Piano Concerto almost entirely on Baban, not only quoting the tune's melody and rhythmic structure, but also letting the phrase structure of Baban determine the form of the entire sixteen-minute work.

EXAMPLE 3.15. Piano Concerto (1992), opening

The Piano Concerto opens with a quotation of the beginning of the Baban melody (Example 3.15), providing material for a fifteen-measure introduction in which Chen announces her source material. Thereafter, the concerto is laid out in proportions that precisely correspond to those of Baban, but greatly expanded. Beginning in measure 16, Chen expands each Baban beat to twelve concerto beats. For example, the first phrase (3–2–3) translates in the concerto into sections of 36–24–36 beats. The pitches of the tune are now only loosely referenced.

Figure 3.2 shows the organization of Part I. Note that midway through the seventh phrase, the tempo slows and each Baban beat becomes equivalent to eight concerto beats instead of the original twelve. After the completion of the sixty-eight-beat pattern, Chen repeats the entire structure of Baban for Part II of the concerto, as shown in Figure 3.3. In the final section, the tempo increases and each beat of original tune corresponds to twenty concerto beats.

A comparison of Figures 3.2 and 3.3 shows that as the number of concerto beats per Baban beat changes, the average tempo also changes: from 120 to 70 to 180 per quarter note, thus creating the fast-slow-fast structure of a typical Western concerto. These tempo changes *overlap* the statements of the Baban form, but the change in the number of concerto beats per Baban beat creates a consistent correspondence throughout the piece: one minute of the concerto equals eight quarter-note beats of Baban.[34]

The last section of the concerto incorporates a climactic passage in which the winds articulate the Baban rhythmic pattern on repeated pitches both forward and backward and at two rhythmic levels simultaneously. As Example 3.16 shows, the woodwinds play the rhythmic pattern 3–2–3, 3–2–3, 4–4. . . , in eighths and quarter-note triplets, while the brass play the pattern in reverse order (lines 8 → 1), 4–4, 5–3, 4–4. . . , at the same two speeds.[35] Slightly later the piano performs the entire sixty-eight-beat rhythmic pattern, striking the

Compositional Processes

FIGURE 3.2. Piano Concerto (1992), organization of Part I

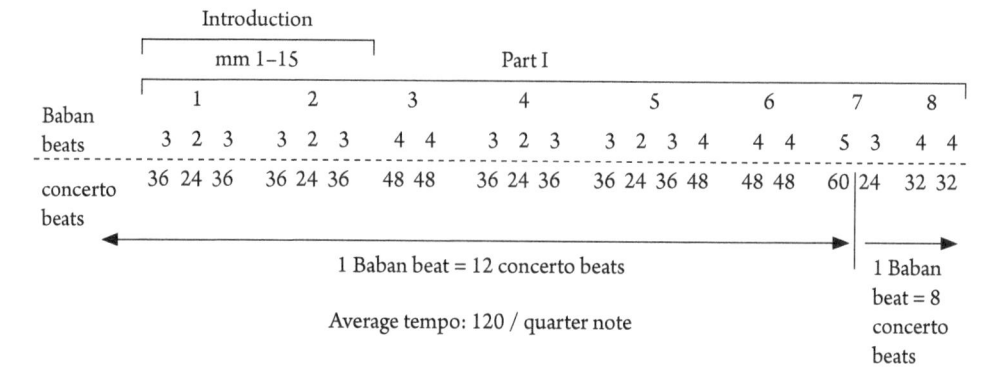

	Introduction mm 1–15		Part I					
	1	2	3	4	5	6	7	8
Baban beats	3 2 3	3 2 3	4 4	3 2 3	3 2 3 4	4 4	5 3	4 4
concerto beats	36 24 36	36 24 36	48 48	36 24 36	36 24 36 48	48 48	60 | 24	32 32

1 Baban beat = 12 concerto beats

Average tempo: 120 / quarter note

1 Baban beat = 8 concerto beats

Average tempo: 70 / quarter note

FIGURE 3.3. Piano Concerto (1992), organization of Part II

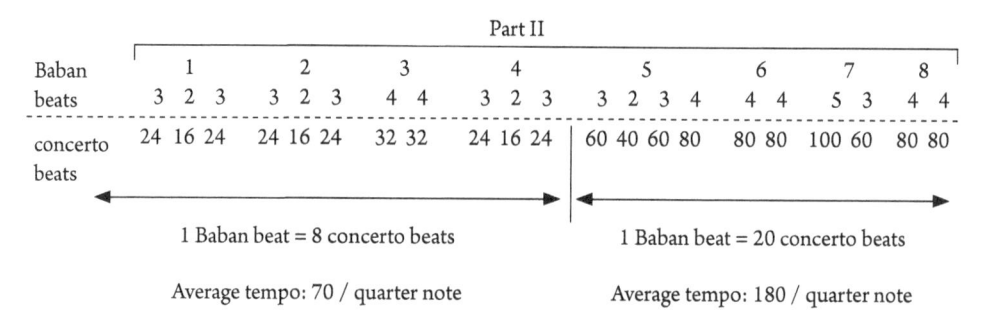

	Part II							
	1	2	3	4	5	6	7	8
Baban beats	3 2 3	3 2 3	4 4	3 2 3	3 2 3 4	4 4	5 3	4 4
concerto beats	24 16 24	24 16 24	32 32	24 16 24	60 40 60 80	80 80	100 60	80 80

1 Baban beat = 8 concerto beats

Average tempo: 70 / quarter note

1 Baban beat = 20 concerto beats

Average tempo: 180 / quarter note

highest note on the instrument repeatedly in groups of 3–2–3, 3–2–3, 4–4.... At the same time, fragments of the tune make their appearance in various wind instruments.

The Piano Concerto is the first work in which Chen Yi systematically explored the process of form variation. Her complex expansion of Baban into large-scale sectional divisions is at once innovative and yet at the same time rooted in traditional Chinese practices, where the principle is called *fangman jiahua* or "slowing and adding flowers." In this tradition the notes of the qupai are slowed, and ornamental pitches are inserted between them. In her dissertation, Chen Yi cites an example of traditional Jiangnan Sizhu music that illustrates this practice. "I got to know [during folk music classes at CCOM] the traditional way to play in the ensemble with different instruments," she says.

EXAMPLE 3.16. Piano Concerto (1992), mm. 544–52

"This variation method inspired me later to design the textures in my orchestral writing when I composed for Western instruments."[36]

The process was further reinforced by the music history courses she took at Columbia. The elaborations over a long-note melody (cantus firmus) in medieval music reminded Chen of the process of form variation in Chinese music, although in fact the relationship is quite distant. A closer analogy might be to *irama* changes in gamelan music, where a skeletal melody (the *balungan*) is slowed to accommodate additional notes in the ornamental lines.[37]

In our study of Chen Yi's music, we have found evidence of Baban in numerous later works including *Sparkle, Song in Winter, Chinese Myths Cantata, Qi, Sound of the Five, The Golden Flute,* Percussion Concerto, *Ba Ban* (a piano solo work based heavily on the solo parts of the Piano Concerto), *Chinese Fables, Si Ji, From the Path of Beauty,* Prelude and Fugue, *The Soulful and the Perpetual* (an arrangement of *Early Spring,* movement 2), *Prospect Overture, UMKC Fanfare, Bamboo Dance, Three Dances from China South,* and *Four Spirits.* Nor can we guarantee that we have detected every instance of Baban's presence. These works, listed in chronological order, span twenty-four years, from 1992 to 2016, showing that the influence of this ancient tune on Chen Yi has not waned.[38]

In some pieces Chen used Baban as structural underpinning in a similar manner to the Piano Concerto, although the tune's form does not always guide the entire composition. In other cases, it is the beginning of the melody that finds expression, the most notable example being *The Golden Flute* cited earlier in this chapter. In still other cases, Chen used only the rhythmic pattern articulated on repeated pitches as she did near the end of the Piano Concerto. A few examples will suffice to show her creative application of traditional variation principles to develop through various procedures works with very different affects.

The orchestral work *Si Ji* and the octet *Sparkle* draw on Baban's structure to determine metric changes, with the tune's beats doubled in length. *Sparkle,* for

Compositional Processes

EXAMPLE 3.17. *Song in Winter* (trio or quartet, 1993), mm. 56–61. The Baban rhythmic pattern appears in the repeated notes of the right hand, marked off by an interpolated chord in the left hand at the end of each iteration. The lyrical flute melody, inspired by Beijing opera, enters just after the Golden Section and floats over the driving structure of the keyboard.

Golden Section

example, opens with measures of 6/4, 4/4, and 6/4, each with repeated figuration, reflecting a doubled 3–2–3 unit. Furthermore, in this piece, completed in the same year as the Piano Concerto, Chen contrasts the Chinese-inspired A section with a B section using a twelve-tone row.

In other works, Chen features Baban's rhythmic pattern without reference to the tune's pitches, as in *Song in Winter* (1993), where the keyboard player articulates the sixty-eight-beat pattern in the right hand at an extremely fast tempo (see Example 3.17), or in the Prelude and Fugue for chamber orchestra (2009), where the repeated notes appear in the crotales in the second movement (mm. 133–44). In both cases, she marks the end of each Baban line by an accented punctuation and introduces a new contrapuntal melodic line right after the Golden Section. In the last movement of the *Chinese Myths Cantata* (1996), Chen belts out Baban's rhythmic pattern in repeated notes in the strings, brass, and percussion.

EXAMPLE 3.18. *The Soulful and the Perpetual* (saxophone and piano, 2012), mvt. 2, beginning. The Baban rhythmic pattern appears in the saxophone, with a single beat interpolation separating subphrases (boxed) and a more elaborate interpolation at the end of each line (dotted boxes).

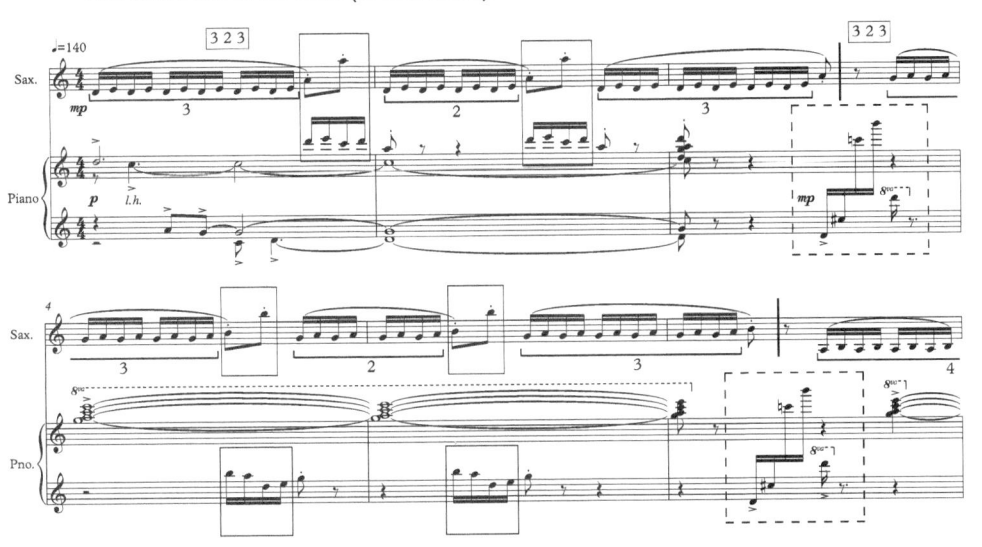

One of the most sophisticated uses of the Baban tune is the second movement of *The Soulful and the Perpetual* for saxophone and piano (2012). As Example 3.18 shows, the Baban rhythmic pattern appears complete in the saxophone, but Chen interpolates a single beat between subphrases (boxed) and a melodically more expansive sixteenth-note figure at the end of each line (dotted boxes). In the central B section, the Baban pattern appears as an ostinato in the piano part, expanded to double time as in *Si Ji* and *Sparkle*; and at the Golden Section, the ostinato changes from straight sixteenth-notes to quintuplets. This piece is one of Chen's most abstract works. In it, the presence of Baban is disguised; neither its rhythm nor its melody appears overtly. Yet, as in the Piano Concerto, written twenty years earlier, Baban controls the work's overall form.

In addition to Baban, Chen sometimes used other folk song sources to control movement forms. For instance, the *Prospect Overture* (2008), the first movement of the Symphony No. 3 (2004), and the first movement of *Ba Yin* (2001) are all based on the form of "Shui long yin," a Shaanxi shawm band piece from the oral tradition that Chen discovered in Stephen Jones's book on Chinese folk music. Using the recording from Jones's book, Chen calculated the piece's tempo changes, documenting mathematically the gradual increase from its

FIGURE 3.4. *Happy Rain on a Spring Night* (2004)

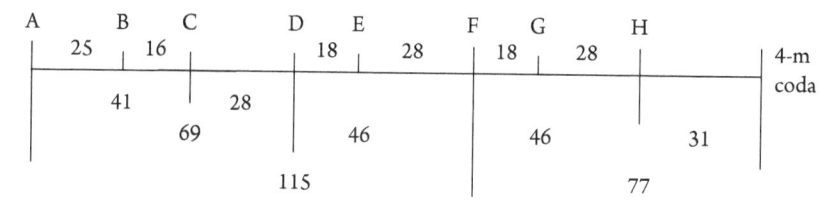

```
A     B    C         D    E         F    G         H
|  25  | 16 |         | 18 |   28    | 18 |   28    |         | 4-m
|      41   |    28   |                  |         |   31    |   coda
|           69        |        46        |        46         |
|              115                       |            77     |
```

A. Proportions of sections in the work. Letters = rehearsal letters; numbers = lengths of sections in terms of number of measures. Calculations and diagram by the authors

Sections	long part: short part	total: long part
A–C	25:16 = .64	41:25 = .61
A–D	41:28 = .68	69:41 = .59
D–F, F–H	18:28 = .64 (Reverse GS)	28:46 = .61 (Reverse GS)
A–F	69:46 = .67	115:69 = .60
F–end (without coda)	46:31 = .67	77:46 = .60
A–end (without coda)	115:77 = .67	192:115 = .60

B. Relationships among the sections

very slow opening to its extremely fast ending. In doing so, she discovered the Golden Section. "I then used the orchestra with accelerated tempo changes to match the structure of the folk piece."[39]

Chen Yi's fascination with the proportions in both Baban and "Shui long yin" reflects her long-term interest in mathematical structures. Indeed, when Chen plans out the overall form of a piece early in her compositional process, she often devises mathematical relationships for the section lengths. Frequently she bases this process on the Golden Ratio, which is found in many natural objects and in simple geometric figures (such as the pentagon).

One of the works in which Chen rigorously used the Golden Ratio simultaneously on four levels is *Happy Rain on a Spring Night*, a quintet for flute, clarinet, violin, cello, and piano (2004). Figure 3.4 shows the proportional relationships among sections, as delineated by rehearsal letters. Relationships between long and short sections (a:b) are all close to the Golden Section, as are the proportions between the whole and the longer segment (a+b:a). Chen is hardly unique among composers in her interest in the Golden Section. She was particularly excited, for example, to read Roy Howat's book detailing Debussy's use of this mathematical phenomenon.[40]

* * *

Periodically during this chapter, we have noted works that Chen developed as reorchestrations or adaptations of earlier compositions. Indeed, she continues to feel a close affinity to her earlier music and, though techniques such as twelve-tone rows appear less frequently in recent works, she still draws on influences from her years in China and her first experiences in the United States. In the following three chapters we aim to demonstrate not only how Chen reimagines these early influences, but also how the overriding stylistic traits we have highlighted throughout this chapter play out in selected works for orchestra, chamber ensembles, and voices.

CHAPTER 4

Solo and Chamber Music Works

Chen Yi's Chamber Works and the Practice of Self-Quotation

In this chapter and the next two, we discuss selected works in the areas of chamber, orchestral, and choral/vocal music. Our aims in choosing the specific works were to embrace a wide chronological range and variety in instrumentation, and to avoid, with a few exceptions, discussing in depth pieces that have been analyzed by others in readily available, published, English-language sources.

One overriding issue affecting all genres is the interrelationship among independently titled pieces. Chen Yi often revisits earlier works to create alternative versions. Two examples can serve to illustrate this often complex and imaginative process.

Example 1. In 1995 Chen composed *Romance for Hsaio and Ch'in* for strings and two violins, and then created alternative versions for violin and piano, cello and piano, and erhu and piano. Two works from 1998 reuse the *Romance*. The first is the quintet *Sound of the Five* for cello and string quartet, whose third movement is an altered reorchestration of the 1995 piece. Also in 1998, Chen created the two-movement *Romance and Dance* for string orchestra and two violins. The *Romance* remained the same; for the "Dance," Chen used the finale of the *Fiddle Suite* (1997). Then in the same year, she revised the slow movement of the *Fiddle*

Suite for use as the second movement of the Percussion Concerto (discussed in Chapter 5). In 2004 Chen orchestrated *Sound of the Five* to create a Suite for Cello and Chamber Winds.

Example 2. The most complex interweaving of diverse works involves about a dozen pieces spanning the years 1996–2012. Within this group of compositions, the most persistent influence began with *Ba Yin* (2001)—a work for saxophone quartet and strings in three movements: "Praying for Rain," "Song of the Chu," and "Shifan Gong and Drum" (analyzed in Chapter 3). *Ba Yin*'s first and last movements reappear reorchestrated in *Wu Yu*, a mixed sextet: flute, clarinet, bassoon, violin, cello, and percussion (2002). *Wu Yu* also offers alternative instrumentation as a septet (omitting bassoon and percussion but adding oboe, viola, and contrabass). In 2003 Chen drew again on the "Shifan Gong and Drum" movement of *Ba Yin* for the finale of *Ballad, Dance, and Fantasy* for cello and orchestra, but with major changes, including an expanded opening and a new ending. She later provided an alternative scoring of the first two movements of *Ballad*, called *Ode to the Earth* (2006), in which a ruan (moon lute) replaces the solo cello. *Ba Yin*'s finale, "Shifan Gong and Drum," continued to intrigue Chen, serving as the source material for the finales of three additional pieces: the piano trio *Tunes from My Home* (2007–8), the recorder concerto *Ancient Chinese Beauty* (2008), and the chorus and string quartet work *From the Path of Beauty* (2008). All of these pieces show alterations from the model, sometimes with revised openings and endings as in *Ballad*, and sometimes with major recomposition of the original. The most dramatic change was Chen's creation of a scat rendition for voices in *Path of Beauty* (see Chapter 6). The vocal parts in this movement correspond closely to the solo recorder passages in *Ancient Chinese Beauty* (composed in the same year), although the *Path of Beauty* version has been shortened. The effect is strikingly different from any of the instrumental pieces. The recorder concerto also draws from two other sources, a five-minute, single-movement sextet from *Han Figurines* (2006), which itself was adapted from the opening portion of the slow movement of the *Chinese Myths Cantata* (1996) and from the second movement of *The Golden Flute* (1997). *Han Figurines* also provided the source material for the second movement of *The Ancient Beauty* (2006),[1] a piece for four Chinese instruments and strings, and for the fifth movement of *Path of Beauty* (2008). The first two movements of the trio *Tunes from My Home* also inspired other works. Chen revised and orchestrated the first movement for *Symphonie "Humen 1839"* and used the same movement for the "Prelude" of the chamber orchestra piece Prelude and Fugue (both composed in 2009). The "Fugue" movement of this piece is built on the second movement of *Tunes from My Home* and includes a long central section derived from the quartet *Qi* (1997). The Fugue then provided material for part of the orchestral tone poem *Blue, Blue Sky* (2012).

One reason Chen reuses older material is to provide alternative performance options. More crucially, however, the process helps stimulate her creativity. Many composers find the compositional task eased by beginning with material they previously found successful. Lou Harrison, for example, often revived old works (sometimes from decades earlier) that he felt had potential to be developed in new ways.[2] When Janice Giteck consulted him for help in breaking through a composition block for a commission for the San Francisco Symphony, Harrison advised her to start with something old. She found the advice revelatory, providing a starting place for the new piece.[3] Unlike Harrison, Chen only rarely turns to decades-old pieces, but one notable exception is her use of the folk song "Awariguli," a process that began with a set of nine variations for solo piano that she composed in China in 1979. In 1994 she arranged the same tune for chorus (*A Set of Chinese Folk Songs*, no. 8) and then in 2000 used one of the original piano variations for the violin cadenza in the third movement of the *Chinese Folk Dance Suite*. In 2011 Chen returned to her 1979 piano piece and reedited it for publication. Other examples of cross-borrowing between works quite distant in time include *Wind* (2010), an orchestration of the second woodwind quintet, *Feng* (1998); *From the Path of Beauty* (2008), which draws on two works originally written in the 1980s; and the finale of her newest piano concerto, *Four Spirits* (2016), which is a reworking of *The Golden Flute* (1997).

Chen's reuse of earlier materials not only forms an integral part of her compositional process but also reflects "the age-old Chinese musical practice of creating new compositions by arranging existing musical materials."[4] Says Chen: "Once I did deep research into a model, I used it again and again." Particularly influential, as we have seen, have been the Shifan Gong and Drum procedure that inspired *Ba Yin* and its many derivatives, and the ancient tune Baban that appears in various guises in nearly two dozen works (both discussed in Chapter 3). Sometimes an old piece simply fits a new context, she told us—like viewing the same image from a different angle. Such compositional interrelationships are not uncommon in the works of contemporary composers, although they are understandably rare for those who, unlike Chen, have taken sharp turns in their creative approaches. Western music history, we should note, is rife with habitual self-borrowers. To cite only two famous examples, J. S. Bach and George Frideric Handel constantly reworked compositions from decades earlier. In Chen's case, these reworkings reflect her aesthetic choices at a given point in her career, and they offer a fascinating glimpse at the evolution of her attitude toward her own work.

Works from the 1980s

DUO YE (PIANO SOLO, 1984; ALSO PIPA SOLO PLUS REVISED VERSIONS FOR CHAMBER ORCHESTRA AND FULL ORCHESTRA)

Although *Duo Ye* has been discussed by several writers, we include it here because the work has played such a significant role in Chen's early career. Furthermore, the many published and unpublished analyses of the piece frequently conflict with one another; we offer Chen's preferred analysis, as communicated by her to Tang Jianping and reinforced in messages to us.[5]

Chen composed *Duo Ye* for piano in 1984, inspired by the visit of the CCOM composition students to a village of the Dong peoples in Guangxi Province. There the students watched the villagers dance in a circle around a bonfire, chanting the vocables "Ya Duo Ye" in response to a leader who stood aside while extemporizing a text to improvised short tunes. Example 4.1a shows the opening of the piece, exhibiting a call-and-response texture between the two hands that mimics the leader-villagers exchange. The left hand, says Chen, represents a "dancing rhythmic chorale."[6]

Chen based her piece around the "Ya Duo Ye" motive, which features the intervals of M2, m3, and P4, as shown in the upper notes in measures 2–4 (D–E–G–E) in Example 4.1a. This interval set not only forms the basis for the melodic lines in this piece, but also appears frequently in many of Chen's other works.

The interaction of the two parts at the beginning of the piece also exemplifies the shifan luogu tradition. The right hand expands in terms of the number of pitches per grouping: 2–3–5–7. The number of beats also expands: 3–5–7–7 (the pick-ups are not counted). The last group should have spanned nine beats to strictly follow the traditional form, but here Chen Yi's musical sensitivity overrode strict adherence to the formula. A whole note at the end of the fourth statement or an expansion of the eighth-note line simply felt too long to her. The left hand, meanwhile, contracts: 7–5–3–1. A few measures later Chen introduces changing time signatures that also reflect shifan luogu patterns: 9/8, 7/8, 5/8, 3/8, 2/8 (with 5/4 measures interjected after the 9/8 and 7/8 measures).

Duo Ye's middle section provides a stark contrast to the opening. First Chen presents an unmeasured recitative-like passage that opens with a motive built on the three main intervals (some of them in inversion) but also evoking a tune from Beijing opera (Example 4.1b). Then she introduces an ostinato in the left hand encompassing all twelve chromatic pitches that accompanies a mountain song in the right, shown in Chapter 3 (Example 3.4). Note that the beginning

EXAMPLE 4.1. *Duo Ye* (1984)

A. Beginning

B. Beginning of the central section

C. Mm. 151–55, rhythmically migrating ostinato

of that ostinato highlights the guiding intervals M2, m3, P4 (the notes C–B♭–G–F as the upper notes of the line and C–F–D as the lowest notes).

Demonstrating an organizational procedure Chen would use often in future works, the final section brings together all of the motives explored earlier, presenting them in new guises. The "Ya Duo Ye" motive appears highlighted in accented unison octaves or in fortissimo outbursts in the bass. And in the coda, Chen uses an ostinato in much the same way we discussed in Chapter 3: a group of six sixteenths is repeated eleven times, then nine, seven, five, three, and once, each time transposed to a new pitch level. The transpositions are by P4 or m3, recalling the defining intervals of "Ya Duo Ye," which serves in part to bring cohesion and unity to her compositional process. The six-note repeated pattern takes up three-quarters of a measure of 2/4 and thus migrates a half-beat earlier at each rendition, much like the forward-migrating ostinato from *Feng* discussed in Chapter 3 (cf. Example 4.1c with 3.5b). Chen Yi rounds out the form by ending with a recollection of the piece's first two notes (E–C♯).

Thus *Duo Ye*, one of Chen's earliest compositions, which has followed her throughout her career in its frequent performances in piano, pipa, chamber orchestra, and full orchestra versions, already shows defining characteristics of her style: the mixture of Chinese folk music and Beijing opera influences with a Western twelve-tone row, the use of ostinati, and her preoccupation with mathematical concepts in the layout of phrases and meters.

WOODWIND QUINTET (1987)

Chen composed the first of her three woodwind quintets in 1987; it is the first major work from her Columbia years.[7] Although the quintet represents one of Chen's most thorough explorations of twelve-tone row manipulation (see Chapter 2), its stimulus came from a Chinese source: a trip to the Zhoushan Islands to collect folk songs in the 1980s. On that trip Chen climbed Buddha Mountain (Putuoshan) near Shanghai and heard nuns singing in heterophony.[8] She recalls being "stunned by the huge and extremely low roars" of the waves as they hit the bottom of the Chaoyin cave and captivated by "swept waves with golden edges (perhaps reflections from the fish)" on Baibusha Beach. The French horn evokes the roars from the cave, as well as an instrument from a different Chinese region: the Tibetan *rag dung* (a collapsible long metal trumpet). "The screaming woven texture played on high woodwinds," says Chen, constituted a reminder of her excitement from the "powerful waves of the sea."

The quintet opens with the flute alone playing five renditions of the tone row, but these full statements are interspersed with partial rows as shown in Example 4.2a. Thereafter the other instruments enter with layered statements

EXAMPLE 4.2. Woodwind Quintet (1987)

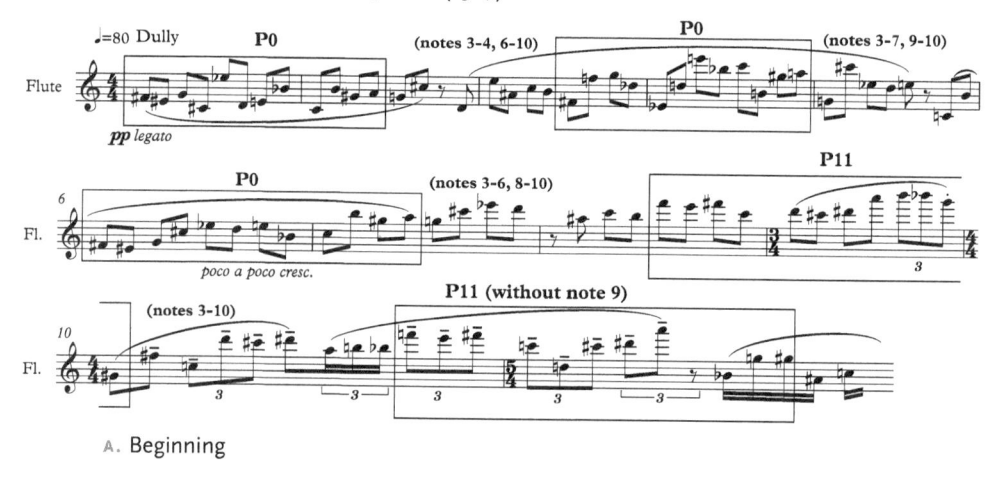

A. Beginning

Notes of the tone row:
Flute: 10-12, 3-4
Oboe: 3-5
Clarinet: 6-9
Horn: 5
Bassoon: 1-2

B. Mm. 118–19. Simultaneous ostinati contain all twelve notes of the row (P8, beginning on D; all instruments at sounding pitch)

of the same row. The opening section of the piece features polyrhythms (not shown in Example 4.2a)—first three against four, then three against four against five—a translation of the heterophonic singing of the nuns.

Typically for Chen, the central section stands in stark contrast to the first. The texture thins, the tempo slows, and the tone row disappears. Replacing the row motive is a quotation of a melody drawn from a Chinese Buddhist prayer (similar to the one shown in Example 3.11c).[9] Also typical of Chen's style is the last section, which is not a recapitulation, but rather a combination of materials presented earlier. The praying tune recurs up to the end of the piece in various guises. The tone row never reemerges in its original linear form, but it makes its presence felt in other ways. One notable passage, shown in Example 4.2b, consists of four short ostinati in polyrhythms with simultaneous groupings of 3, 4, and 5, recalling the polyrhythms of the opening section of the piece. Each of the instruments contains small fragments of the row: notes 1–2 in the bassoon, 3–5 in the oboe, 5 in the horn, 6–9 in the clarinet, and 10–12 and 3–4 in the flute.

Works from the 1990s

THE POINTS (PIPA SOLO, 1991)

The virtuoso pipa player Wu Man met Chen Yi and Zhou Long at CCOM after the institution reopened in 1978. At age 13, Wu became the youngest student in the conservatory's middle school program; Chen and Zhou were in the college division.[10] Wu completed a master's degree in 1987 (the first conferred on a pipa player) and in 1990 she moved to the United States, where she reconnected with Chen and Zhou. The following year, Claire Heldrich, codirector of the New Music Consort, consulted Chou Wen-chung about programming for a concert featuring Chinese instruments. Chou not only showed Heldrich scores by various Chinese composers, but also recommended that she invite Chen to compose a piece for pipa specifically for Wu Man.[11]

Chen had become familiar with pipa technique through interactions with her roommate in the Beijing opera troupe, but she needed more input on specialized pipa notation practices. So during Chen's residency at the Yaddo colony in July 1991 (which also came about through a recommendation from Chou), Wu visited Chen, and the two artists collaborated intensively for a week. Chen would ask for a particular sound, recalls Wu. "Show me how you can make it. Then I put down the fingering, put down the special notation for pipa."[12] Wu also demonstrated various specialized techniques, such as the *xiangjiao* vibrato, in which "the left hand pushes and pulls on the . . . string in the upper ledges

EXAMPLE 4.3. *The Points* (1991), end of the first yong stroke and beginning of the second one

to perform a vibrato with a small, wobbly sound."[13] Wu premiered *The Points* on Columbia's NEWworksOCTOBER series on October 17, 1991. It has since become a commonly required piece for pipa competitions.[14]

The Points was inspired by the Eight Principles of Yong (*yongzi ba fa*), in which all eight common calligraphic strokes of Chinese *Zhengkai* calligraphy are contained in a single character (yong 永 = eternal).[15] Each section of the piece, ranging from a few measures to more than sixty, exemplifies an individual stroke. Chen attempted to capture not only the direction of the strokes, but also the speed and pressure a calligrapher would exert to create them. Rests or fermatas mark the ends of most sections.

The piece is extremely virtuosic. For example, one section contains sixty measures of sixteenth notes at a presto tempo with frequent jumps in the left hand. The second point (m. 14ff) references material taken from Qinqiang (a type of folk opera from Shaanxi Province; Example 4.3). Here, Chen says, the pipa imitates the huqin playing opera melodies in a kind of "instrumentalized song."[16] *The Points* ends with the sudden appearance of the *lunzhi*, "a circular strumming motion, creating a strong tremolo sustained for thirty-six beats," bringing the last stroke to a "finishing flourish."

Harmonically, *The Points* falls well within the contemporary Western framework, which Chen made possible by having the pipa retune in order to easily create dissonant intervals. Instead of the normal A–D–E–A tuning, the lower two strings are raised by a semitone (A♯–D♯), allowing for half steps and tritones on open strings. The scordatura tuning also facilitates the folk song style of Qinqiang, which features a scale with an expressive flat seventh, typically played with a wide vibrato.

In the same year (1991), Chen composed Suite, for a quintet of Chinese instruments, using *The Points* as the basis for movement 1. This Suite, written for the five musicians of Music From China, contains three continuous movements. Movement 2 later provided the source material for the beginning of the second movement of *The Golden Flute*.

SONG IN WINTER (TRIO: HARPSICHORD, DIZI, ZHENG; OR QUARTET: FLUTE, ZHENG, PIANO, PERCUSSION, 1993–94)

Chen also calls for retuning a Chinese instrument in *Song in Winter*, written for the Alea III ensemble and harpsichordist Joyce Lindorff, premiered in Boston on February 4, 1994. In this case, the zheng (a zither) retunes some of its twenty-one strings in order to sound all twelve half steps of the equal-tempered scale.[17] Chen's compositional stimulus was nature, particularly pine and bamboo, often featured in Chinese paintings and admired in Chinese literature "as symbols against evil influences."[18]

One reason Chen has the zheng retune is to perform a twelve-tone row, which sounds briefly at the beginning, recurs in the middle, and then returns near the end, highlighting important structural moments in the form. This row, which Chen also used in her Symphony No. 2 (written in the same year), features prominent half steps and tritones (see Chapter 3, Example 3.11, double bass, m. 12–14). In *Song in Winter*, the ostinato in the keyboard that follows this opening figure again uses a shifan luogu mathematical principle: its notes appear in the repetition scheme 1, 2, 3, 5, 3, 2, 1 with successive patterns increasing the number of pitches from two notes to eight (Example 4.4).

The middle section begins quietly. After exploring the twelve-tone line at length using a variety of rhythms and textures, as well as inventive displacements of pitches to create a distinctive melodic character, this section culminates with the passage discussed in Chapter 3 in which the keyboardist hammers out the Baban rhythmic pattern on repeated notes, each of its eight lines marked by a punctuating chord, while the flute enters at the Golden Section playing a melody inspired by Beijing opera (Example 3.17).

In this work, Chen continues to combine concepts derived from her study of twelve-tone writing with Chinese influences, but here the influence of tone rows is much less pervasive than in the woodwind quintet. Although Chen would occasionally use melodic lines encompassing all twelve pitches in later works, this important part of her academic study gradually diminished.

QI (FLUTE, CELLO, PERCUSSION, PIANO, 1997)

Qi, a ten-minute quartet commissioned by the New Music Consort, the San Francisco Contemporary Music Players, and the Los Angeles Philharmonic Association, draws together and sums up compositional processes from the late 1980s and early 1990s. Chen dedicated the work to Chou Wen-chung for

EXAMPLE 4.4. *Song in Winter* (1993), quartet version, piano part only, beginning

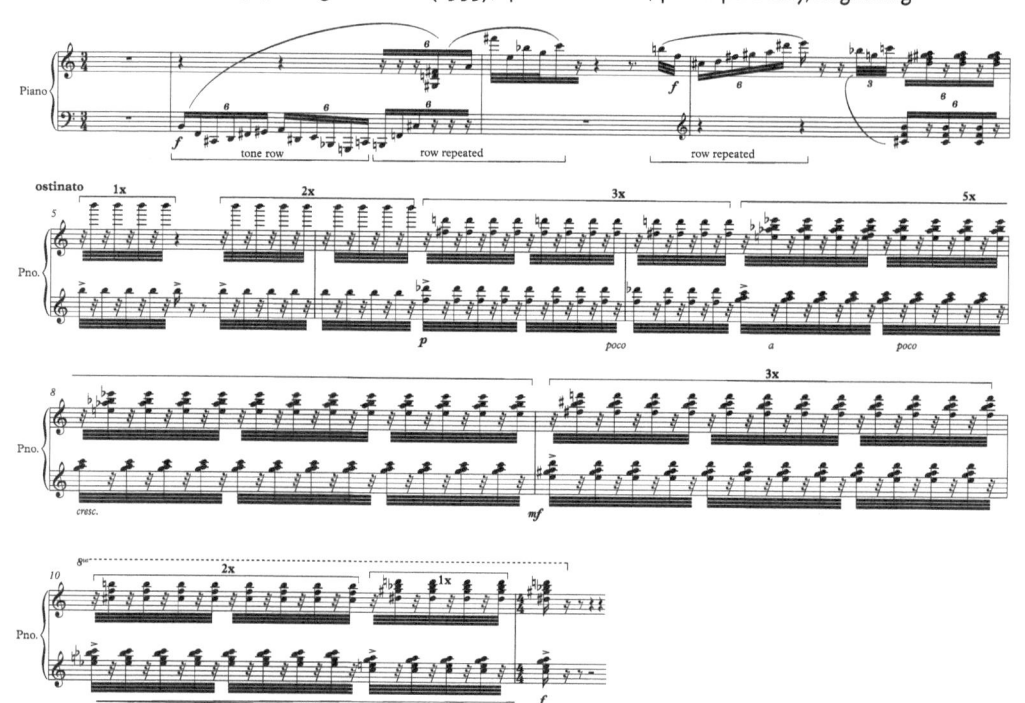

his seventy-fifth birthday. Following his guidance, she envisioned qi (literally "air," figuratively "material energy" or "life force") as reflecting "the space in Chinese paintings . . . , the dancing lines in Chinese calligraphy," and the spirit of the human mind.[19] The work's Western instruments stand in for Chinese ones: the flute, Chen says, should be played with the breathy tone quality of the dizi or the clay *xun*; the cello imitates the erhu and Chinese plucked instruments, such as the pipa; the percussion patterns often suggest Beijing opera; and gestures in the piano at times mimic the arpeggiated sounds of the zheng.

Qi begins with the cello alone presenting the main thematic material, which combines motives from three disparate Chinese sources into a single line (Example 4.5a). The opening tritone again draws its inspiration from the low singing of the leader of the Yao people Chen had heard on her 1980 field trip to Guangxi Province (see Example 3.11a and related discussion of Symphony No. 2). In *Qi* Chen recalls the oldest folk song she heard on that trip, dealing with the Chinese myth of the giant Pan Gu creating heaven and earth. Chen had used this low tritone (as well as the creation myth) the previous year in her *Chinese*

EXAMPLE 4.5. *Qi* (1997)

A. The opening cello line

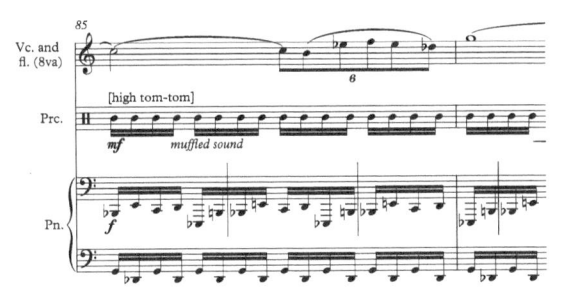

B. Letter G (m. 85)

Myths Cantata, which we discuss in Chapter 6. The major and minor seconds that follow the tritone come from the cadential figuration of choral folk songs of the Zhuang people—who also reside in the Guangxi region. The cello melody then ends with a flourish of fast notes, which Chen identifies as her "imitation of the shape of mountain song-singing, which is close to the sound of speech."

Several other compositional processes we have noted earlier appear in this work. In fact, the only one absent is the twelve-tone row. In Chapter 3, we noted the ostinato figuration in the piano beginning in measure 25 that reflects the telescoping rhythm characteristic of the shifan luogu percussion ensemble (Example 3.5a). This ostinato marks the beginning of section C (see the diagram in Figure 4.1). Another ostinato pattern marks the beginning of section G, a crucial moment when the tempo doubles (Example 4.5b). Here the six-note pattern in the right hand crosses the beat; it appears sixteen times and then is transposed up a seventh and played another twenty-one times. As is common in Chen's works, the fast ostinato figure interacts with a slower melodic line in the flute and cello.

Baban's rhythmic pattern appears twice in *Qi*, in much the same way as in *Song in Winter*; that is, as repeated notes striking the sixty-eight-beat pattern 3–2–3, 3–2–3, 4–4, and so forth. These renditions of Baban's rhythm, first in the percussion and then in the piano, immediately precede sections J and L, building a rhythmic climax approaching important structural moments. In the

Solo and Chamber Music Works

FIGURE 4.1. *Qi* (1997)

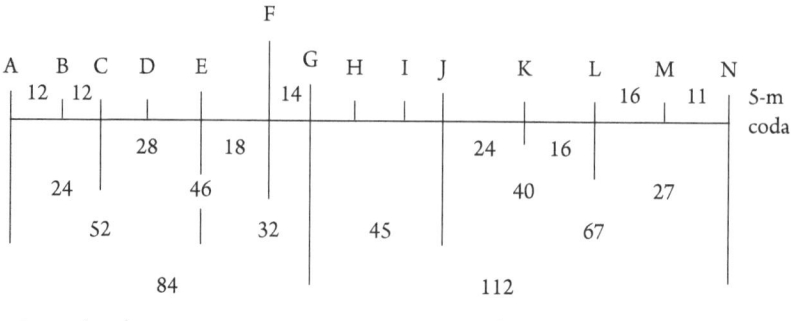

```
                          F
A   B   C   D   E    |   G   H   I   J     K      L    M    N
  12  12             |  14                      16    11   5-m
    |     28    18   |                24    16              coda
    24        46     |              40            27
       52            |    32    45          67
          84                       112
```

Part 1 (A–F): 70 × 2 = 140   Part 2 (F–N):
                                    F–G 14 × 2 (28) + G–N 112 = 140

A–G: quarter note = 56
G–N: quarter note = 112

A. Diagram, by the authors, of the form of the quartet

Sections	long part: short part	total: long part
C–F	28:18 = .64	46:28 = .61
A–F	24:46 [reverse GS] = .52	70:46 = .66
A–G	52:32 = .62	84:52 = .6
J–L	24:16 = .67	40:24 = .6
J–N	40:27 = .68	67:40 = .6
G–N	45:67 [reverse GS] = .67	112:67 = .6

B. Some proportional relationships among the sections

second instance, the end of each Baban line is punctuated by a rhythmic attack in the left hand as in *Song in Winter*. Years later Chen would use a similar procedure in "The Perpetual" (shown in Chapter 3, Example 3.18).

Qi exemplifies one of Chen's most rigorous applications of the Golden Section (Figure 4.1). Like the Piano Concerto, *Qi* is divided into two parts (A–F and F–N), with a tempo change traversing the sectional division. The first part (A–F) and the beginning of Part 2 (F–G) are twice as slow as G–N and therefore must be counted twice to compare the actual sounding length of the two sections. This calculation reveals that the two large sections of the piece are equal in duration. Within this overall binary form, however, relationships among sections generally reflect the Golden Section (3:2), as shown in Figure 4.1. Sections A-B and B-C, however, are equal; they form an introduction that models the balanced two-part form of the entire piece.

Works from 2000 to 2009

NING (VIOLIN, PIPA, CELLO, 2001)

The concert Hún Qiáo (Bridge of Souls), presented in St. Paul, Minnesota, on May 30, 2001, was the inspiration of violinist Young-Nam Kim, artistic director of the Chamber Music Society of Minnesota. Kim's aim was both to pay "homage to the victims and survivors of war atrocities"[20] and to bring about reconciliation among "three countries that hated and loved together," in the words of pipa player Wu Man.[21] The Society commissioned pieces from four composers: Chen Yi (China), Hi Kyung Kim (Korea), Michio Mamiya (Japan), and Andrew Imbrie (USA). Chen's was the only piece to call for a non-Western instrument. Once again, she wrote for Wu Man (dedicatee of *The Points*), but this time she coupled the pipa with cello and violin. Funding from the Barlow Endowment and the Hoeschler Fund[22] not only paid Wu Man's fee, but also enabled the appearance of famed cellist Yo-Yo Ma. Young-Nam Kim himself played the violin part. This commission initiated Chen's relationship with Yo-Yo Ma, for whom she would later write *Ballad, Dance, and Fantasy*.[23]

In *Ning*, Chen chose to memorialize the more than 200,000 Chinese victims of the six-week-long Nanjing massacre by Japanese forces that began in December 1937. The traumatic experience of escaping from Japanese bombs haunted Chen's parents ever afterward;[24] in fact, her mother often screamed in her sleep from repeated nightmares. The Chinese character "Ning," Chen reminds us, not only stands for the city of Nanjing—the capital of the country at the time—but also means "serene and peaceful." Her aim was to call the departed souls "back to a resting place" and "look forward to the peace of the world in the future."[25]

On the surface, *Ning* appears to be one of Chen's more abstract works, yet typical Chinese markers, such as sliding tones, grace notes, and pentatonic scales, appear within it. Much of the "Chineseness" of the work, however, comes about through the special effects created by the pipa, which is retuned, as in *The Points*, with the lower two strings raised a half step. *Ning* opens with a violent cello cadenza (Example 4.6a)—"hysteric crying and miserable sobbing" (the sobbing effect later enhanced by baroque-style descending two-note "sigh motives")—but it eventually settles into "gripping meditation and illusive fantasy."[26] Example 4.6b shows the beginning of the most striking moment of death and desolation, appearing about two-thirds of the way through the work, that is, near the Golden Section. Out of this desolation, emerges an oblique reference to the famous Chinese song "Jasmine Flower" ("Mo li hua"), fragments of which had appeared in earlier portions of the piece (Example 4.6c).[27] In Chen's reference the tune is heavily modified, with changes in rhythm and even some

EXAMPLE 4.6. *Ning* (2001)

A. The opening cello line

B. Portrayal of desolation (mm. 146–51)

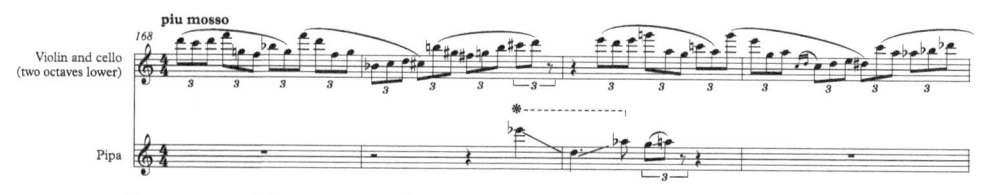

C. Emergence of the "Jasmine Flower" (mm. 168ff.)

pitches—so changed in fact that many listeners might miss the allusion. Chen may have felt, however, that the tune is so well known by Chinese people that virtually all of them would recognize it. The text translates as: "What a beautiful jasmine flower / Sweet-smelling, beautiful, stems full of buds / Fragrant and white, everyone praises / Let me pluck you down / Give you to someone else / Jasmine flower, oh jasmine flower."[28] Thus the simple innocence of the Chinese victims rises from the jaws of death. In a review of a New York performance in 2002, Allan Kozinn found *Ning* "a melancholy and sometimes terrifying visceral evocation of China during [the period just prior to] World War II."[29]

Ning constitutes part of a group of pieces on political themes Chen composed at the turn of the century, beginning with *Eleanor's Gift* marking the fiftieth anniversary of the United Nations' Declaration of Human Rights (1998) and continuing through four works written in 2001–2 in response to the 9/11 terrorist attack: the choral work "Know You How Many Petals Falling," the orchestral piece *Tu*, the string quartet *Burning*, and the mixed quintet . . . *as like a raging fire* . . . .

THREE BAGATELLES FROM CHINA WEST
(FLUTE/PIANO, AND OTHER ARRANGEMENTS; 2006)

Chen Yi points to *Three Bagatelles* as a turning point in her compositional development, a time when she began to explore extended settings of folk songs in her instrumental music, as opposed to short quotations from songs or simply folk song inspirations. The piece was commissioned by flutist Marya Martin, but it became so popular that Chen created numerous alternative versions for both Western and Chinese instruments, as detailed in Chapter 3. Each of the three movements draws on folk materials from a different minority ethnic group: in movement 1 the Jingpo people from southwest China; in movement 2 the Yi people—one of China's largest minority groups—who reside mostly in the mountainous areas in the western part of the country; and in movement 3 the Miao culture, a composite of many smaller linguistic groups, including the Hmong.

Indeed, *Three Bagatelles* contrasts sharply with Chen's previous uses of folk material, where small fragments of folk tunes might appear in the context of a larger Western-inspired composition. Although Chen had made arrangements of folk songs for chorus during her San Francisco years, in this piece she used regional songs—several of which she herself transcribed from recordings—as the basis for an instrumental work, setting them for European instruments and then decorating them, creating variations on them, and combining them in unique ways. In the first bagatelle, the flute plays a Jingpo farmer's song and imitates the *lerong*, a double-pipe bamboo instrument held obliquely in front of the player. One of the two pipes contains finger holes. Inserted transversely into the lower part of the other pipe is a small cylindrical tube that creates a reedlike sound.[30] The piano in this movement imitates a three-tongued jaw harp (*kouxian*),[31] which Chen chose to portray by leaps of sevenths, reinforcing the concluding interval of the tune (Example 4.7a). Following an extended presentation of the original song, Chen composed variations and elaborations on it, reinforced the piano part with octaves, and also inserted an extended flute cadenza.

Movement 2 opens with the pianist playing a twenty-three-bar melody based on the Yi folk song "Ashima" (a girl's name, literally meaning "more precious than gold"), to which Chen added punctuating minor ninths after each subphrase (Example 4.7b). The pianist repeats this melody throughout the movement, while the flute plays a version of the song "Nai Guo Hou" (Playing Tune), which Chen had heard on the bawu, an instrument shaped like a flute but containing a free reed and therefore closer in sound to a clarinet. The "Nai Guo Hou" tune contains passages of rapid notes, ending with long notes that the player bends downward in pitch (Example 4.7c). The simultaneous melodies in the two instruments are independent both modally and rhythmically. The movement is bimodal; and the two instruments make no attempt to coordinate rhythms or tempos. After the initial presentation of the bawu tune, Chen continues the flute part in the same style, creating variations in the typical Chinese tradition and leading ultimately to a haunting climax as the flute climbs to nearly the top of its range.

The finale follows similar principles with different regional inspirations. The piano part imitates an ensemble of lusheng, a Miao instrument composed of a cluster of bamboo pipes, each of which contains a free reed. The instruments, which come in different sizes, generally contain five or six pipes that sound in tight clusters. Meanwhile, the flute plays a Miao tune "Dou Duo" (or "Han Ge" meaning "shouting song"). After its initial presentation, Chen created her own music inspired by its style, while the piano part becomes increasingly intense rhythmically until it is interspersed with arpeggiated sextuplets to bring the work to a close.

In composing her *China West Suite* for two pianos or piano and marimba in 2007, Chen expanded the finale of *Three Bagatelles* for the new work's fourth movement. In addition, the suite's opening movement draws on "Ashima" and is thus related to the second of the bagatelles. In the suite's third movement, Chen used a process similar to that in *Three Bagatelles* by combining two Tibetan tunes, one a composite developed from several folk song sources, the other a lyric melody more directly created from a single borrowed tune.[32]

EXAMPLE 4.7. *Three Bagatelles from China West* (2006)

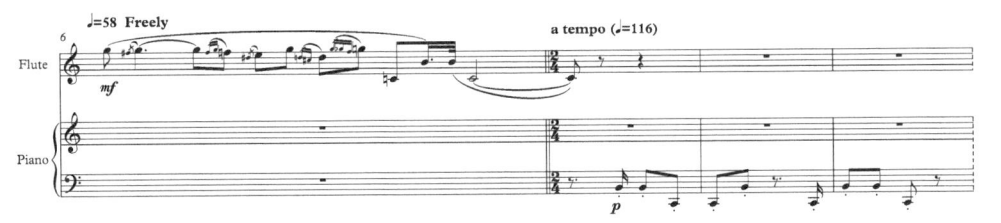

A. Bagatelle No. 1, mm. 6–9. The flute part shows the beginning of the *shange* (mountain song) tune. The piano imitates the kouxian.

B. Bagatelle No. 2, beginning. The piano plays "Ashima" interspersed with left-hand punctuations.

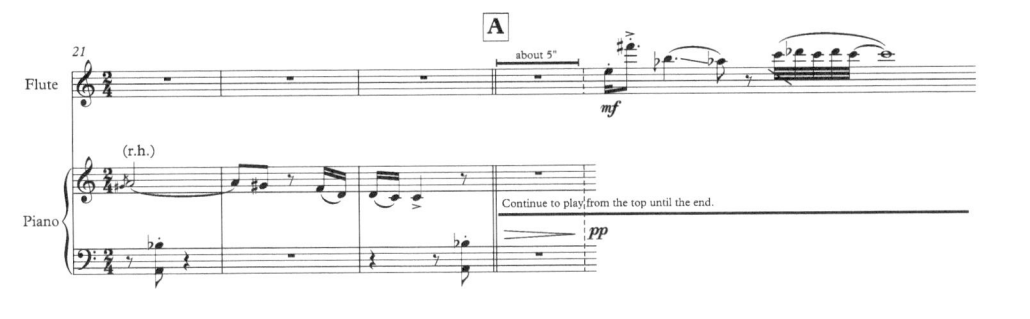

C. Bagatelle No. 2. The flute enters playing "Nai Guo Hou," while the pianist repeats "Ashima."

TUNES FROM MY HOME
(PIANO, VIOLIN, CELLO, 2007–8)

In the piano trio *Tunes from My Home*, Chen Yi found a compromise between referencing folk song styles and creating variations on borrowed melodies. She wrote the work for the Newstead Trio, whose pianist, Xun Pan, comes from a Cantonese-speaking family in Guangdong. To make Xun "smile and feel at home,"[33] Chen used three well-known Cantonese tunes that he would surely recognize: "Hantian lei" (Summer Thunder), "Sailong duojin" (Racing the Dragon Boat), and, most extensively "Ema yaoling" (Prancing Horses), whose captivating motive dominates most of the first movement.[34] As in the opening of *Qi*, discussed earlier, Chen combined the first two tunes to create a new composite melody (Example 4.8a). Beginning in m. 9 in the piano part, Chen reassembles the two segments of "Racing the Dragon Boat" originally split apart by "Summer Thunder." Beat 1 is a transposed version of measure 2 in the strings; beat 2 is a transposition of measure 6. This now-unified tune becomes an ostinato that Chen transposes by sequence. The same pattern recurs at various points later in the piece, sometimes in truncated form, sometimes intensified by the addition of open fifths.

The third tune, "Prancing Horses," is based on the Cantonese Yi Fan mode, which contains six pitches, the third and sixth of which are variable. This mode, as used in *Tunes from My Home*, includes the pitches B C♯ (D–D♯) E F♯ (G♯–A). Example 4.8b shows the measures in which Chen Yi first introduces the melody. During the course of her presentation, she uses both forms of the variable pitches: a D later becoming a D♯ and a G♯ becoming an A.

For the slow second movement, Chen transformed the opening four notes of the "Summer Thunder" motive introduced in movement 1 into a dreamy, languid melody by slowing the tempo, altering the rhythm, and adding "flowery" ornamental grace notes (Example 4.8c). This motive forms the basis for a loose fugue. Buried in the contrapuntal material, Chen hides the "Prancing Horses" motive as well. A piano ostinato appears periodically, featuring a repeating pattern consisting of three notes in the right hand against four in the left; the two patterns coincide after eight repetitions in the treble and six in the bass (8×3 = 6×4), after which Chen transposes the complex up a step twice. Ostinati, Chen reminds us, represent for her a recollection of her Beijing opera years. Typically, "a group of us would play a very simple ostinato, which would be repeated endlessly until the actors changed to the next section of dialogue or the next part of the performance." Her application of this process, however, is far more complex than her direct opera experience: typically, she creates

EXAMPLE 4.8. *Tunes from My Home (2007–8)*

A. Mvt. 1, beginning: "Summer Thunder" and "Racing the Dragon Boat" motives

EXAMPLE 4.8. Continued

B. Mvt. 1, mm. 26–31: "Prancing Horses" motive in the strings

C. Mvt. 2, beginning, left hand. Right hand plays same melody two octaves higher.

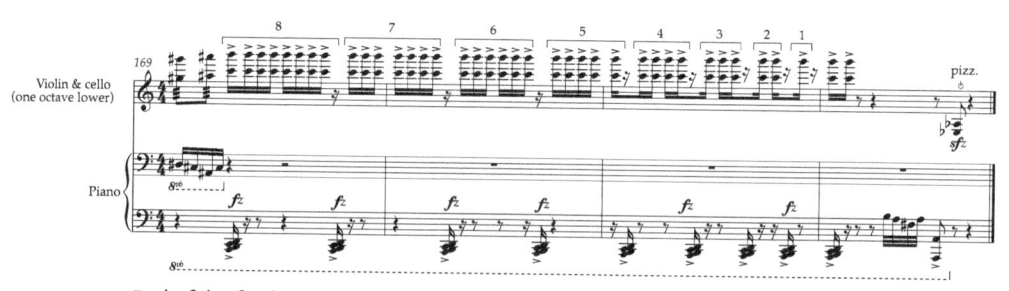

D. End of the final movement

ostinati with polyrhythms as in *Blue, Blue Sky* (Example 3.6) or the Woodwind Quintet (Example 4.2b), extended in length as in *Three Bagatelles*, or, as here, with repeated patterns containing different numbers of notes. "I don't want you to memorize my ostinato and sing along!" she says.

The final movement of *Tunes from My Home* is a revamping of the finale of *Ba Yin* ("Shifan Gong and Drum"). In this case Chen altered one section near the beginning and changed the final portion, but she preserved the dramatic ending with its repeated-note pattern of 8–7–6–5–4–3–2–1 and percussive clusters (Example 4.8d).

Three Recent Works

NORTHERN SCENES (PIANO SOLO, 2013)

In recent years, Chen Yi has continued to draw on influences that have motivated her since the 1980s while at the same time incorporating new ideas, some of them drawn from popular culture. *Northern Scenes*, written for pianist Susan Chan at Portland State University, represents the more abstract side of Chen's compositional personality while also retaining references to her Chinese heritage.

For the pitch materials in this piece, Chen constructed four hexachordal scales containing primarily major and minor seconds and minor thirds. The upward scales are mirrored in inversion (see Example 4.9a). Scale 4 is an exception in that it contains major thirds and a second octave with a new starting pitch of D. Note that the first interval in each scale increases in size by a half step (in the ascending version: C–D♭; then C–D; then C–E♭; and finally C–E).

As Example 4.9b shows, the piece begins with scale 1 in its descending form, followed by two clusters that include all but one of the pitches of configuration 1 (ascending and descending combined). The clusters also evoke the sound of the sheng. Scale 2 makes an appearance in measure 4. The intervening flourish in measure 3 consists of the pitches of scale 1, but out of order (pitches 1 4 5 6 2 3 6). By presenting the notes in this rearrangement, Chen creates a melodic line beginning with a tritone, semitone, and whole step, a pattern she later transforms into a contrasting declamatory melody for the B section (Example 4.9c). Comparing the distinctive flourish in measure 3 with the melody of section B (Examples 4.9b and c) shows the intricate relationship Chen creates between distant moments in the work: the first four sixteenth-notes of measure 3 (C–F♯–G–A) appear in the B section in retrograde and transposed up a step in the right hand (B–A–G♯–D) and then in transposed retrograde inversion in the left hand (B♭–C–D♭–G).

EXAMPLE 4.9. *Northern Scenes* (2013)

A. Hexachordal scales forming the basis of the composition. The example is adapted from sketches for the piece provided by the composer and incorporating her corrections to those sketches.

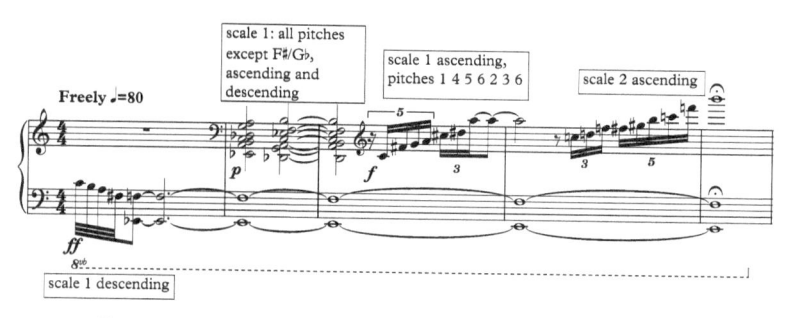

B. Beginning

C. Melody of the B section, built from a retrograde of the first four sixteenth-notes in Example 4.9b, m. 3, transposed up a step, and then imitated in inversion in the left hand

These hexachordal scales, manipulated in imaginative ways, form the basis for the entire composition. Thus *Northern Scenes* illustrates the balance of head and heart we cited in Chapter 3: a sophisticated theoretical construction undergirds an expressive, emotional work that on the surface gives the impression of freedom and improvisation.

BAMBOO DANCE (PIANO, 2013) AND *THREE DANCES FROM CHINA SOUTH* (DIZI, ERHU, PIPA, ZHENG; 2014)

Chen composed *Three Dances from China South* for the thirtieth anniversary of Music From China and dedicated the work to Susan Cheng, who had played such a pivotal role in her early years in New York. As in several earlier works, Chen calls for the zheng to retune many of its twenty-one strings so that all twelve chromatic pitches are available (though not in the same octave). Once again Chen draws from disparate minority Chinese cultures. In the first movement, "Lions Playing Ball," she quotes a folk tune accompanying a dance from the Chaozhou region of Guangdong Province, which she treats through the type of variation techniques she has refined over the course of her career. This tune had provided inspiration for Chen as early as her viola concerto of 1983 (*Xian Shi*). She used it again in a few later works, such as *Spring Festival*, a short piece for high school band (1999), and the first movement of the *Chinese Folk Dance Suite* (2000).

In the second movement, Chen moves to Hainan Island, calling to mind a dance of the Li people that traditionally celebrates the harvest. The ceremony involves pairs of people holding bamboo rods, which they clap in a steady pulse. The previous year Chen had composed a piano piece, *Bamboo Dance*, in which she evoked this same ceremony using a four-note staccato motive followed by a more lyrical one, both marked by falling sevenths (Example 4.10a). For *Three Dances* she orchestrated the first half of the piano piece. Following the clapping motive (in both pieces), Chen again evoked the Baban rhythm, this time interjecting the four-note staccato clap after each Baban phrase (Example 4.10b shows the beginning of this section), much as she had done in *The Soulful and the Perpetual* discussed in Chapter 3 (see Example 3.18). After the rendition of Baban's sixty-eight beats, *Three Dances* diverges from its piano model, repeating most of Baban again, but ending with an exploration of the four-note clap.

In the finale, Chen again recalls the lusheng ensemble of the Dong minority in Guangxi Province that had inspired many of her compositions since she first encountered the ceremonies associated with this ensemble in the 1980s. Over the rhythmic articulation of the lusheng reference, she overlays a slower

EXAMPLE 4.10. *Three Dances from China South* (2014)

A. Opening of the piano piece, *Bamboo Dance* (2013), adapted for the second movement of *Three Dances*

B. Mvt. 2, mm.15ff, showing the beginning of the Baban rhythm with intervening four-note clapping cells (boxed)

C. Mvt. 3, mm. 9–11. The pipa participates in the lusheng reference while the zheng and dizi play a melody from a Guangxi folk song.

lyrical melody adapted from a Guangxi folk song called "Swallow Flying with Mud in its Mouth" (Example 4.10c).

* * *

The foregoing discussion of selected chamber works from 1984 to 2014 shows Chen's compositional path to be one of accumulation rather than redirection. Whereas some composers abandon early influences and make sharp turns toward new modes of expression, Chen tends to gather together musical inspirations that stimulated her over the years, combining them in new ways. The compositional train she drives moves resolutely in one direction, picking up passengers and supplies along the way, compelling them to interact with creativity. A few elements (such as twelve-tone writing) have disembarked during the journey, but in general the sources of inspiration show a consistency that she has been able to cultivate over many decades. Unlike some other composers, Chen continues to feel an affinity for her early works. *Duo Ye* is as appealing to her now as it was in the 1980s. Baban, which first appeared in the Piano Concerto of 1992, continues to influence her most recent works. And mathematical structures continue to fascinate her as a means to facilitate coherence and stability. In the next chapter, we will see how Chen has applied these same compositional stimuli to works for large instrumental ensembles.

CHAPTER 5

Works for Large Instrumental Ensembles

CHEN YI HAS COMPOSED an impressive number of compositions for large ensembles: full orchestra, Chinese orchestra, string orchestra, wind ensemble, and concertos with various solo instruments. In the works catalogue at the end of this book, which covers pieces up to the time of our writing, we list about fifty compositions for large ensembles (with or without soloists), of which about twenty are concerti. Although only three of these pieces bear the generic title *symphony*, others, more colorfully named, are in effect in the same genre.

Ge Xu (Antiphony), 1994

Chen composed several major orchestral works in the early 1990s, including the Piano Concerto (1992) and Symphony No. 2 (1993) discussed in Chapter 3, as well as *Ge Xu*, written for the Women's Philharmonic as part of her residency with that organization. The title, which translates as *Antiphony*, was inspired by a traditional fall gathering at the Lunar New Year of the Zhuang people, the largest ethnic minority in southern China. In her notes, Chen writes about the antiphonal singing that takes place at this ceremony: "Distinct groups or individuals make up the texts" as a friendly competition.[1] For her pitch material, however, Chen drew not only on a Zhuang tune, but also on songs from the Miao and Yi peoples, mixing influences from different minority cultures as we have seen in other works, such as the *Chinese Folk Dance Suite*.

In the case of *Ge Xu*, Chen used three distinctive tunes, which she presents separately at the outset and then combines at the end. She quotes enough of the tunes for them to be recognizable but modifies them by adding ornaments, extending them in length, altering the rhythm, and/or modifying their intervallic structure to fit the contemporary melodic or harmonic vocabulary of the work. The first tune, a mountain song, "Fei Ge" (Flying Song) of the Miao people, exemplifies this process. Example 5.1 shows the original melody (a) and Chen's adaptation of it in the violin (b).[2] She replicates the first three notes precisely, but as the tune progresses Chen moves further from the model, not only decorating it with "flowers" but also expanding the rising perfect fourth E–A to a tritone and contracting the concluding major third (C♯–A) to a minor third and then inverting it to a complementary major sixth. The result is an expansive melody that reflects the shape of a borrowed tune, while avoiding what for Chen were the undesirable tonal implications of the perfect fourth and major third in the original *shange*. Such modifications and elaborations of borrowed tunes permeate Chen's compositions. For example, in *Momentum*, written for the Peabody Symphony in 1998, Chen drew the opening theme from her Beijing opera experiences but altered the m7 and P4 of the original to a M7 and a tritone (Example 5.1c),[3] creating a more contemporary soundscape for the primary theme.

For the second theme of *Ge Xu*, Chen drew less literally from her source. Here, she references an instrumental piece of the Bouyei people, traditionally played on the *shuangxiao*, a vertical flute with two pipes and three finger holes on each of them. One pipe sounds the tune, while the other may play in unison or sound a pedal tone.[4] The melody features a tritone at the start followed by rising and falling seconds. Chen captures the melody's characteristic intervals with a prominent theme played by the French horn but makes no attempt to replicate the melody's overall contour (Examples 5.1d and e).

Ge Xu's final tune, "A Xi Tiao Yue" (Dancing Tune of the Yi People), contrasts to the first two in its lively, rhythmic character, distinguished by rests and offbeat interjections (Example 5.1f). Chen quotes the rhythm of the original, but only loosely refers to its pitch material; instead, she recalls the minor third that began theme 1.

Ge Xu includes other stylistic features characteristic of Chen's music, for instance an ostinato that migrates rhythmically (mm. 36–40) and another one in polyrhythms (4 against 5 against 6) that appears first in m. 17 and is similar, though not identical, to the one in *Blue, Blue Sky* and *Dragon Rhyme* shown in Chapter 3 (Example 3.6). A climactic moment near the end features a percussion cadenza inspired by African drumming, where Chen makes reference to the Fibonacci series: repeated notes articulate groups of 2, 3, 5, and 8 (mm. 111–14).

EXAMPLE 5.1. *Ge Xu* (1994)

A. Mountain song, "Fei Ge," beginning. For the full melody, see Guo, "Chinese Musical Language," 146.

B. *Ge Xu*, opening, violin: first theme, derived from "Fei Ge." Notes taken from the original tune are shown in boxes. The fourth note and the last one are slightly altered; they reflect the shape of the tune, but with the interval sizes altered by half steps.

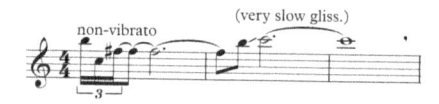

C. *Momentum* (1998), opening (piccolo)

D. Bouyei instrumental tune. For the full melody, see Guo, "Chinese Musical Language," 148.

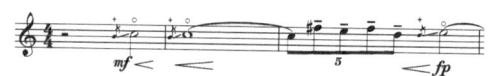

E. *Ge Xu*, mm. 24–26, horn: second theme

F. *Ge Xu*, mm. 67–69, violins: third theme

Two Related Works from the Late 1990s

FIDDLE SUITE (1997)

One of Chen Yi's most compelling works is the *Fiddle Suite* from 1997, commissioned by the Fromm Foundation. This work for solo huqin exists in several formats: with string quartet, string orchestra, full orchestra, or an orchestra of Chinese instruments. The term *huqin* refers to a family of bowed two-stringed instruments, whose small body may be round, hexagonal, or octagonal. The bow hair passes between the two strings, thus requiring a virtuosic technique in which the player activates one string by pulling upward with the bow while sounding the other by pressing down. The huqin comes in various sizes (and therefore different ranges). Chen calls for three of them. The most common huqin is the erhu, which, at a medium pitch level, excels in cantabile lines. That instrument is used in the opening movement. The lower-pitched *zhonghu* was developed more recently to expand the range of the traditionally treble-dominated Chinese orchestra; it serves as the counterpart to the Western viola. Chen calls for this more mellow instrument in the second movement, where it "recites" an eleventh-century text by Su Shi. For the finale, Chen scores for the high-pitched *jinghu* from Beijing opera to bring the concerto to a lively dancelike close.[5]

The opening movement is lyrical, as befits the erhu timbre, and features imitation between the soloist and the cellos near the beginning, underlaid by a polyrhythmic ostinato (5 against 6). In the middle section, Chen draws on the shifan luogu tradition by writing arpeggiated lines that expand from seven notes to nine, eleven, thirteen, and fifteen, while intervening lines in the cello simultaneously shorten. Overall, the movement is in a loose A B A' form.

The most unusual movement of the suite is the second, in which Chen derived her melodic material directly from the tonal inflections of a poetic text. The movement begins with Chen's wandering chromatic in the background, leading into the entry of the zhonghu, which literally declaims the entire Su Shi text. As she had explored the previous year in the *Chinese Myths Cantata* and would do later in *Happy Rain on a Spring Night* (2004), Chen translated the tonal inflections of the poem into the solo instrument's melodic line, often exaggerating the inflections and creating an expansive tessitura (Example 5.2a; see also Example 3.7a). In most works, Chen would utilize only small parts of a poem; in the Fiddle Suite, however, she adopted the inflections of the entire Su Shi text, which form the basis for the full movement.

In the exciting finale, Chen quotes the *qupai*, "The Night Deepens" (discussed in Chapter 3), but she reshaped the original melody and adjusted it to

EXAMPLE 5.2. *Fiddle Suite* (1997)

A. Mvt. 2, mm. 6–15: wandering chromatic in the orchestra, followed by recitation by the zhonghu

B. Mvt. 3, jinghu part, mm. 31–34. Note the resemblance to Baban's opening phrase; Example 3.1a.

a late-twentieth-century expressive language. One simple technique involved expanding the typical m7 interval of Beijing opera to a M7, in a similar manner as in the example from *Momentum* shown earlier. The following four-note melody bears close resemblance to the beginning of Baban, though with an initial leap of a sixth instead of a fifth (compare Example 5.2b with 3.1a).

PERCUSSION CONCERTO (1998)

The *Fiddle Suite* provided material for the Percussion Concerto, composed a year later for the renowned virtuoso Evelyn Glennie, who is severely hearing impaired.[6] Glennie's connection to Chen Yi came through an old schoolmate, Shui Lan, director of the Singapore Symphony, who gave the percussionist one of Chen's orchestral CDs. Glennie decided to commission Chen and then promptly announced on Chinese television that Chen was writing the piece. "So I cannot stop now," Chen joked in a June 1998 interview.[7]

For the new work Chen rescored two movements from the *Fiddle Suite*; its finale became the concerto's opening movement and the distinctive slow movement became the concerto's middle movement. In this case, however,

Chen calls on the soloist to actually sing the Su Shi poem. The pitches through which she rendered the exaggerated tonal inflections of the spoken text are essentially the same as those in the *Fiddle Suite*, but at times she altered the rhythm, simplified the vocal line, changed the surrounding accompanimental material, and moved parts of the zhonghu line to the orchestral instruments (compare Example 5.2a from the *Fiddle Suite* with Example 3.7c from the Percussion Concerto). Chen's intention is that the percussionist declaim the text half-sung, half-spoken (in a fashion similar to Sprechstimme); the pitches need not be precise.

The Percussion Concerto's finale, "Speedy Wind," is a tour de force, exploiting Glennie's formidable technique. It begins with the Baban rhythmic pattern, each beat being transformed into a measure (Example 5.3a). The repeated pitches in the orchestra, featuring seconds and sevenths, evoke opera percussion. As discussed in Chapter 3, Chen normally marks Baban's lengthened fifth line by a musical delineator that highlights the added four-beat "conjunctive" phrase extension, and she typically emphasizes in some manner the position of the Golden Section, which occurs midway through this added phrase (see Example 3.14). In this finale from the Percussion Concerto, the position of the conjunctive phrase is signaled by a change from eighth notes to triplets and a dramatic thinning of the texture (the percussionist plays alone). Chen then heralds the Golden Section itself with an accented interjection by the orchestra, a return to eighth notes, and a change in the solo player's instruments from Chinese tom toms to *dagu* (a large drum; Example 5.3b). Chen was still attracted to twelve-tone rows as ostinati and introduces one in the center of the movement (Example 5.3c). She emphasizes, however, that more important than having all twelve pitches are the open strings on the first and fourth beats of the figuration (boxed), which make the G and A stand out more prominently than the other notes, thus reinforcing the major ninth. Later in the movement, a rhythmic figuration foreshadows the wonderful "Shifan Gong and Drum" movement of *Ba Yin* (2001), which would be so influential in later pieces.

The Percussion Concerto met with rave reviews at its world premiere in Victoria (Singapore Symphony, 1999), its US premiere in Washington, DC (2001), and its European premiere in London (2003). Matthew Rye perhaps summed up its effect most succinctly in a review in the UK's *Daily Telegraph*: The piece largely avoided gimmicks, he wrote, and produced "a hybrid of Chinese and Western sounds, Beijing opera meets Hollywood thriller."[8]

EXAMPLE 5.3. Percussion Concerto (1998), mvt. 3

A. Beginning, showing Baban's rhythmic pattern

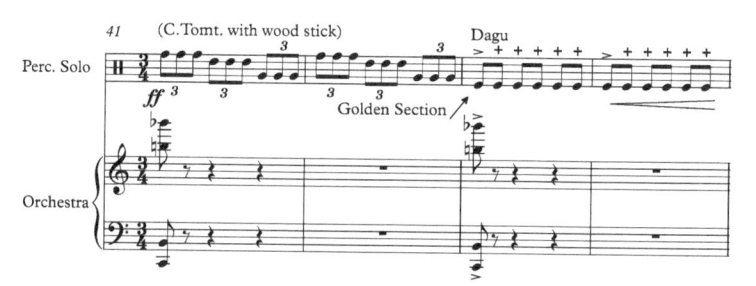

B. Conjunctive phrase in Baban's fifth line, and the Golden Section

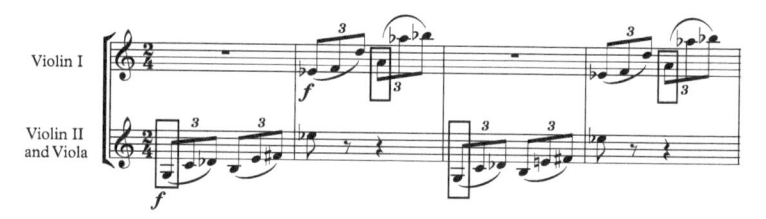

C. Twelve-tone ostinato in the orchestra, beginning in m. 73

Two Works from the Early 2000s

BALLAD, DANCE, AND FANTASY (2003)

Chen Yi had first written for famed cellist Yo-Yo Ma in the trio *Ning*, composed in 2001 for the Chamber Music Society of Minnesota (Chapter 4). So she was delighted to be commissioned to compose a work for him again, this time a cello concerto to be premiered by the Pacific Symphony based in Orange County, California, in a "Tradewinds from China" concert, part of the orchestra's 2004 American Composers Festival.

In the concerto's three movements, Chen traces a journey along the ancient Silk Road, starting from central China and moving westward through the Middle East to Europe. In Chapter 3 we discussed the romanticized Silk Road legend that inspired this work and showed the Shaanxi folk song that informed the cello part in the opening movement, with which Chen intended to symbolize "an old master telling an ancient story of the earth" (Example 3.10). The asynchronous microtonal passage in the second violins beginning in measure 9 creates an atmospheric background wash of sound to accompany the expressive melodic line of the soloist, which is filled with single, double, and triple grace notes and slides, creating an impression of improvisation. The central part of the movement contains one of Chen's most complex ostinato patterns in the accompanying strings (Example 5.4). The first violins play a figure in quintuplets repeated ten times and then transposed down a half step (except for the first note) while the second violins simultaneously play a pattern in sextuplets (also repeated ten times and then transposed *up* a half step). Complicating the polyrhythm is the viola line, which rhythmically aligns with the first violins but has a repeating pattern of seven pitches. Against this multilayered ostinato the solo cello intones a lyrical slow melody that introduces groups of four and three. Chen had previously used this same ostinato figure in the first movement of the *Fiddle Suite*; its effect in both cases is to provide a blurry background to a slower solo line.

Prior to the first performance, Chen Yi met with Yo-Yo Ma. Instead of asking her about the interpretation of her new work, as she expected, he had her sing the original folk songs that inspired the melodies and write down the names of the provinces from which they came. For the first movement "he created some special fingerings to imitate the rough, wild, and passionate folk singing style and thereby captured the spirit of the folk music," recalls Chen. "It became a truly invaluable experience for both of us."

Moving westward, the second movement draws inspiration from the predominantly Muslim Uighur culture of northwest China, which Chen had previ-

EXAMPLE 5.4. *Ballad, Dance, and Fantasy* (2003)

A. Beginning of the ostinato section in mvt. 1, mm. 45–49

B. Mvt. 2, beginning, violin 1 and percussion 1 only

C. Mvt. 2, mm. 26–29, solo cello part only, referencing Uighur mugham system

ously explored in the *Chinese Folk Dance Suite* of 2001.⁹ Although she uses 7/8 meter again, this work is not in any way an arrangement of the earlier piece. As might be expected, however, some of the rhythmic motives and melodic gestures are similar (compare Example 5.4b with 3.12). Following an introductory section, Chen references the culture's twelve *mughams*: that is, modes and melodic formulas that guide improvisation and composition (Example 5.4c). Her intention was to highlight mugham 12 in particular, but she notes that her newly composed melody bears similarities to other modes as well.

The finale of the concerto, "Fantasy," is a revised and expanded version of the "Shifan Gong and Drum" movement of *Ba Yin* but with the cello imitating an electric bass with descending glissandos at phrase endings. At the concert, Chen recalls, Ma joined the orchestra in playing his solo part as if a rock 'n' roll band were transporting the Chinese village celebration to the West.

SI JI (2005)

The fifteen-minute orchestral work *Si Ji*, composed two years after *Ballad*, does not bear the title "symphony," but it certainly could have. It is divided into four movements played without any breaks, providing the typical contrasts in a symphony. The sections, in this case, illustrate the seasons, inspired by four poems from the Song Dynasty by Su Shi (1037–1101) and Zeng Gong (1019–1083).[10] *Si Ji* was the second work commissioned by the Swiss multinational health care company Roche (founded in 1896) as part of an arts program developed in conjunction with the Lucerne Festival, its artistic director Michael Haefliger, the Cleveland Orchestra, and Carnegie Hall.[11] (The first commission was awarded to British composer Harrison Birtwistle, whose *Night's Black Bird* premiered in 2004.) Chen again showed her long-lasting debt to Chou Wen-chung by dedicating the work to him.

Although *Si Ji*'s four sections contrast in tempo and dynamics, the entire work is unified by its references to Baban, which, as we have seen, had inspired Chen repeatedly since her first use of it more than a decade earlier. In the first movement, "Spring," she uses Baban's sixty-eight-beat pattern (Chapter 3, Example 3.14) to govern the movement's structure in a manner similar to, but not as complex as, that in the Piano Concerto. Here, as in the octet *Sparkle*, the time signatures reflect the Baban rhythmic pattern with each beat doubled: for example, the first phrase of the original melody, 3–2–3, becomes 6/4–4/4–6/4. Melodically, Chen highlights the first four, or interestingly— and non-obviously—sometimes the first *five*, pitches of Baban, as shown in Example 5.5a. This motive appears throughout the four movements, varied in ways we have shown in other works, most notably *The Golden Flute*: Chen

EXAMPLE 5.5. Use of Baban opening motive in *Si Ji* (2005)

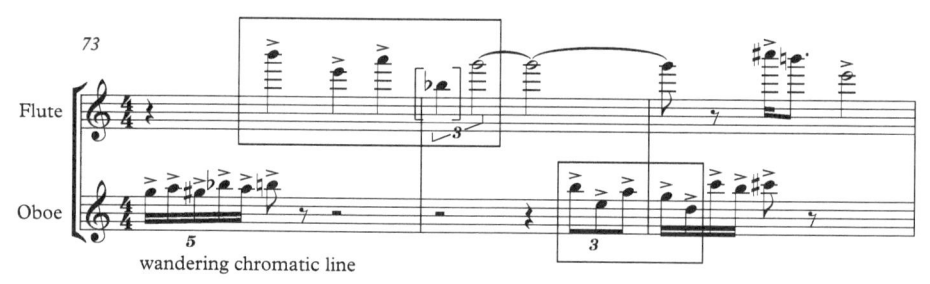

Baban opening phrase

Trumpets, m. 5

A. First five pitches quoted

Flute

Oboe

wandering chromatic line

B. Extra note inserted (bracketed) and motive imitated in rhythmic diminution (boxed)

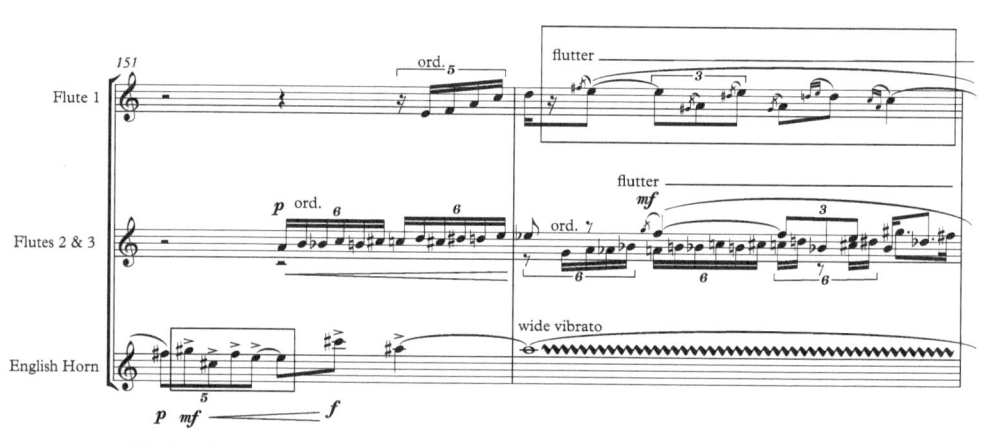

Flute 1

Flutes 2 & 3

English Horn

C. Motive altered into a quintuplet (m. 151), decorated with grace notes (m. 152), and with first two notes repeated (m. 152), coupled with wandering chromatic

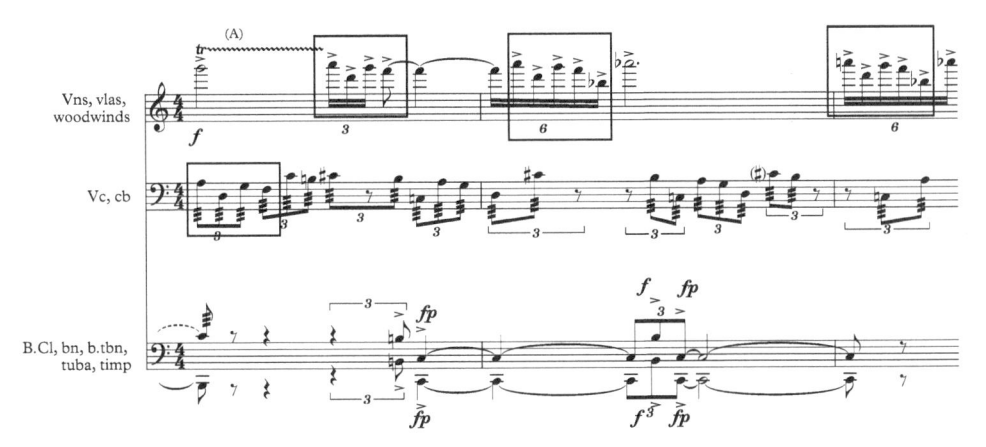

D. Climactic section of the final movement, mm. 197–99

sometimes expands it by the insertion of a foreign pitch, uses it in imitation and with rhythmic diminution, decorates it with ornamental grace notes, extends it by repeating pitches, or alters it rhythmically (Examples 5.5b and c). The motive finally reaches a dramatic climax in the last part of movement 4 (Winter), where Chen punctuates it with descending major sevenths (Example 5.5d).

The Cleveland Orchestra performed *Si Ji* several times in 2005: first in Lucerne in August and then in Cleveland and New York in October. The work was phenomenally successful, reflected in its selection as a finalist for the 2006 Pulitzer Prize.

Ancient Chinese Beauty (recorder concerto, 2008)

Chen Yi composed *Ancient Chinese Beauty* for the renowned Danish recorder player Michala Petri in anticipation of the sixtieth anniversary of uninterrupted diplomatic relations between Denmark and China, to be celebrated in 2010. Petri premiered the work in Beijing on April 4, 2008, and repeated it in Latvia and Denmark later the same year.

In this instance, Chen took inspiration from Chinese visual arts. The first movement celebrates the vivid ceramics of the Han Dynasty (206 BCE–220 CE); the second, the "fierce-looking totem patterns on bronze wine vessels." Chen compares the final movement (a minor revision of the "Shifan Drum and Gong" movement of *Ba Yin*) to the "dancing lines and layers in ink calligraphy."

For the opening movement, Chen recast a sextet, *The Han Figurines*, that she had composed two years earlier for "the adventurous new-music ensemble"

Opus 21 in Kalamazoo, Michigan.[12] The dramatic change in instrumentation to a recorder concerto required a major reworking of the material, although the length of the movement corresponds to that of the sextet and the thematic material is basically identical. The first minute or so of *Han Figurines* is in itself an altered recasting of the slow second movement of the *Chinese Myths Cantata* from 1996, in which the zhuihu "speaks" in the voice of the goddess Nü Wa (see Chapter 6). Here the recorder soloist directly takes on the goddess's persona. Was Chen perhaps expressing her admiration of the extraordinary talent of Michala Petri?

The beginning of the first movement shows Chen's personal adaptation of the pentatonic modal system (Example 5.6). The alto recorder begins as if it were going to sound the gong mode, while the second violins imply an inverted shang mode. In both cases, however, the mode is disrupted after a few notes. In the recorder part, the fourth note should be A to continue in the mode; in the violins, the fifth and sixth notes should be a half step higher, that is, C♯ B. (Although this analysis is ours, Chen Yi enthusiastically endorses it, though she says the process was subconscious.)[13] The two lines outline dissonant intervals (M9, m9), thus bringing the Chinese influence into alignment with a contemporary Western language. The compositional process here resembles the one we previously noted in Chen's alterations of borrowed melodies in *Ge Xu* (Example 5.1); in both cases, she references her Chinese musical heritage but tweaks it to meet her own aesthetic choices. The movement contains other stereotypical Chinese markers, such as sliding tones and grace notes, as well as Chen's ubiquitous wandering chromatic lines and dissonant clusters played in tremolos. In her notes, Chen highlights the contrasting themes of Han sculpture that inspired these varied figurations: "the enraptured storyteller, the vivid acrobat and the moving dancers with long sleeves."

In the second movement, "The Ancient Totems," the soloist switches from the bright alto recorder to the lower-pitched, more mellow tenor instrument (similar to the change of huqin instruments in the *Fiddle Suite*). Totem, she writes in her program notes, is an auspicious symbol to express "an irresistible force and a historical inevitability." The movement contains slides, microtonal trills, harmonics, and repeated notes that gradually accelerate.

The transformation of *Ba Yin*'s finale into the last movement of *Ancient Chinese Beauty* creates an extremely virtuosic challenge for the recorder player (who now reverts to the more agile alto instrument). As in *Ba Yin*, the movement alternates between sections featuring the soloist alone (sometimes with interjected chords in the orchestra) and those in which the orchestra plays

EXAMPLE 5.6. *The Ancient Chinese Beauty* (2008), opening, solo recorder and violin 2 only

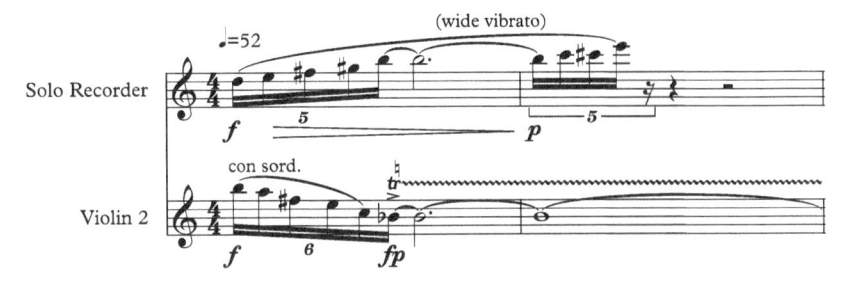

the shifan luogu patterns with various intervals representing different instruments (see the discussion of *Ba Yin* in Chapter 3). As with the earlier work, in each rendition of the tutti sections Chen changes the order of presentation of these intervals to represent a different leading instrument. Listening to this captivating movement, it becomes obvious why Chen Yi was so attracted to her original "Shifan Drum and Gong" creation. With each transformation—from saxophones and orchestra in *Ba Yin* to a sextet or septet in *Wu Yu*, to a cello concerto in *Ballad, Dance, and Fantasy*, to a piano trio in *Tunes from My Home*, to a recorder concerto in this work, and finally to a choral/string quartet version in *From the Path of Beauty*—the movement takes on a new character but retains its infectious energy.

The 2010s

DRAGON RHYME (2010)

Chen Yi composed the fifteen-minute band piece, *Dragon Rhyme*, on a commission from the National Wind Ensemble Consortium Group (composed of thirty-five bands).[14] The Hartt College Wind Ensemble (led by Glen Adsit) played the premiere performance in Carnegie Hall on May 30, 2010. The piece draws on two previous works: the finales of Symphony No. 3 (2004) and *Symphonie "Humen 1839"* (2009), which Chen Yi composed jointly with Zhou Long. The image of the dragon not only captures the power of a large ensemble of wind and percussion instruments but also reflects the symbol of this beast in Chinese lore: it is, says Chen, "auspicious, fresh, and vivid."[15]

The piece is a fine example of Chen's adaptation of procedures she had refined since the 1980s, including sophisticated ostinato and variation techniques, as well as recollections of her experiences in the Beijing opera troupe. *Dragon Rhyme* opens with a complex multilayered ostinato featuring a 4 against 6 polyrhythm, different length repetition patterns, and irregular substitution of rests for notes. She later used it, with minor changes, in *Blue, Blue Sky* (Chapter 3, Example 3.6a). Such polyrhythmic ostinati date back as far as the Woodwind Quintet (1987) (Example 4.2b). Other examples abound. *The Golden Flute* (1997), for instance, begins with one characterized by 4 against 7. The effect, as with the complex ostinati in *Ballad* and the *Fiddle Suite* discussed earlier, is an indistinct atmosphere resulting from the blending of the individual lines.

Like *The Golden Flute* and *Si Ji*, *Dragon Rhyme* centers around a single theme that permeates its two movements. First introduced in full in m. 40 (Example 5.7a), this theme calls to mind the jue mode (which would include the pitches D♯, F♯, G♯, B, C♯), if one discounts the pick-up E. Its disjunct shape highlights important intervals that characterize Beijing opera tunes. For the previous ten bars, Chen had teased the listener by anticipating elements of the tune. Later in the piece she dramatically transforms the motive using her now well-honed variation skills; it appears slurred, fragmented, augmented, altered rhythmically and in terms of intervals, treated canonically, and harmonized with fourths and seconds (Examples 5.7b and c). Other ostinato motives appear within the work as well, including one in the percussion that recalls the shifan luogu figurations of *Ba Yin* and its derivatives.

BLUE, BLUE SKY (2012)

Blue, Blue Sky, written in 2012 for the tenth anniversary of the Beijing Modern Music Festival, draws on elements from several previous works, but is not a direct arrangement of any of them. For the opening (Example 5.8a), Chen used the Tibetan tune "Du Mu," on which she had also based the opening movement of the *China West Suite* for two pianos (2007). At measure 18 she introduces the ostinato with irregularly spaced missing pitches from *Dragon Rhyme* discussed in Chapter 3 (Example 3.6a), but the surrounding material differs. In this case Chen overlaid the ostinato with an augmented and simplified version of the "Du Mu" opening melody in the horns (Example 5.8b).

The center section begins with an adaptation of the slow movement of *Tunes from My Home*, a "fugue in delicate and sensitive expression"[16] titled "Nostalgia," which Chen had already orchestrated as the second movement of Prelude and Fugue (2009). She quotes her previous work for only twelve measures, however, and even in that quotation diverges from the source material in several places.

EXAMPLE 5.7. *Dragon Rhyme* (2010)

A. Main theme and its anticipation (oboes, mm. 38–40)

B. Theme slurred (oboe) and fragmented (clarinet)

C. Theme augmented (horn) and altered in terms of intervals and rhythm (flute), mm. 110–11

EXAMPLE 5.8. *Blue, Blue Sky* (2012)

A. Main theme, from "Du Mu" (flute, m. 2–3)

B. Augmented version of theme in the horns (m. 20ff), which appears simultaneously with the ostinato taken from *Dragon Rhyme* shown in Example 3.6a

Flashbacks

CHINESE RAP (2013), RECALLING SYMPHONY NO. 3 (2004)

In two works from the 2010s, *Chinese Rap* and *Four Spirits*, Chen Yi looked back to earlier works and to influences that in some cases dated back to her earliest days in New York. *Chinese Rap*, written for violinist Helen Kim and the Kennesaw State University Symphony Orchestra, draws on Chen's remembrances of the subway music she encountered when she first arrived in the United States. The strong impression of that experience has surfaced directly in only a few compositions, one of which was the Symphony No. 3 (composed for the Seattle Symphony in 2004), which had a direct impact on *Chinese Rap*. The symphony bears a self-reflective program charting Chen's own geographic and musical journey. Movement 1, "The Dragon Culture," evokes her Chinese heritage and references the dragon as the symbol of "power and spirit." In the middle movement, entitled "The Melting Pot," Chen mixes this Chinese background with New York's pop culture. In the finale, "Dreaming," she notes that "only in the world of dreams can I forget that I am far away from my homeland."

The "Melting Pot" movement of the symphony opens with a percussion riff and random pizzicato pitches in the contrabasses, repeated for thirty seconds, representing Chen's interpretation of a background drum-set (Example 5.9a). Over this ostinato, the flute plays a melody inspired by a folk song from Shandong Province that Chen had previously used in her string quartet, *At the Kansas City Chinese New Year Concert* (2002).[17] In the quartet, she combined it asynchronously with a second melody in a procedure she had used as early as 1997 in the choral work "Spring Dreams" and would later explore in works such as *Three Bagatelles* (2006; see Chapter 4.) In the Symphony No. 3, Chen reinforces the asychronicity by specifying different tempi for the cymbal/contrabass part (quarter=108) and the flute (quarter=96). The contrapuntal layering then increases as Chen adds bimodal melodies first in the celli and then in the violins. As the layering becomes denser, the percussion line increases in length, its dotted rhythms more clearly evoking rap. Then, as the movement progresses, Chen makes a specific reference to the 1996 song, "Woo hah!! Got You All in Check" by Busta Rhymes, in which the rapper interjects the exclamation "Woo hah!" at the ends of lines or sections. Chen grabbed this two-note motive as a memory of subway music. She hints at it in the beginning of the opening movement and then brings it fully to the forefront in "Melting Pot," where she interjects "woo hah!" exclamations, at first intermittently in the trumpets, and later repeatedly in the horns and tuba, punctuating a repeated note figure that evokes a rap accompaniment (Example 5.9b).

EXAMPLE 5.9. Symphony No. 3 (2004), mvt. 2 ("The Melting Pot")

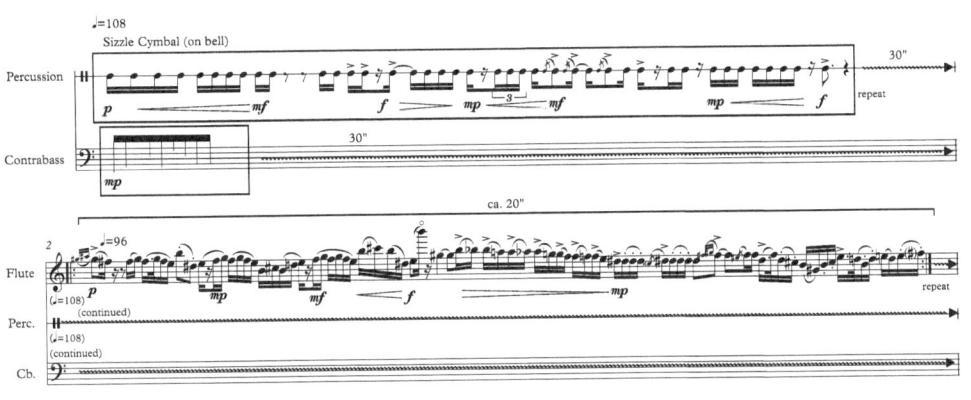

A. Beginning

B. Mm. 75–78, showing rap percussion and the "Woo hah!" interjections in the horns

In 2013 Chen returned to the inspiration of subway music, as well as to the Chinese tradition of quyi (musical storytelling), when she created *Chinese Rap* for violin and orchestra. Actually, says Chen, "some performers in quyi tradition tell stories in rap style with a pair of bamboo clappers in hand, while others play accompanying percussion or plucked instruments between sung sections." *Chinese Rap* opens with the same percussion motive as in the symphony, but this time the repetitions are notated in the same tempo as the surrounding material. The melody that then appears in the clarinet bears a distant relation to that in the symphony, but its many grace notes and slides suggest Chinese plucking techniques (Example 5.10a). Chen had used this material in a duet for violin and piano entitled *From Old Peking Folklore* (2009), but it takes on a very different complexion in this new piece, superimposed on the rap percussion line. Here Chen has truly created a transcultural melody, drawing from popular music styles of the West but deliberately singing them with a Chinese accent. In the next section, the tune morphs into a pentatonic melody as an introduction to the main theme (thus highlighting its Chinese character), after which the solo violinist enters with a reference to quyi singing (Example 5.10b). In a later episode Chen recalls the instrumental interludes typically inserted between sections in a quyi performance, evoking the tradition's bamboo clappers and other accompanying instruments and even suggesting the beginning phrases of Baban (3–2–3, 3–2–3) with repeated dissonant chords in the strings and interjected claps in the woodwinds (Example 5.10c; compare with the similar procedure in *Bamboo Dance*, Example 4.10b). After a virtuosic cadenza bringing together the movement's many themes and ending with an exclamation by the soloist on Chen's favorite M7 interval, she concludes, as in many other works, with a recapitulation that introduces variations on the previous motives and an energetic coda.

FOUR SPIRITS (2016)

Chen continued to draw on Symphony No. 3 three years later in *Four Spirits*—a concerto for piano and orchestra in four movements. Here, she makes reference to Chinese legends associated with four regions of her home country: "The Blue Dragon in the East," "The Black Xuanwu in the North," "The White Tiger in the West," and "The Red Phoenix in the South." For the opening movement, Chen used parts of Symphony No. 3's third movement, "Dreaming," but greatly expanded it from a six-minute miniature to an eleven-and-a-half-minute tour de force for both orchestra and soloist. The main theme of this movement, shown in Example 5.11a, bears a close similarity to that of *Dragon Rhyme* (Example 5.7a). At its introduction in *Four Spirits* at measure 8, Chen reused material

EXAMPLE 5.10. *Chinese Rap* (2013)

A. Background melody in the clarinet, mm. 8–10

B. Mm. 43–49. The melody is transformed into a pentatonic tune in the marimba and bassoons as an introduction to the theme. The main melody enters in the solo violin.

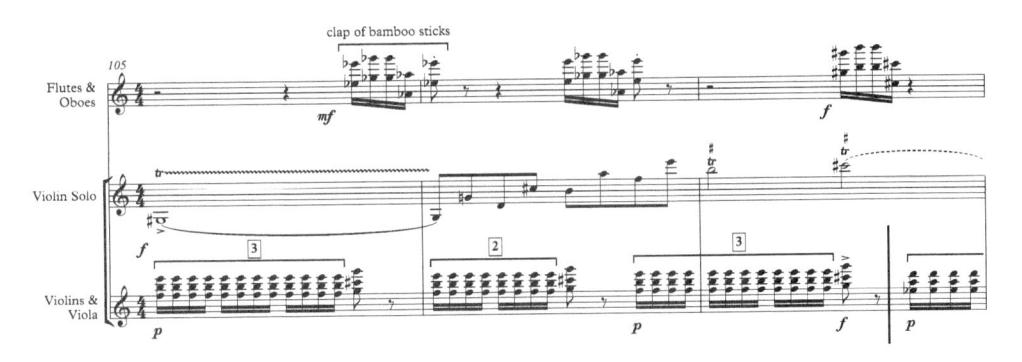

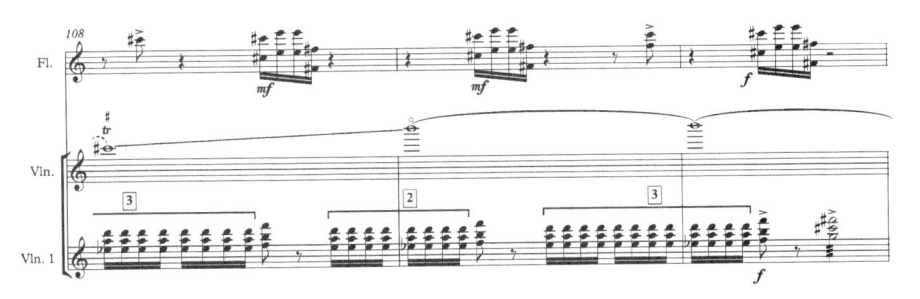

C. Mm 105–110, selected instruments only, showing reference to the first phrases of Baban (3-2-3, 3-2-3) and the bamboo clapping sticks. Compare with Example 4.10.

EXAMPLE 5.11. *Four Spirits* (2016), mvt 1

A. Main melody, oboe, mm. 8–9. Compare Example 5.8a, main theme.

B. Mm. 148–50. The melody is transformed into a quiet zheng evocation in the solo piano.

from the symphony for eleven measures and then diverged into new music. The opening section combines this lively melody with some of Chen's favorite devices: polyrhythmic ostinati and wandering chromatic lines. The central part of the movement introduces great contrasts, the most striking of which is a quiet interlude in which the theme is transformed into a delicate passage that might remind Western listeners of windchimes but for Chen imitates the arpeggiations of a zheng (Example 5.11b).

The concerto's second movement, named for Xuanwu, a powerful god of Taoism associated with northern China, is an orchestration of the piano piece, *Northern Scenes* (discussed in Chapter 4). Clusterlike low background chords create a mysterious, gloomy panorama. The third movement is largely new, but does make reference to another piano piece, *Ji-Dong-Nuo*, from 2005. In a technique similar to one used in the quintet... *as like a raging fire...*, Chen has the soloist play an ostinato pattern at the extreme ends of the keyboard; this effect, contained in a section in the middle of the movement, begins with the piano alone and builds to a climactic orchestral tutti. For the final movement, Chen took a long look back to *The Golden Flute* concerto of 1997. In transcribing its last movement for piano and orchestra, she instituted substantial changes and omitted the cadenza, but her revisitation of the early work, which once again references the opening notes of Baban, reaffirms her unwavering attraction to this ancient Chinese qupai.

* * *

The compositional techniques we have noted in Chen's works for large ensembles are consistent with those in other genres: evocations of Chinese inspirations both aural and visual, creative modifications of Chinese traditional musical materials, flowery and structural variation processes, rhythmically complex ostinati, the persistent influence of Baban, mixtures of musical inspirations drawn from various regions of China, and the combining of Chinese inspirations with those she encountered in her adopted country. Chen's continual reworking of her earlier works shows the consistency of her compositional language, marking her music with an identifiable unique voice. Over successive decades, as she developed and refined her stylistic vocabulary, her goals remained constant while the realization of those goals became gradually more sophisticated.

CHAPTER 6

Choral and Solo Vocal Works

Choral Music

Since primary school, Chen Yi has been involved in choral singing, which she describes as being "in unison always, or in two parts"[1] during those early years. "We were good in music. We always performed in violin ensemble off-campus, and we were sent to the airport to greet foreign visitors." Chen was the head of her class in academics during both primary and middle school, but during the latter she was also "head of the choir, to train them to sing in two parts." In Maoist China and especially during the Cultural Revolution, singing focused on "music for the masses." Many of these revolutionary songs originated during the 1930s. Some were adapted from folk songs with new words, some borrowed familiar tunes from Europe, and many were newly composed with simple, diatonic melodies (generally in major keys). Many revolutionary songs composed during the Cultural Revolution, which are called *yuluge*, have texts drawn from speeches or writings by Chairman Mao, such as those from *Quotations from Chairman Mao Tse-Tung* or the *Little Red Book* as it was commonly known in the West, that everyone in China carried around and basically had memorized. "So in this way, millions of people learned Chairman Mao's thoughts through singing his songs because the songs are easy to remember." Because this music was intended to arouse the people to action, "much of it was unaccompanied song intended to be sung in the streets by thousands of people."[2] According to Chen, "that's why Chinese are singers, but not in choral singing style." Only during the past two decades in China have "many good school teachers . . . started to teach choral singing [again], and now it has become more popular."

Chen's adult experience with singing has been largely as an observer, for example, during her eight years leading the orchestra for the Guangzhou Beijing Opera Troupe. Chen explains: "I have never been trained. But when you teach, you sing too." However, on one remarkable occasion, which is documented on video, Chen showed her extraordinary skill as a singer. For a Polish television series about living composers (cited in Chapter 2), Chen made her professional singing debut performing the second movement of her vocal work, *As in a Dream*, with violin and cello. In this performance, Chen sings with purity of tone but adds modest vibrato to warm the sound on higher sustained notes. Her performance is musical with appropriate dramatic touches and much subtlety in handling the details of the score, such as ornaments, glissandi, and inflections. She demonstrates her wide range (A below middle C up almost two octaves to G♯) on the challenging angular line, which she executes with precision and spot-on intonation. Near the end of the episode, composer Rolf Liebermann offers glowing commentary about Chen's performance: "She impressed me very much with her absolute ear at the beginning, which is really astonishing. . . . She's a real musician." Singers, and even instrumentalists, are encouraged to use this video as a performance model.[3]

Before Chen arrived in San Francisco in 1993, she had composed only one choral work, *Three Poems from the Song Dynasty* (1985, mixed chorus), recorded when Zhou Long worked in the radio station in Beijing. This recording by the Central Philharmonic Society Chorale with conductor Yan Liangkun was her calling card for Chanticleer. Founder Louis Botto and music director Joseph Jennings "loved the piece" and supported her three-year appointment as Composer-in-Residence. Although Chanticleer is a male chorus, it is not the typical voicing, TTBB (two tenor and two bass parts), but rather twelve male voices with vocal ranges from soprano to bass. Thus, compositions written for Chanticleer are more suitable for mixed or SATB chorus than for traditional male or TB ensembles and are published under this rubric by Theodore Presser.

Chen's relationship with Chanticleer was productive during her residency and has continued to be important throughout her career. Although Chen was required to compose only one work for Chanticleer during her San Francisco years, she wrote several: *A Set of Chinese Folk Songs* (ten movements); arrangements based on popular Japanese and Korean folk songs, "Sakura, Sakura (Cherry Blossoms)" and "Arirang"; *Tang Poems* (original a cappella version); and *Chinese Myths Cantata*, a major multimedia work (discussed in detail below). In addition, Chen created an orchestral accompaniment for *Singin' in the Dark* (*Songs of the American Frontier*), three American folk songs in a cappella settings by Alice Parker. Since leaving San Francisco, Chen's collaboration with Chanticleer has generated two more commissions: *From the Path of Beauty* (2008), jointly with the Shanghai String Quartet, and "I Hear the Siren's Call" (2012), a retelling of the myth about sirens luring sailors to their death on the rocks. Chanticleer's repertoire also includes works by Chen that were commissioned by other ensembles, for example, "Spring Dreams," about which their blogger wrote ("July: Recording Chen Yi," July 24, 2010):

> Another fantastic day in the recording studio. The biggest project for the last day was Chen Yi's "Spring Dreams" which we have sung all over the world in the last year or so and which now occupies a permanent place in our ongoing repertoire ... because people like it so much. It's a soundscape evoking the sight and sounds of a beautiful garden which has been destroyed in a storm.

After being in the United States for several years and completing her doctorate, Chen gained increased cultural self-awareness. She attributes this growing realization to her opportunity and ability to compare native Chinese culture with the new experiences and understandings she encountered in New York. "I soaked [up] all this kind of nutrition," she points out. "Inspiration is most important for new creation.... You are not limited to your own [creative ideas or culture] as before.... Then you treasure your old culture the most.... When you compare, then you know what's yours." In addition to her skills as a composer, Chen's engagement with philosophical and educational ideas helped prepare her for the opportunities ahead.

A Set of Chinese Folk Songs (1994)

Soon after Chen arrived in San Francisco, Botto and Jennings from Chanticleer hosted a meeting with her and a group of local choral directors and middle school teachers. "I said I could write a whole set of Chinese folk song arrangements. Then you could sing, I could coach." This dialogue was the impetus for *A Set of Chinese Folk Songs*, which Chen composed for Chanticleer but adapted for student involvement. She explained further: "I wanted to do this because forty percent of the kids in the public school string orchestra are Chinese.... Ten folk songs covering different regions, different minorities, and in different tempos. [The kids] said, 'Oh, [for] the first time we have learned we *do* have a good heritage.'" Chen regards folk songs as an effective educational strategy for sharing and fostering Chinese culture.

A Set of Chinese Folk Songs opens with "Fengyang Song" (Gong and Drum Song), an "easy" and "straightforward" setting, which has become Chen's "number one song; I guess ten thousand people have sung it." Its accessibility has made the first volume of the set even more popular than the other two.

Chen worked effectively to engage as many students as possible in music making. Although she was expected to work only with teacher Joan Murray[4] and the string orchestra at the Aptos Middle School, she helped establish a before-school choir; gave composition lessons; collaborated with Joseph Jennings to prepare the students for side-by-side performances with Chanticleer; and created arrangements to accommodate the available resources in each school participating in Chanticleer's Singing-in-the-Schools program (see Table 6.1). Near the end of her residency, Chen helped the board of Meet The Composer raise additional funds for future projects by playing tapes of the school children singing with Chanticleer in a presentation to donors.

Although each of these ten songs has a distinctive character due to the source material and Chen's compositional choices, they have in common a readily apparent folk melody. In "Fengyang Song," soprano sings the pentatonic melody after a two-measure introduction by alto, tenor, and bass, who establish an ostinato imitating the marching of a traditional gong and drum ensemble. The second verse (starting in m. 16) is presented in canon at the octave, an approach adapted from Chinese folk singing. The song concludes with a codetta where all four parts imitate the gong and drum ensemble in a diminuendo suggesting that they are marching away into the distance.

"Riding on a Mule" also opens with vocal percussion, using one of the set rhythm patterns (*luogu dianzi*) from Beijing opera in the upper two voices and the syllables (*luogu jing*) associated with learning these traditional patterns (see Example 6.1a). "I borrowed the syllables' sound [from] Beijing opera . . . just to be lively." Each Chinese character or syllable is associated with—and captures the characteristics or flavor of—a percussion instrument or group of instruments (see Table 6.2.). During the introduction Chen also establishes a five-bar ostinato phrase in the bass part, comprised of a repeated three-beat figure plus an expanded figure of four beats, with reciting syllables borrowed from east Indian folk percussion music in the accompaniment (Example 6.1a). Chen learned about these syllables from an Indian composer while teaching in the 1992 Summer Courses for Young Composers, Polish section of the International Society of Contemporary Music, in Kazimierz, Poland. "I loved the sound of those percussive syllables from their percussion instruments, as well as their vivid rhythmic structure, and found them similar to Peking Opera percussion sound. . . . I think that the two types of syllables got along very

Choral and Solo Vocal Works

TABLE 6.1. *A Set of Chinese Folk Songs* (1994) for chorus with optional instrumental parts

Published order for SATB in 3 vols by T. Presser (a cap or w/ optional piano)	Language [All include phonemes or chenci]	Ethnicity	Province or region	Order of alternate rental version composed for Chanticleer &/or children with varied instrumentation	Instrumentation & voicing for school / for Chanticleer	School version for str orch or str quintet (no singers)
Vol. 1				**I. Prelude: Fengyang Song**	str, dr, cyms	
1. Fengyang Song [Gongs & Drums]	Ch	Han	Anhui	1. Fengyang Song	SSA, str, dr, cyms / CTTB	✓
				II. Sanshili Pu	str	
2. The Flowing Stream	Ch	Han	Yunnan	2. The Flowing Stream	SAT / CTTBB	✓
3. Guessing	Eng, Ch	Han	Yunnan	3. Guessing	SSAA / CCTT	
4. Thinking of My Darling	Ch	Han	Shanxi	4. Thinking of My Darling	SSSAA / tenor solo, CCTT	
				III. 2 songs combined as interlude	str	✓
Vol. 2						
5. Mayila [girl's name]	Ch	Hasake (= Kazak)	Xinjiang	5. Riding on a Mule	SAT / CTBB	
6. Jasmine Flower (Mo Li Hua)	Ch (Jiangsu dialect)	Han	Jiangsu	6. Diu Diu Deng	SAAT / CTBB	
				IV. Prelude: Mayila	str	✓
7. Riding on a Mule	Ch	Han	Shaanxi	7. Mayila	SSA, str / TBBB	
8. Awariguli [girl named after a flower]	Ch	Uighur	Xinjiang	8. Jasmine Flower	SATB / CCTB	
				V. Interlude: Jasmine Flower	str	✓
Vol. 3						
9. Diu Diu Deng	Ch (Minnan dialect)	Han	Taiwan	9. Awariguli	STB / CTBB	
10. Mountain Song	Ch, Eng	Miao	Guizhou	10. Mountain Song	SATB, str / CCTB, echo ensemble	
& Dancing Tune	Eng, mostly syllables	Yi	Yunnan	& Dancing Tune (Finale)	SATB, str, dr, cyms / soprano solo, CTB	

TABLE 6.2. "Riding on a Mule" from *A Set of Chinese Folk Songs* (1994), showing instruments associated with luogu jing (syllables)

luogu jing	equivalent instruments
kuang	Tutti: large and small Beijing opera gong, small Chinese cymbals, and Beijing opera drum (*bangu*)
cei	small pair of Chinese cymbals
yi	a rest[1]
dei	small Beijing opera gong, with the bending tone up at the end of the sound
cang	large Beijing opera gong
ba	Beijing opera drum (*bangu*)

[1] Not woodblock as indicated by Law, "The A Cappella Choral Music," 43.

well."[5] Given the duple meter of the folk song, the bass produces unexpected phrase overlaps with the melody. A role reversal occurs in the short codetta with the bass parts singing two perfect fourths and ending on B–E, the two pitch centers used during the song. The upper three parts (SAT) take over the bass ostinato in a slight variant, now structured as the three-beat figure followed by truncations to two-beats and three-beats (each eliminating the full-beat rest). The final two-note diminution suggests that the pattern might continue (Example 6.1b).[6]

In a 2004 BBC interview (rebroadcast in 2014) Chen notes that Chinese traditional music includes four different categories—musical storytelling (quyi), Chinese instrumental music, folk opera sung in dialects, and folk song—which correspond to the folk music courses she took at the Beijing Central Conservatory (cited in Chapter 2). She then identifies four general types of folk songs, each of which she has used in her compositions: lyrical (*xiaodiao*), mountain (*shange*), work (*haozi*), and dance. The first three categories are those most typically used for folk songs of the Han Chinese,[7] who comprise about ninety-three percent of China's population; however, the same classifications are also used for the fifty-five ethnic minority groups across China,[8] whose folk music Chen often employs in her compositions. These categories can be confusing not only because they often overlap but also because the labels are not self-evident. Lyrical songs or xiaodiao, literally "little tune," is a large grouping, including love songs, songs of daily life, narrative songs, and songs popular among the people, which can be sung by their creators or more likely by entertainers. Mountain songs (shange) may have nothing to do with mountains but are those sung in an open area, for example, a field or near a mountain. In general, they

Choral and Solo Vocal Works

EXAMPLE 6.1. "Riding on a Mule" from *A Set of Chinese Folk Songs* (1994)

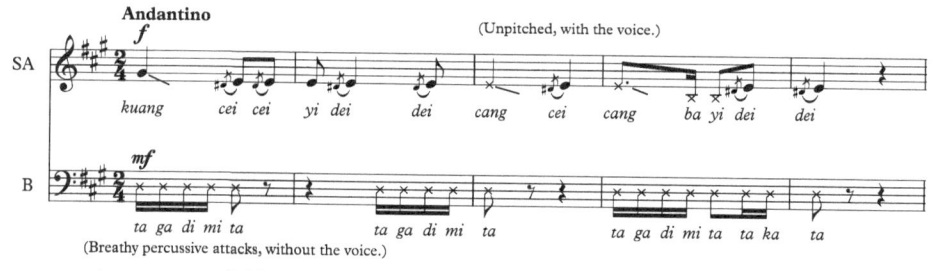

A. Luogu jing syllables (SA, mm. 1–5) and ostinato (B)

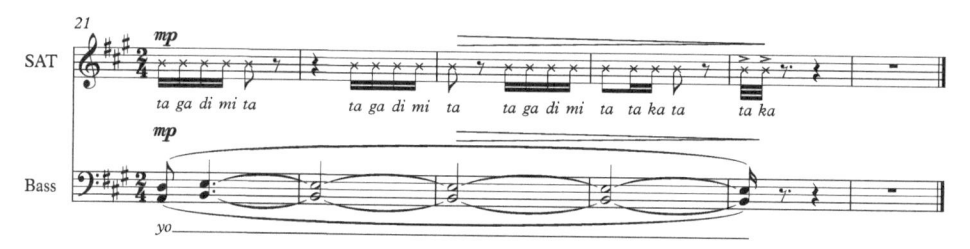

B. SATB, mm. 21–26, showing role reversal and rhythmic variation of ostinato

exhibit freer rhythms and their texts are often improvised with frequent use of vocables and falsetto voice. An outgrowth of shouting to get people's attention in the outdoors, shange often begin or end with a long, high note. Dealing with a range of topics that include herding, farming, and especially love, shange make frequent use of antiphonal singing. Work songs or haozi, literally meaning "crying" or "shouting," are meant to facilitate hard, heavy labor. As might be expected, they feature a strong rhythmic pulse but also many vocables and often utilize call-and-response performance.

When setting folk songs for chorus, Chen most frequently selects lyrical songs (xiaodiao) or mountain songs (shange). In the two examples from *A Set of Chinese Folk Songs* discussed earlier, the primary categories can be identified, but some overlap occurs. "Fengyang Song" is a lyrical song but could also be sung with dance. "Riding on a Mule" is a mountain song because it was originally sung in the open fields by farmers who work with the mules, but its light love song elements suggest a lyrical song as well.[9]

Chinese Mountain Songs (2001)

Clearly drawn from one classification of folk songs, *Chinese Mountain Songs* (2001), a set of five folk songs for treble voices, are particularly instructive in terms of how Chen retains the original folk song elements and their style in her settings. As was the case for *A Set of Chinese Folk Songs*, she again brings together material from different geographic regions and ethnic groups as part of her commitment to honor her culture and to educate singers and audiences. The most important element for projecting the region and ethnicity of origin in a folk song is the linguistic dialect; the particular vocables or *chenci* used are second in importance. Chinese folk singing regularly includes vocables, but different phonemes characterize the traditions in various provinces. In her folk song settings, Chen retains these ethnic markers; however, when including chenci in compositions that are not folk song arrangements, she often mixes vocables from various provinces as a means of enhancing the meaning or character of the music. Chenci are prominent in each of the five settings, with the text of "A Ma Lei A Ho" (song 2) totally comprised of syllables and that of "Mt. Wuzhi" (song 4) using only phonemes except for the location names.

In "Gathering in the Naked Oats" (song 3, see Example 6.2), Chen uses onomatopoeic vocables associated with an expanded form of the Shanxi folk song: "*Si lou*" mimics the sound of cutting hulless oats with a sickle or scythe; "*Ge beng*" imitates the sound of digging taro with a shovel. These referential gestures are sung with the same pitches and rhythms, but the sounds of the syllables clearly distinguish the two activities. This setting exemplifies most of the common features of a mountain song and how Chen retains these traditional traits while adding a dimension of her own creativity. The text is only two lines, telling about a man harvesting oats (or Chinese buckwheat)[10] and his girlfriend digging up the root vegetable. Chen highlights the dialogue and love song elements between the two characters by limiting the scoring to only two parts. The sopranos, taking the man's role, sing the first phrase, which begins with a typical held note. The altos answer with the second phrase, which completes the original fourteen-measure tune. Throughout the remainder, Chen focuses on the onomatopoeic chenci in alternation, varying their interaction and especially the length of the silences between the two-note gestures. In the final section, the two parts sing together, beginning with a combined recollection of the last gesture of each of their text phrases. This passage is followed by a new element on the phonemes "yo wei," moving freely from each singer's lowest to highest notes over two measures and with a crescendo from *p* to *ff*. Chen selected these two unrelated chenci solely for their sonic qualities in order to

EXAMPLE 6.2. *Chinese Mountain Songs* (2001), no. 3. "Gathering in the Naked Oats," mm. 16–32

give the passage a "strong Chinese folk song flavor."[11] The final phrase is quiet with singers a perfect fifth apart in unison rhythm on vocables, which have increasingly longer silences between the gestures.[12] Although Chen's setting does not use a high tessitura, the standard folk song transcription[13] is a perfect fifth higher, in keeping with the high range of mountain songs. Chen also captures the rhythmic freedom of this shange with her marking "from slow to fast" (mm. 8–12) as well as with the playful and irregular metrical treatment of the vocable interchange (mm. 16–24; Example 6.2). Chen retains the pentatonic mode of the original folk song, the *zhi* mode (see Figure 3.1). Although this folk song portrays types of work, it is not a work song (haozi), which would have a much stronger rhythmic pulse to assist heavy physical labor.

Throughout this collection, Chen concentrates on the monophonic aspect of Chinese folk song while also adding some vertical elements, largely perfect fourths and fifths. The transparent settings slip easily between unison singing and vertical perfect intervals. Sometimes, as in "When Will the Scholartree Blossom?" (song 1), the perfect intervals take the role of background support, but at other times they move in near parallel motion with the primary melody. Notably, Chen deviates from these two intervals much less in folk song settings than in other works. "I don't want to stay with something too pure," she says. She also features antiphonal or imitative relationships between parts in this collection, a strategy that is particularly apparent in "Gathering in the Naked Oats" and "Mt. Wuzhi."

Chinese Myths Cantata (1996)

Written as the culmination of Chen's three-year residency in San Francisco, *Chinese Myths Cantata* was commissioned by the Women's Philharmonic (JoAnn Falletta, conductor)[14] and Chanticleer. In addition to these two ensembles, *Cantata* is scored for four Chinese traditional instruments: erhu (doubling on zhuihu),[15] yangqin, pipa, and zheng, which are "organically embedded in the orchestra, [and therefore] the concertino loses its exotic effect after a few minutes."[16] Accessibility was enhanced with visual projections, painted backdrops, staging, and the inclusion of Chinese dancers (for the premiere, the Lily Cai Chinese Dance Company).[17] Chen noted that she "wrote down all the program notes first, including all this lighting design and stage design," theatrical aspects she had learned during her years with the Guangzhou opera company.

For this large-scale work, Chen selected three popular Chinese myths, which children in China "hear from their grandmas or babysitters."[18] The first movement tells the story of the giant, Pan Gu, who was nurtured in a large egg for 18,000 years before breaking out to create the universe. In the second, the goddess and shape-shifter Nü Wa, who has a human face and the body of a snake, creates humans out of mud because she wants companions. The third movement recounts the thwarted love story of the Weaving Maid, daughter of a celestial god, and the Cowherd, a human farmer. They were happily married until her father separated them with the Silver River (or Milky Way). They were forced to live apart as the stars Vega and Altair, one on each side of the Milky Way, except one day each year.[19] This movement concludes with an a cappella setting of "Song of Weaving Maid and Cowherd," an anonymous poem from the Han Dynasty (206 BCE–220 CE) that reflects on the sadness of the separated lovers.

The opening of the first movement is a fount of material for the entire composition. The significance of the "chaos" motive goes beyond its pitch content: a tritone and minor seconds. Chen had first heard this gesture during the influential field trip in Guangxi Province that also inspired *Duo Ye* and the Symphony No. 2 (Chapter 2). She and a few classmates had walked nineteen miles to reach a small, remote Yao village where they heard an elderly farmer with a deep bass voice present the story of Pan Gu creating heaven and earth. Chen noted the tribal leader's singing and then utilized this intervallic gesture at the beginning of *Cantata* (see Example 6.3a). Here a single bass voice sings the word "chaos," first in English and then in Mandarin (*hùndùn*),[20] immediately signaling the transnational nature of the work. The motive's intervallic material, E–B♭–E♭–D, is also prominent in modernist Western classical music. The

EXAMPLE 6.3. *Chinese Myths Cantata*, mvt. 1

A. Opening of mvt. 1, "Pan Gu Creates Heaven and Earth"

B. Variation of chaos motive, mm. 7–9, contrabassoon

motivic variant in the contrabassoon retains the opening tritones but is more expansive: B♭–E–C–B♮–F–F♯ (Example 6.3b). As Chih-Suei Shaw points out, the use of the tritone or *diabolus in musica*, as it was nicknamed in the late medieval era, in this context enhances the text since this interval can "represent a state of 'chaos' in Western classical music."[21]

In overall design, the second movement has two main sections, separated by a six-bar transition: a woodblock solo (see Figure 6.1). Each of the main sections is further subdivided in part by reaching ever broader and more intense climaxes. If the transition measures are grouped with the second main section, this movement is proportioned according to the Golden Section, that is, the ratio between the small and large segments is (virtually) the same as between the large section and the whole (Section 1: Section 2 = Section 2: whole or expressed in measures, 62:100 = 100:162).

Chen's compositional process almost always involves an initial mapping of an overall structure, which is often based around proportional relationships in general and the Golden Section in particular, including its implementation in Baban (see Chapter 3). Each of these tangible elements of Chinese culture and traditional music has been exceptionally influential on Chen's approach to composition, grounding her philosophically and structurally with her Chinese heritage. In *Cantata*, Chen utilizes only the rhythmic beat pattern of Baban late in the third movement (mm. 115–31).

The opening subsection of the second movement (mm. 1–21) is atmospheric—all about the image, gesture, and setting the scene. It is full of marvelous, imaginative sounds with an orchestration dominated by the four Chinese string instruments and the four percussionists. The music personifies Nü Wa and is suggestive of her movement: unpredictable with snakelike gestures (see Example 6.4.). Chen scores this movement for zhuihu (a special type of erhu), which has an amazing capacity to sound like a human voice—or in this case the voice of the goddess Nü Wa. How appropriate that the zhuihu takes the role of Nü Wa since its resonator is usually covered with skin of a python or other snake. Within the sparse texture, the zhuihu or Nü Wa takes focus and commands attention. For the angular material in the zhuihu's first melodic gesture, Chen links this shape to the tonal inflection of the statement "wǒ shì Nǚ Wá " (in Mandarin) meaning "I am Nü Wa." Throughout this movement, as is typical in many of her compositions, Chen creates melodies from exaggerated and inflected speech gestures.[22]

The second subsection (mm. 21–42) is closely linked with the first, developing material both dramatically and musically. Nü Wa continues to slither about and realizes she is lonely. Compositionally, Chen creates a superb balance among the retention of familiar, stable gestures; elaboration of musical ideas; and the introduction of new material—or at least what often sounds new but in fact may have at least some connection with earlier material. The third segment opens with the zhuihu still playing the role of Nü Wa. The E♭ clarinet mirrors her motive up an octave, reinforcing the idea of Nü Wa seeing herself reflected in the pond—first, literally (Example 6.5a); then with rhythmic augmentation and extension (Example 6.5b). This important motive (Example 6.5a) might be described as four notes of a chromatic scale (G♯–A–B♭–B); however, the B♭ is strategically displaced down an octave creating a disjunct and distinctive phrase. The next echoed gesture by zhuihu and E♭ clarinet (Example 6.5b) starts a whole step higher and has its own shape and ornamentation but is still based on a chromatic fragment. However, the expected C is extended up an extra half step and pitches are rearranged, resulting in the following quasi-chromatic series (A–A♯–B–C♯ instead of C). These musical gestures along with the motives in Example 6.6 derive from the first moment of this movement: the rising arpeggio by yangqin, which can be arranged as another chromatic fragment (B–C–C♯–D) (Example 6.6a). This simple but fundamental musical germ occurs in many different guises throughout the movement, reminding us that Nü Wa is a shapeshifter. Examples 6.5 and 6.6 show five iterations from the large range of possibilities for a motive of successive half steps and—by metaphoric linkage—the many changing faces of Nü Wa.

Section 2 is all about Nü Wa creating humanity, first individual humans and then—when she grew tired—groups of people via mass production. Section 2 is divided into two segments that align dramatic and musical elements. The first is further divided into seven phrases of increasing length and density,

FIGURE 6.1. *Chinese Myths Cantata*, movement 2, formal structure with Golden Section

mm	1-A 1–21	1-B 21–42	1-C 43–62	2-D 62–67 (trans)	2-E 68–118	2-F 119–162	163 (trans) → Mvt 3
Myth	setting the scene & intro Nü Wa	Nü Wa moves around & feels lonely	Nü Wa sees own reflection mirrored in pond	Nü Wa ponders	Nü Wa creates individual humans from mud: 7x	Mass produces humans w/ swirling vine	
WW	sparse hi & low add to climax		E♭ clarinet echoes		sparse; pics & E♭ clarinet - hi trichord punc +Bns—related to m. 15 more; related to figures in 1-A & B		
Br		only in final cres.	sparsely used esp. final cres.			join WW figures then 6 rips ↑, telescoping pattern	
Perc	Whole tone Glock gestures gliss.			wood block solo	sparse, as accents, some with the hi WW	building density	hi Glock tremolo +backgr

FIGURE 6.1. Continued.

					yangqin solo
Chinese Instru	**zhuihu** = Nü Wa speech-like shape of Mandarin + Cantonese, Eng, Sp all 12 pc unpredictable yangqin & zheng repeated gestures Y↑ & Z↓	↑ ↑	↑	Begin each of 7 subsections as a **unit** w/ many variations and developments	
Voices				solo voices only—singly then in counterpoint phonemes; repeated notes w/ grace notes & gliss 2-E4—bass Beijing opera (*Sprechstimme*) recitation 2-E7—long, lyrical melody	chorus + AUDIENCE
W Str	only db M9 punctuation	AB tremolo hi harm gliss TT & P4; asynchronous			hi trill gliss tremolo, repeated pattern

EXAMPLE 6.4. *Chinese Myths Cantata*, mvt. 2, opening, zhuihu part

II. Nü Wa Creates Human Beings

[wo shi Nü Wa]

EXAMPLE 6.5. *Chinese Myths Cantata*, mvt. 2, mirrors

A. Zhuihu mirrored by E♭ clarinet, mm. 43–45

B. Echo with rhythmic augmentation and extension, mm. 49–51

EXAMPLE 6.6. *Chinese Myths Cantata*, mvt. 2, "changing faces" of Nü Wa

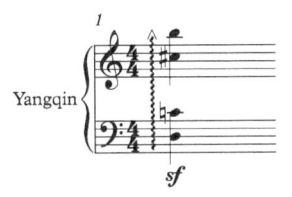

A. Yanqin, mm. 1, pitches reordered to chromatic segment: B C C# D

B. Voice 1, mm. 98–99, reordered to chromatic segment: G A♭ A B♭

C. Zhuihu, mm. 53–54, reordered to chromatic segment: B C D♭ D

demonstrating Chen's imaginative development strategies. Each phrase begins with the group of Chinese traditional instruments followed by the addition of the chorus. Zhuihu remains the chief carrier of melodic material, thus keeping Nü Wa the focal point. At first, the chorus, which Chen reserves until the arrival of the first human, performs one voice at a time, on vocables using repeated pitches with grace notes or glissandi, borrowing from motivic material heard earlier in pipa and zhuihu. These solo voices also adopt the timbre of the zhuihu, which highlights Nü Wa as the model and source of these living beings.

When Nü Wa began mass production in the final section (2-F) she "dipped a long vine into the pond, swirled it around, and swung it through the air. When drops of mud spattered on the ground, they turned into many little people!"[23] The portrayal of the swirling vine is heard first in trilled glissandi by the Western strings and then by the upward rips of the entire brass section, glissing from lowest to highest possible note. Everything builds toward the final climax and completion of creation. Singers, who are spread through the audience, make their way toward the stage and begin encouraging the audience to add their voices on recited chenci, such as "yo, yo, yo" or "yi, yi, yi" or to giggle or speak freely. The instrumentalists, except for the wind players, finally join in, creating a climactic "swirl of voices."

Throughout the movement, links with Chinese traditional music, especially Beijing opera, are apparent, for example, prominent use of slides, grace notes, large glissandi, reciting style, and the exaggerated singing style of Nü Wa through the zhuihu. Some of the percussion patterns also have strong connections with Beijing opera. One of the most striking is the woodblock solo, used during a stop in the action and music to show that a character is thinking. Just as in Chinese opera, the pace and dynamics shift rapidly in the woodblock solo (see Example 6.7).[24] This solo begins with a tight, *ppp* trill, and then a one-measure crescendo to *fff* accompanied by a sudden shift to a slower rhythmic gesture that quickly returns to the original trill and a diminuendo. The six-measure transition occurs while Nü Wa ponders after seeing her face mirrored in the water and recognizing herself. This action can be viewed as a contemplative exploration of female subjectivity, which fits with ideas and imagery in writings by Simone de Beauvoir and Luce Irigaray.[25]

Irigaray returns often to the metaphor of a mirror in her feminist critique of the psychoanalytic approaches of Sigmund Freud and Jacques Lacan. In *Speculum of the Other Woman* (1974), she attempts "to invert and traverse ... the mirror of self-reflection governing men's representations of women."[26] Springing from Lacan's discussion of Alice from Lewis Carroll's *Through the Looking Glass*, Irigaray attempts "to go through the looking glass ... to a Wonderland beyond phallocentrism, in which women may be able to talk and represent themselves in quite different ways."[27] Australian philosopher Elizabeth Gross summarizes Irigaray's thinking: "Our received images of femininity have been masculine—inverted, projected images of male ideals and fantasies, images of the male 'other' rather than a female subject."[28] Irigaray's project is to conceptualize woman as a subject in her own right so that she is not understood only as the inverse of man or as a deficient man. She identifies metaphorically the *flat mirror* as "what privileges the relation of man to his fellow man"[29] and a *curved mirror* (or *speculum*) as essential "for the relation of woman to 'herself' and to her like"[30] because it disturbs "the staging of representation according to too-exclusively masculine parameters"[31] and allows for woman as an autonomous being.

In this movement, pitch material and timbre have metaphoric significance, pointing toward the all-encompassing nature of Nü Wa and the environment she inhabits, which in the mythological story was the locus for creation of human life. Chen tweaks some details of the orchestration for the second movement, beyond the change from erhu to zhuihu, that serve to widen the overall range and timbre of the orchestra. Piccolo replaces *both* flutes, creat-

EXAMPLE 6.7. *Chinese Myths Cantata*, mvt. 2, mm. 62–68, woodblock solo

ing a timbre closer to that of the Chinese transverse flute, dizi; the clarinets take up E♭ and bass clarinets, with the penetrating E♭ perhaps evoking the guan or the suona; and contrabassoon substitutes for the second bassoon to remind us of the low singing of the village elder heard at in the opening of the first movement. Not only is a wider register possible with these orchestration changes, but Chen also utilizes both high and low extremes. Principal oboe's first entrance is its lowest possible pitch (B♭ just below middle C); two bars later contrabassoon emulates this extreme with its lowest note (also a B♭).[32] At the high end of the spectrum, the piccolos and E♭ clarinet have a recurring stratospheric trichord cluster (B♭–B–C) at their highest or nearly highest notes (Example 6.8). From mm. 86 to 95, all three instruments play as the trichord occurs with less time between each recurrence, and with piccolo 1 sounding its highest note, a piercing C four octaves above middle C. Both the trichord and brass section rips (mentioned earlier) use this telescoping approach, sounding closer and closer together—something Chen often does, borrowing from folk percussion repertoire.[33]

Another aspect of this movement that contributes to the metaphor of inclusiveness is the frequent presence of all, or almost all, twelve pitch classes. Vertical examples occur primarily in the later stages of the movement as choral clusters (m. 131 onward). Early in the movement this event is primarily a linear array, for example, in the initial long phrase for zhuihu where mm. 4–11 include all twelve notes (see Example 6.4). This treatment is not at all conventional twelve-tone serialism as pitches are repeated and recur, and the standard permutations do *not* occur.[34] However, the impact of Chen's approach projects completeness to Nü Wa's realm.

By the time of the first performance of *Chinese Myths Cantata*, Chen's profile in the United States was already on the rise, building on the reputation she had established before leaving China in 1986: a full-evening concert in Beijing and her orchestral works released by the China Record Company.[35] Chen's prestige was impressive even during her conservatory years. Wu Man, "recognized as the world's premier pipa virtuoso,"[36] who entered the Central Conservatory in 1978 in the middle school division, remembers Chen Yi and her siblings: "In the campus, we know [them]. They're kind of famous, the whole family. Two

EXAMPLE 6.8. *Chinese Myths Cantata*, mvt. 2, mm. 93–95, piccolo 1 & 2, E♭ clarinet, sounding B♭ B C, another smaller chromatic segment

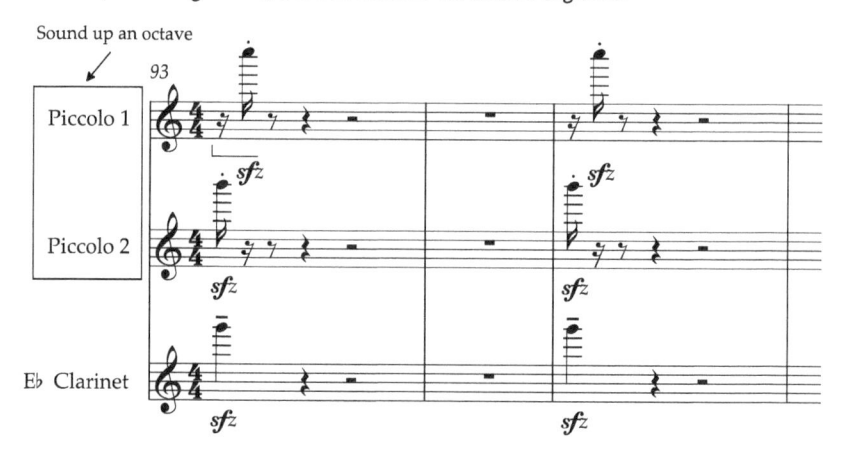

sisters, one brother . . . [are] all very good in their own profession. . . . Chen Yi was a star student in her class."[37] Along with Symphony no. 2 and *Ge Xu*, both for orchestra, the success of *Chinese Myths Cantata* further contributed to her growing prominence in the United States and beyond. In a *New York Times* feature article the weekend prior to the premiere of *Chinese Myths Cantata*, Matthew Daines identified Chen as the "latest star" in "an emerging school of Chinese-American composers,"[38] all earning doctorates from Columbia University and each a student of Chou Wen-chung.

From the Path of Beauty (2008)

To celebrate their thirtieth and twenty-fifth anniversary seasons, respectively, Chanticleer and then the Shanghai String Quartet independently approached Chen about a commission. The idea of a collaboration between these two outstanding professional ensembles was Chen's suggestion. "I knew that it would work if I plan for the whole structure of the song cycle carefully, to have balance, suitable combinations and contrast."[39] From the beginning, she envisioned a work in which the two ensembles performed together and separately, but with equality among all participants.

The work was inspired in part by a Chinese philosophy and art book, *The Path of Beauty: A Study of Chinese Aesthetics* by Li Zehou, one of the foremost philosophers in post-Mao China during the 1980s.[40] In this work, Li presents leading art forms throughout China's history and discusses them in relation to Chinese culture and artistic values. Just two years after the original Chinese version of this book was published, Chen received a copy as a gift from Wang Shu, her orchestration professor at the Central Conservatory, when she completed her undergraduate studies. Then in 2001, she received a gift of the English version from Professor Chou Wen-chung, when he visited UMKC.[41] More than just a translation, the English publication (1988) is an expanded version, integrating material from the original with two revised editions and adding material for Western readers, especially many color illustrations.[42]

In *From the Path of Beauty*, Chen does not follow the historical chronology of Li's book or attempt to represent the array of visual, literary, and performing arts found there. Rather, she draws inspiration from her encounter with the book and grounds herself in her Chinese artistic cultural heritage. Chen avoids attempts at literal representation, striving instead for a deeper connection with the "philosophical and spiritual underpinnings of Chinese culture."[43] The phrase, which was used by the publisher to describe Li's book, seems equally apt when applied to Chen's composition.

We find a strong affinity between Chen and Li, as expressed in his "Afterword," where he articulates his assessment of Chinese sensibility: "Human nature . . . blends emotion with rationality, individuality with social conscience, awareness and feeling with imagination and understanding. We might say it is the sedimentation of rationality in emotion, of imagination and understanding in awareness and feeling, of content in form."[44] Li earlier clarified his aesthetic appraisal of form. "Beauty is not ordinary form but 'significant form'—natural form that has acquired a socially defined content. So, while form defines beauty, beauty is not just form. There is no beauty without form, but form by itself is not beauty."[45]

Chen also avoids prompting a predisposition toward concrete meanings for the movements involving the chorus by using text that is exclusively chenci drawn from various Chinese folk song traditions. This strategy helps create a transnational direction for the composition and leaves more space for audience members' imaginations and insights. The seven titles give just a hint of the inspiration and overall characteristics of each movement.

The gradual unfolding of the opening movement from a quiet choral unison on the E above middle C seems fitting, not only for a movement that reaches back to more than a millennium BCE for its title, "The Bronze Taotie," but also for the launch of a thirty-five-minute major work. See Table 6.3 for an overview of the seven-movement composition and the art forms referenced. Chen focuses on chant-like repeated notes—to be performed "spiritually"—alluding to an ancient totemic time. Opening up the musical space first with a

TABLE 6.3. From the Path of Beauty (2008), overview

7-mvt version	7-mvt scoring	4-mvt string quartet version	Links with Chinese arts & history[1]	Connections with other Chen Yi works
1. The Bronze Taotie	SATB chorus a cap (div a 12 clusters near end)	rescored for strings as mvt 1	Inspired by bronze taotie ritual vessels, commonly with stylized animal mask carvings of this greedy wild animal; function may have been totemic, protective, or symbolic of metaphysical forces; Shang Dynasty (ca. 1600–ca. 1100 BCE)	This movement is available as a separate octavo publication
2. The Dancing Ink	strQ	retained but as mvt 4	Exaggerated shapes and gestures in Chinese cursive script calligraphy during Tang Dynasty (618–907), which marked a high point for this art	Uses fragments of Baban tune; combined with Mm2 interweave or wandering chromatic; mvt title used elsewhere but with different music
3. The Ancient Totems	strQ & chorus	(not present)	Includes reference to singing and reciting as performed in Chinese opera; also to percussion patterns in opera; totems, an auspicious ceremonial symbol, were added to bronze wine vessels to protect against evil and described as having "ferocious beauty" expressing "an irresistible force."[2]	Reworking of the 2nd mvt of the recorder concerto, The Ancient Chinese Beauty (2008), with soprano more closely linked to recorder solo part; both mvts use same name
4. The Rhymed Poems	strQ	retained as mvt 2	Instrumental rendition of musical reading of two poems by Li Qingzhao; Song Dynasty (960–1279)	Reworking of As in a Dream, originally composed 1988 for solo voice, violin, & cello in 2 mvts, which are merged into 1 mvt; viola generally takes the vocal part

TABLE 6.3. Continued

5. The Clay Figurines	strQ & chorus	(not present)	Inspired by exaggerated gesture of clay storyteller; most of these figurines have a gleeful expression; Han Dynasty (206 BCE–220 CE)	Significant reworking of *The Han Figurines* (2006) for mixed sextet, which was also the basis for 1st mvt of the recorder concerto (*The Ancient Chinese Beauty*); both mvts use same name
6. The Secluded Melody	strQ & chorus	retained as mvt 3 with identical string parts; choral parts omitted	StrQ pitch material inspired by qin music from Six Dynasties era (497–590), "Jieshi Diao You Lan" (Secluded Orchid in the Jieshi Mode), especially its pan tonal quality; the melody is newly composed and not based on traditional qin repertoire	StrQ = strings (but no dbl bass) in *Sprout* (1982/86); voices are a new, added layer
7. The Village Band	strQ & chorus	(not present)	Singers and strings imitate a typical village ensemble of percussion and wind instruments; based on the pattern of Yu he ba (The Sum Is Eight), from a folk percussion ensemble music fixed form	Drawn from 3rd & final mvt (Shifan Gong and Drum) of *Ba Yin* (2001) for saxQ & strs; this music also appears as 3rd mvt of the recorder concerto (*The Ancient Chinese Beauty*); after strQ takes opening section for saxQ alone (= recorder cadenza), voices take the saxQ/recorder part in modified form

[1] This column includes information from Chen Yi's preface to the full score for *From the Path of Beauty*.
[2] Chen Yi's preface to the score for *The Ancient Chinese Beauty*.

minor second, then octaves and perfect fifths, the music reaches a climax with an eleven-note cluster chord (m. 23), followed by the twelfth pitch class in the low bass, which brings back the repeated-note chanting. One simple, but prominent, three-note motive (descending whole step and minor third) occurs throughout at various pitch levels and using notes twice as fast as most of this movement. This unison[46] trichord acts as a cadential formula, not unlike those in Gregorian chant, at phrase endings. First introduced in measure 6, the sopranos and altos conclude the movement with this trichord atop a six-note stack of perfect fifths, and the same interval pattern is also presented vertically when the cluster begins with tenors and basses (m. 21), creating a tightly integrated movement.

The second movement title, "The Dancing Ink," refers to calligraphy, specifically the cursive script at its peak during the Tang Dynasty and in parallel with a zenith in Chinese poetry, especially in the writings of Li Bai (701–62). His poems have been characterized as having "virtually no rules or inhibitions: everything was spontaneous, composed on the spur of the moment, yet always novel and beautiful."[47] This description seems perfect as a summary of this movement for string quartet. The music, moving in sweeping gestures, is very active and a huge contrast with the first movement's restraint. It sounds free yet contains internal structure and unity through almost constant reference to the four- to seven-note motives derived from Baban (see Chapter 3). Near the end of this movement, first violin presents a longer solo segment of the Baban tune in ornamented Beijing opera style, which serves as a link to the following movement.

Voices and strings join together for the first time in "The Ancient Totems," where references to Beijing opera are prevalent, especially in the ornamented soprano part and later in other voice parts. Tenor and bass parts imitate percussion gestures created by accelerating repeated-note patterns that in Chinese opera indicate a character is thinking. Chen shapes this movement largely through careful attention to timbre and the use of several distinctive textures, often blocks of sound. The muted strings begin with high artificial harmonics using asynchronous entries and rearticulations but sustaining a high, ethereal cluster (C–E♭–F–F♯). From measure 8 to 37, the atmospheric examples of sound mass—blocks of sound that place the central compositional focus on timbre—use various special playing techniques to create a spectrum of tone colors to project a mystical ambiance: tremolo harmonics; clusters with microtonal trills; cluster combining harmonics and natural pitches; artificial harmonics; and *sul ponticello* (that is, bowing on or very near the bridge, which creates more audible harmonics and a somewhat nasal or metallic timbre) in combination with trills in lower strings, a minor second apart, and four-note parallel ostinato figures in the violins, a minor second apart. Finally, in a gesture to round out the form, violins return to the artificial harmonics of their first entrance (now unmuted and normal playing technique) combined with a sustained viola trill and long upward glissando in the cello, extending the motivically important minor seventh by an added octave.

The singers also participate in sound mass components, at first altos and tenors in a six-note cluster (mm. 5–7, 8–13, 22–24, 34–36) and then altos, tenors, and basses in a nine-note cluster (mm. 19–22) with parallel glissandi. The concluding segment features six-note and then ten-note clusters with upward sweeps and with dynamics (crescendo-diminuendo) providing the shape. Chen's selection of chenci for the singers forms an integral element of the shifting textures and timbres as particular sounds are associated with specific musical ideas. For example, "Yo" or "Yo Wei" are used prominently for Beijing opera singing style, "Wu" is linked with clusters, and the more articulated "Dou" is used for imitation of percussion gestures.

"The Rhymed Poems" for string quartet alone is rich and sophisticated. Perhaps ironically, the movement that addresses sung poetry does not include the chorus. For this movement, Chen adapts an earlier work, *As in a Dream*, originally composed in 1988 for solo voice, violin, and cello. In the new conception, the viola takes the vocal part; second violin generally takes the violin part; and the cello part is largely retained. First violin plays several roles, performing some high passages originally for cello, adding texture with newly composed material (often harmonics, sul ponticello, or trills), and covering the violin part while the second violin adds texture (often with tremolo). Subtle transformations occur in small details of rhythm and phrasing.

Chen scores the final three movements for chorus and string quartet and creates her usual balance of continuity and contrast. The string quartet parts in "The Clay Figurines" are a significant reworking of *The Han Figurines* (2006) for mixed sextet, which was also the basis for the first movement of her recorder concerto (*The Ancient Chinese Beauty*; see Chapter 5); however, the voice parts are newly composed and transform the movement with an original layer of richness. Chen was inspired by the Han Dynasty clay figure of a storyteller making broad gestures,[48] and she brings the idea of exaggerated action prominently into the main motive for the singers, an upward leap of a major seventh that is animated by the rhythm and syllables used (Example 6.9). When Chen introduces a new major section (m. 40) where the voices have her signature wandering chromatic figure coupled with new phonemes, she retains the rhythmic motive from measure 1, still using the leap of a major seventh and giving

EXAMPLE 6.9. *From the Path of Beauty*, mvt. 5, mm. 1–3, chorus

more attention to the initial bass interval of a rising major second. Further variation occurs in the coda with an expansion of the sevenths to minor and major ninths (complementary intervals) plus occasional downward leaps to bring the movement to a conclusion.

Throughout this movement, all of the performers focus on upward motion, which supports the positive energy of storytellers, who, in the ancient world kept alive the history and myths of their people in a way that helped to explain life and culture. As a composer, Chen takes on the role of bridging Chinese and Western cultures and keeping ancient Chinese cultures alive. The terracotta ceramic figure (ca. 21.75 inches tall) that inspired this movement holds a drum under his left arm with a striker in his right hand; he appears to be singing his narrative and perhaps even dancing. The sculptor demonstrated the integration of various art genres; Chen's composition adds still another layer.

The string parts of "The Secluded Melody" are virtually identical with *Sprout* (1986 version) except here no double bass part is present. *Sprout* was inspired by the mood and panmodality of a traditional guqin piece, "Jieshi Diao You Lan" (Solitary or Secluded Orchid),[49] but is not directly based on this ancient melody. The vocal parts are a new addition. The overall impression is slow, euphonious, and mellifluous with a contrasting middle section that is a lively dance (mm. 37–63), yielding an overall ABA' structure. This movement links with the previous one by virtue of the prominent upward leap of a seventh, but the effect here is much calmer due to the slower pace and even rhythms. The movement concludes on a sustained *pp* C♯ major triad with an added major sixth (A♯), an exceptionally tonal reference among Chen's works and one that foreshadows the jazz aspects of the scat in the next movement.

The concluding movement, "The Village Band," is a fun romp and a tour de force especially for the singers. According to Honggang Li, the violist in the Shanghai String Quartet, Chanticleer told the quartet members that *From the Path of Beauty* "was the most difficult piece they have ever done,"[50] and this movement alone could make that disclosure true. The movement is one of several pieces based on the third and final movement (Shifan Gong and Drum) of *Ba Yin* (2001) for saxophone quartet and strings (see Chapters 3 and 5).[51] The string quartet takes the opening section originally written for saxophone quartet. When the voices enter, they pick up the saxophone quartet parts in modified form while the string quartet shifts to the string parts of *Ba Yin* and the telescoping rhythmic structure derived from shifan luogu percussion repertory. Starting in measure 54, the singers have a virtuosic scat style on running sixteenth notes, focusing on syllable groupings such as "Da Ba Da Ba Da Ba" and "Ta Ka Ta Ka Ta Ka." From measure 79, Chen mixes in additional melodic ideas and new syllables, including "Yo Hei Yo Hei Yo" where "Yo" is accented and "Hei" is staccato. This selection of chenci melds with the articulations—an approach integral to this movement and typical for Chen.

Sarah Tyrrell summarizes *From the Path of Beauty* as crossing disciplines and "linking China's rich visual and literary arts legacy and its dynastic history with illustrative musical materials."[52] Honggang Li acknowledged another aspect of Chen's intertwined artistic languages: "What I really like about Chen Yi's music is how she is able to balance traditional elements and modern elements, mixed together. . . . It is refreshing and new, but also has tradition in it."[53] Further, he commented that for the Chinese elements "some are hidden a little bit; some are very obvious." However, as with many pieces, Chen has an agenda beyond the aesthetics of the composition itself, hoping her work contributes to "improving cultural understanding between two countries, and also world peace."[54] Chen makes this composition both local and global by paying tribute to former San Francisco Supervisor Gordon Lau and Deputy Mayor Peter Henschel, who were important in the Sister Cities' friendship between San Francisco and Shanghai, and by honoring the home cities of the two commissioning ensembles.

The premiere of *From the Path of Beauty* in San Francisco (March 13, 2008), home base for Chanticleer, was widely anticipated by residents who remembered fondly many performances of Chen's music during the 1990s. Critic Joshua Kosman described the atmosphere for the premiere weekend as filled with "the old emotions—excitement, satisfaction, gratitude."[55] The weekend included four performances in the Bay area plus one at the University of California Irvine just south of Los Angeles. During 2008, the two ensembles toured together for several high-profile performances (Metropolitan Museum of Art, New York City; Ravinia Festival near Chicago; and Tanglewood Music Festival near Boston); the Shanghai String Quartet gave the premiere of the four-movement quartet version at the Smithsonian Institution, Washington, DC, April 23, 2008) and additional performances in Woodstock, New York, and Ottawa, Canada. More joint performances occurred the following year, including on the Friends of Chamber Music series in Kansas City, Missouri, and on a tour in China where the performers appeared on May 3 and 5, 2009, in two of the most important concert venues: the Shanghai Concert Hall and the new National Centre for the Performing Arts or National Grand Theater in Beijing, known colloquially as "The Giant Egg" because of its ellipsoidal dome of titanium and glass.

Solo Vocal Works

AS IN A DREAM (1988/1994/2010)

Chen's large catalog of compositions includes only three solo vocal works, each written for female voice with one or two instruments. In *As in a Dream* Chen set two poems by the most famous historical woman poet in China, Li Qingzhao (1084–*ca.* 1151).[56] Originally written for soprano, violin, and cello, she later adapted this work for soprano, pipa, and zheng and then for only zheng accompaniment. The other two vocal works are for voice and piano: *Meditation* (1999/2012), a set of two Tang Dynasty poems, and "Bright Moonlight" (2000), using an original text by Chen Yi herself in English. Despite the English titles, the two earlier settings are in Chinese.

Li's poetry, which Chen had loved since her childhood, seems an appropriate choice for *As in a Dream* since the poems are written in a song form called *ci*, first popularized orally by women singers. By the Song Dynasty (960–1279), the ci was a major literary form that gave special attention to word choices and the inseparable relationship between poetry and music, featuring unequal lines (that is, differing numbers of characters) with set rhyme schemes and linguistic tonal patterns. Ci, originally called *quzi ci* (literally "tuned poetry" or "lyrics of songs"),[57] developed through a merger between banquet music and poetry. The music preceded the poetry, and many ci use the same form. For example, the two poems set by Chen in *As in a Dream* utilize the same standard tune (*cipai*). Rather than providing information about the literary content of the poem, the ci title establishes the fixed tune and identifies the patterns used for writing the ci.

Learning ancient Chinese poetic texts was an important element of Chinese education during Chen's childhood. However, with the closing of schools during the Cultural Revolution, she learned about poetry in secret at home, using her father's collection of books where she encountered *Poems from China*,[58] a collection of poems with English translations, published by Wong Man, her father's physician colleague and dean of the Dr. Sun Yat-sen Medical College in Guangdong where Chen Ernan earned his medical degree. The book contained two of Li's ci, including "Picking Mulberries [with Added Characters]," discussed later in connection with "Bright Moonlight" and *Three Poems from the Song Dynasty* for chorus, but neither of the lyrics set in *As in a Dream*.

Chen's fondness for Li's poetry was based on "the feeling and the rhymes and the form," "the simple, straightforward words," and the "sensitive and sentimental" character of the texts. Further, she acknowledges an emotional connection with Li's poetry because Li was also a woman.[59] Her admiration of Li's ci seems well placed since consensus scholarship evaluates her as the preeminent poet in the "elegant restrained style"[60] of the ci. As the first woman ci poet of high artistic achievement, Li offered a genuine female perspective rather than that of men using assumed female personas.[61] Her early ci are carefree and focus on love of nature and her husband. *As in a Dream* is an excellent example of this outlook. Li's works after the fall of the Northern Song regime in 1127 reflect on the collapse of her country and her circumstances as war refugee and widow. The poem "Picking Mulberries with Added Characters," which Chen set as the first movement of *Three Poems from the Song Dynasty*, comes from the second period.

A classmate of Chen at the Beijing Conservatory, soprano Rao Lan,[62] requested a composition while studying in Germany. The result was *As in a Dream*, dedicated to Rao, who has developed a successful, highly visible international career and, since 2007, has been based in Hong Kong. Although she did not give the first performance of the work, she gave the German premiere in Frankfurt as part of the "Erste Europäische China-Woche" in July 1989 and premiered the version with pipa and zheng on October 9, 1994, at Merkin Concert Hall in New York on a concert by Music From China. In 1999 this live performance was issued on the CD, *Sparkle*, devoted to Chen's compositions.[63]

The first movement of *As in a Dream* narrates a boating excursion by a woman, a surprising scene since typically women in the twelfth century were thought to live almost entirely indoors.[64] The persona in the poem has enjoyed her outing, had enough wine that she "lost the way home" and hits a "thick patch of lotuses." As dusk has already set in, she paddles hard and the noise "startled a whole sandbar of egrets into flight."[65] This lyric is Li Qingzhao's best-known of several poems about women boating. The second movement, among Li's most anthologized ci, focuses on the imagery of the final line: "The greens [leaves] must be plump and the reds [begonias or crab apple blossoms] withered."[66] "This lyric represents *wanyue* sentiment of boudoir repining, and pathos on the transience and fragility of youth and beauty represented by the images of flowers which were damaged by the rain and wind."[67] The female persona reveals her deep distress over the events, which can be interpreted as a metaphor for aging. If also read through an autobiographical lens—the common strategy until this century (shifting only with the influence of feminism)—the image of Li comported well with the view prevalent in male literary culture: that her "primary literary impetus was to give expression to her longing"[68] for an absent husband. Perhaps this evaluation at least partially accounts for why this lyric was among Li's most anthologized ci and remains one of her most beloved even today.

Beijing opera reciting style is the primary musical inspiration for *As in a Dream*, recognizable from the singer's slides, grace notes, and use of exaggerated speech-song quality. Describing the composition in a review of the German premiere, Manfred Dahmer claimed that "here, the most fundamental Chinese techniques of glissando and vibrato become a dense, intricate, and fascinating variety of expression."[69] As a representative of her early US style, Chen has called this work "an experiment" in how to combine atonality with Chinese gestures in order to project a personal style; or, as Chen puts it, "to present the Chinese *yun wei* [lingering charm]."[70] Vocally, this song—like Chinese opera—uses a variety of techniques and modes of production along a spectrum from speaking to singing. Chen describes these and other components for the singer and instrumentalists: "In my eyes and taste, Schoenberg's *Sprechstimme* is close to our Beijing opera reciting style. The singing pitches are designed very carefully according to reciting tones, tunes and gestures of Chinese music style, general rules in atonal style, the singer's ability and favorite notes and expressions, and imitation of Chinese instrumental playing on Western instruments."[71] For this type of speech-song, Chen indicates the rhythm but expects the singer to adhere only to the general melodic outline. These notes are marked with an "X" on the stem (see Example 6.10).[72] The melodic contours that Chen created conform to the pattern of linguistic tones in the text, although in an exaggerated form, which is typical of her approach. The development of this concept led Chen "to discover a new way to construct … melodies,"[73] a strategy she used in many later works, such as *Happy Rain on a Spring Night* and the Percussion Concerto, discussed in Chapters 3 and 5, respectively.

EXAMPLE 6.10. *As in a Dream* (1988/1994/2010), original version in manuscript for voice, violin, cello, mvt. 2, ending

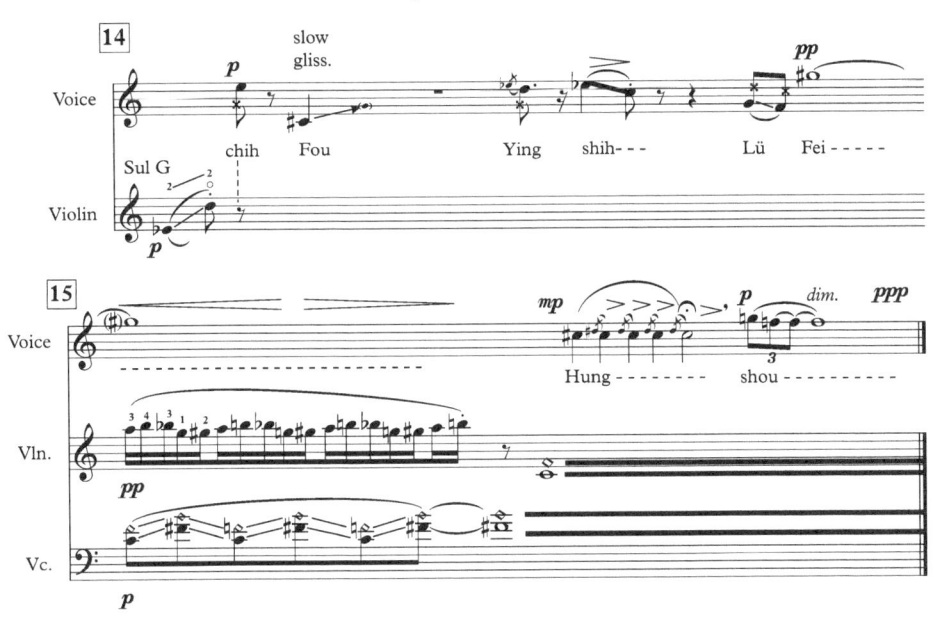

This work avoids linear and vertical intervals that might imply a tone center. Motivic repetition and development dominate the string parts. Even when specific motives are not present, tight, narrow-range filigree characterizes the first movement, and both movements include short ostinato figurations (Example 6.11b). The two closely related violin motives at the beginning provide musical continuity in each movement (Example 6.11a): the first (A) is a pair of interlocking whole steps; the second (B) is an expansion in both interval size and length with three pairs of thirds concluding with a whole step, taking a "tint" from motive A. Development of the motives begins immediately with blending of the two: motive A is embedded within motive B. Rehearsal [2] is almost a combination of the motives in reverse order, but is actually more imaginative. The last six notes of the longer figure yield a presentation of motive A plus a two-note tag from motive B (Example 6.11a). An additional example illustrates the development of motive A (Example 6.11b). In the cello the motive extends to a fifth note, with a final rising whole step, which retains the primary interval. The violin expands to seven notes and uses augmented triplets. Both figures disregard the bar lines, and their interaction shifts due to the differing number of notes in the ostinati as well as their independent rhythmic values.

Choral and Solo Vocal Works

EXAMPLE 6.11. *As in a Dream* (1988), mvt. 1, opening introduction

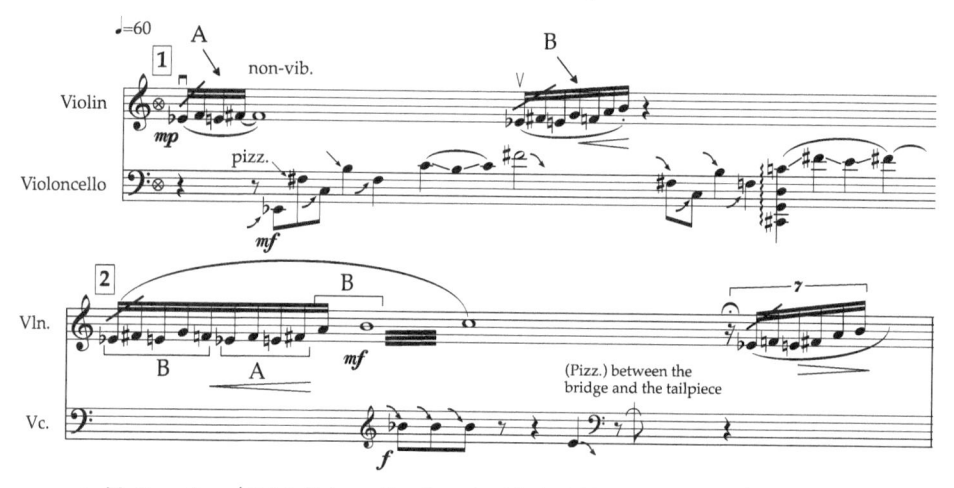

A. Motives A and B (violin); motive A embedded within motive B (violin, [2])

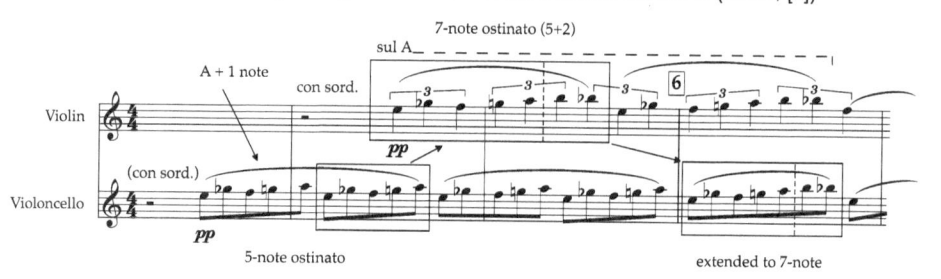

B. Motive A augmented at different values (and extended to five and seven notes) and in counterpoint between cello and violin, before & after [6]

The asynchronization of these instrumental lines creates the impression of improvisation, freedom, and flexibility.

The second movement again begins with a concentration of pitches, which over the first four measures gradually expand to include all twelve pitch classes. Nevertheless, this composition does not involve serial procedures. The systematic exposing of additional pitches starts from the violin dyad (C♯ D) plus a D♯ in the cello and expands somewhat symmetrically by adding half steps to complete the unordered pitch-class set of twelve (Example 6.12).

Chen's instrumental writing often supports the narrative of the text. As the boating woman enters the lotuses, the instrumental parts become more animated to underscore her state of delight with an accelerando and crescendo on ascending lines. Then with the singer's word for "compete" (*zheng*), they

EXAMPLE 6.12. *As in a Dream* (1988), mvt. 2, opening; gradual unfolding of all twelve pitch classes

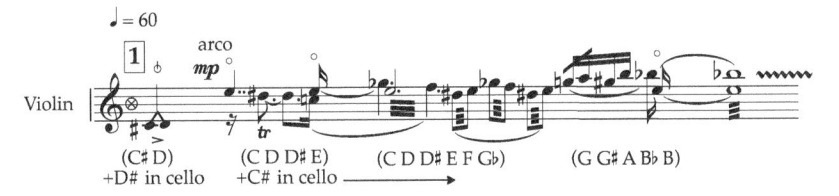

```
♩ = 60
         arco
    [1]   mp
Violin

(C♯ D)       (C D D♯ E)    (C D D♯ E F G♭)    (G G♯ A B♭ B)
+D♯ in cello  +C♯ in cello →
```

match this concept with a close canon using a five-note ostinato. This ostinato (but not the canon) recurs in the second movement at another point of excitement, on the repeated utterance of the urgent question: "Don't you know?" Although the emotional flavor of the two ci is quite different overall, Chen connects them, not just through mutual musical gestures, but also by linking moments of similar intensity with shared musical elements.

As with the vocal part, the range of performance techniques in the instrumental parts is quite pronounced already in the first version for violin and cello with slides, graces, pitch bends, glissandi, pizzicati, and wide vibrato. In the two subsequent versions, changes in the instrumental parts are substantive; however, the voice part is modified only minimally. To complement the sustaining quality of the Western strings, the pipa, and sometimes the zheng, play tremolos. In its two versions, the twenty-one-string zheng has slightly altered tuning that seems particularly important for making specific bass notes available. A comparison of the three versions reveals some of Chen's thought process. (See the discussions of zheng retuning in *Song in Winter* and *Three Dances from China South* in Chapter 4.)

"BRIGHT MOONLIGHT" (2000)

Poet Li Qingzhao also plays a role in another vocal work, "Bright Moonlight," scored for voice (mezzo-soprano) and piano. It was one of sixteen works commissioned by the New York Festival of Song "on a text by a contemporary poet that related to the new millennium or to the future."[74]

Chen wrote her own text in English but used the specific fixed form of Li's ci "Picking Mulberries with Added Characters,"[75] a text filled with longing. A few years earlier, Chen had set this text as the first movement of her earliest choral work, *Three Poems from the Song Dynasty* (1985). Despite the English title of this earlier composition for mixed chorus, it used the original Chinese text, but she had translated the poem into English for her program notes. Because of the change in language in "Bright Moonlight," Chen borrowed the structure

TABLE 6.4. Text comparison between Li Qingzhao's "Picking Mulberries" and Chen Yi's "Bright Moonlight"

Tune: Picking Mulberries [with Added Characters] The Banana Tree Text by Li Qingzhao, English translation by Wong Man[1] Used in Chinese by Chen Yi in *Three Poems from the Song Dynasty*, no. 1 (1985)	Bright Moonlight Text and music by Chen Yi (2000)
Outside my window the banana tree Shadowed the courtyard, Shadowed the courtyard; Every leaf, every blade Leaves some impression on the heart.	Outside my window bright moonlight Kissing the grassland, Kissing the grassland; Near in front, far away, Given to the earth with consonance.
When midnight rain sent sad thoughts to my soul, Dripping lone and sore, Dripping lone and sore; Dreams of the absent one Force me up to listen more.	Look at the window bright moonlight Missing my homeland, Missing my homeland; Near in front, far away, Yearning for the world of consonance.

1. Wong Man, *Poems from China*, 106–107. Chen translates the lyric's title as "The Palm Tree."

but not the linguistic tones of Li's original. The number of Chinese characters in the lines of Li's poem is: 7–4–4–4–5 twice. While the English syllable count (8–5–5–6–9 twice) does not match the number of characters, Chen maintains a similar relationship as can be seen in Table 6.4. She also duplicates the repeated second and third lines in each stanza and creates an added connection between the two halves with the internal rhyme "kissing" and "missing."

Musically, "Bright Moonlight" weaves together traits from Beijing opera and Western art song. The vocal lines draw from, but do not quote, the melodic gestures of Chinese opera, while lyrical, expressive elements, including the intimate emotional focus on yearning, align with a Western Romantic ethos. The blurring of pitches by means of frequent tremolos and rapid passagework in the piano hints of Impressionism but is also reminiscent of Chinese string instruments such as pipa or zheng. The prevailing harmonic vocabulary is complex but with G as a periodic pitch center. The opening seven-note disjunct ostinato pattern (mm. 1–3; also 39–40, 82–end) combines with a left-hand tremolo to sound all but one note of a complete chromatic scale and to create a moonlight atmosphere. The missing B♭ is reserved for the voice to sing almost immediately in its opening melody (see Example 6.13).

Although ostinati are used predominantly as background material in Beijing opera, here Chen foregrounds the ostinato figure that opens and closes the

EXAMPLE 6.13. "Bright Moonlight" (2000), opening, voice & piano

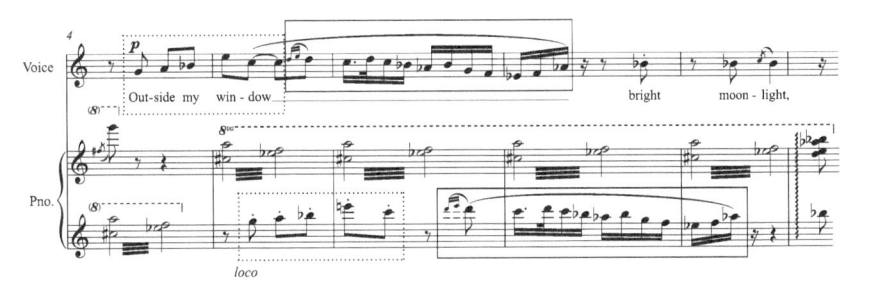

song and marks the return of the varied A section (m. 39). As with Western art song, the interaction between the vocal line and the piano is tight, with the piano anticipating the voice and also echoing the singer. Another feature drawn from typical Beijing opera lyrical singing is the holding tone (*tuo qiang*) where the last note or syllable of a phrase is held or decoratively extended to create a lingering melody with embellishments, examples of which occur periodically throughout the piece (for example, mm. 5–7 where the vocal part is based on folk material in "Lions Playing Ball" from Chaozhou music, Chaozhou region in Guangdong Province). Structurally, the music parallels the poetic text, observing the two-stanza form of the ci: ABA'B'. Overall, "Bright Moonlight" is a more conventional work than either *As in a Dream* or *Meditation*. Notwithstanding the influences from Chinese music, its major stylistic concentration is Western modernist art song.

Mezzo-soprano Wen Zhang describes "Bright Moonlight" as "relatively conservative for performers and audiences"[76] but also identifies the work as "challenging" for the singer due to the demands of low and high registers. The overall range, however, is only middle C to high B♭ with a reasonable tessitura.

Chen's careful attention to the texts for her vocal works continues to be guided by her father's advice. "My father taught me to set poems 'with deep

Choral and Solo Vocal Works

meaning and metaphors, yet simple, easy to understand language' because when the music is sung, it should be understood."[77] Apart from folk song settings, virtually all of the texts chosen for her choral and vocal works are ancient Chinese poems, from as early as the sixth century BCE to the Song Dynasty (960–1279). The only exceptions are texts written by the composer or her use of vocables. When the lyric is in English, Chen generally prepares her own singing translation. "Sometimes I would have to study as many other versions as possible in their English translation forms, in order to do it idiomatically and musically in terms of language and meaning."[78]

CHAPTER 7

Issues

MORE THAN ONCE we heard Chen speak about wanting her music to contribute to a better global community and to "improve the understanding between peoples in the world."[1] In her Alpert award application she stated, "I hope to help resolve social problems and unnecessary conflicts through my music making and teaching." Beyond Chen's desire to educate and bridge cultural differences, some titles of her compositions and her program notes give a clear indication that through her compositions she at times wishes to address explicitly political or social issues. The earliest of these works, *Eleanor's Gift* (1998) for cello and orchestra, is celebratory, honoring Eleanor Roosevelt for her role in securing passage of the United Nations' Universal Declaration of Human Rights fifty years earlier. The topic is global but with a focus on a US woman's leadership. In *Ning* for trio (2001), Chen addressed a particularly brutal chapter in Chinese history commemorating the Nanjing Massacre (1937) with its mass killing of Chinese civilians and widespread rape of Chinese women by Japanese soldiers. In keeping with her own positive outlook and the concert theme of the premiere, *Bridge of Souls—A Concert of Remembrance and Reconciliation*, Chen moves in *Ning* from the horrors and violence of war to a calm ending that evokes hope and reconciliation (see Chapter 4). Four commissions that came in the wake of the 9/11 terrorist attacks resulted in compositions that address this tragedy in various ways: "Know You How Many Petals Falling?" for mixed chorus, *Tu* for orchestra (*Tu* is Chinese for "burning" or "fiery"),

Burning for string quartet, and *...as like a raging fire...* for chamber ensemble. All of these compositions from 2001 and 2002 focused on the fire and fury of this event, and the first two works were dedicated to the heroism of the New York firefighters. Significantly, Chen's "Know You How Many Petals Falling?" is based on the same Tang Dynasty poem by Meng Haoran (689–740) that served as a spark for one of Chou Wen-chung's early works, *And the Fallen Petals* (1954) for orchestra. These compositions by Chen and her mentor also share a common political theme with each driven by a traumatic event: 9/11 in Chen's case and the horrors Chou witnessed during the Second Sino-Japanese War. The final sentence of Chou's program note reveals the elegiac nature of his work: "Thinking of all the young lost in violence and terror who, dying, looked back through a veil of blood at the incomprehensible landscape of their lives, I composed this work in memoriam."[2] Chen's program note similarly evokes the tragic loss of life by firefighters serving to protect people and concludes with the following dedication: "To express the composer's compassion for the victims and their families, to denounce terrorist acts, and to call for the peace of the future."[3] Turning to another conflict, Chen's *Spring in Dresden* (2005) for violin and orchestra commemorates the reconstruction of the Dresden Frauenkirche sixty years after its destruction in World War II by American and British Forces. The church was left in ruins for a half century as a war memorial, but after the reunification of Germany in 1990, its reconstruction was undertaken in 1994. By marking the restoration of this church, Chen captures the positive energy and celebration emerging from the healing and rebuilding rather than the destructive forces of war.

Just as Chen has committed to going beyond the music, we wish to examine a number of political and social issues emanating from her life and music that reach deeper than the scores or their performance. In this concluding chapter, rather than a standard summary we choose to take up questions related to gender, ethnicity and nationality, transnationalism, border crossing, diaspora, exoticism, and identity. Although we can touch on these topics only briefly, we feel they are crucial to address, and we focus on the aspects that seem most relevant to Chen Yi and her music.

Border Crossing, Diaspora, Transnationalism

From a cultural studies viewpoint, location (both physical and metaphorical) and related concepts such as border crossing, diaspora, and transnationalism have become increasingly important as we seek to understand identity and to reveal meaningful strategies for illuminating artistic creation. Divergent perspectives on these terms emerge from differences in disciplinary approaches, changing assessments across time, and the articulations of individual scholars. The boundaries for these concepts are porous, fluid, and "increasingly blurred."[4] Like gender, these lenses are socially constructed.

For an understanding of borders, border crossing, and borderlands, the edited collection *Borderlands and Liminal Subjects* stands out as particularly relevant.[5] Examining both geopolitical and conceptual borders, the essays critique the hierarchical binary pairs (for example, Self/Other, male/female, inside/outside, dominant/subordinate, East/West) created by much of Western philosophy through a recognition of an "interstitial zone"[6] or a state of mind where "we must be willing to break apart our old worldviews and reassemble them into something that allows us to navigate, survive, and bridge the liminal territory between binaries."[7] Further, "the permeability of these Borderland spaces opens up possibilities for reimagining our categories and creating new paradigms that recognize difference and resist hierarchical structures of identity."[8] This borderland—an ambiguous liminal space—is "neither of the categories that it separates and unites, but somehow partakes of both."[9]

Chen has repeatedly crossed the borders between China and the West, both physically and musically, and the musical crossings began early (age three) and have continued throughout her life. Most reviewers, graduate students, and scholars writing about Chen's music emphasize her mixture of Chinese and European/American musical traits, favoring terms such as *hybridity*, *fusion*, or *biculturalism*; however, none of these terms truly captures the essential character of Chen's musical identity. Both cultures are foundational in her compositions; yet the influences and sources of her inspiration create a complex amalgam that might best be described as a new cultural "Third Space," in the parlance of Homi Bhabha: an "interstitial passage between fixed identifications" where "the borders between home and world become confused." In the case of Chen Yi, this "in-between space" is at once representative of, and yet distinct from, each cultural practice.[10]

When Chen became part of the Chinese diaspora in New York City, she joined about 110,000 Chinese people who arrived in that city between 1980 and 1990.[11] Chen was also part of what Su Zheng describes as "the transnational cultural traffic between China and America" that "illuminates a historical (and ongoing) tradition of complex and entangled relationships, indicated not only by imperialist and neocolonialist advancement, expansion, and exploitation, but also by a strong affiliation of Chinese students, visiting politicians, and traveling intelligentsia to American universities and cities that were for them significant extraterritorial centers and major political and intellectual battlefields."[12] Consensus scholarship acknowledges several surges of Chinese migration to the United States, and Zheng demarcates three precise periods: 1849–1950 (from the Gold Rush to the Communist takeover), 1951–79 (up to the end and winding down of the Cultural Revolution), and 1980–99 (post–Cultural Revolution). Each diaspora phase is distinguished primarily by such characteristics as class background, educational level, languages spoken, Chinese locale of the émigrés, and variable politics.

Chinese migrants in the earliest major wave formed a relatively homogeneous group: primarily male working-class laborers, focused first around San Francisco and later in New York's Chinatown. On the West Coast many were gold miners or worked for Central Pacific on construction of the transcontinental railroad. As these jobs dried up, the Chinese moved east. They generally viewed the United States as a temporary, short-term location and longed for a return to China possessing greater prosperity than when they had left home. The Chinese Exclusion Act (first legislated in 1882 and not rescinded until 1943) brought almost a complete halt to the entrance of migrants, especially laborers. As a university student, Chou Wen-chung, however, was permitted to come to the United States in 1946.

With the Chinese Communist Party's takeover on the mainland in 1949 and Mao's establishment of the People's Republic of China, almost everything about the Chinese diaspora in the United States was upended. Particularly disrupted were five thousand Chinese intellectuals who "were stranded in America, including students, tourists, businessmen, government officials, journalists, and priests, most of them from a privileged social class."[13] These transient residents stood in sharp contrast to the established Chinese American diaspora, in both their premigratory backgrounds and their new experiences. The new arrivals often received US government aid and a warm reception by American society, further complicating the polarization between these two immigrant groups. In this second wave many in the diaspora sought their "lost identity" through performing traditional Chinese music.[14]

Political events of 1979 precipitated a rapid increase in Chinese immigration: US quotas doubled for Chinese immigrants and restrictions on emigration eased in both Taiwan and the People's Republic. In 1986, the year Chen arrived in New York, the quotas for China and Taiwan were twenty thousand each, plus five thousand for Hong Kong. The immigrants from the mid-1980s through the late 1990s included many professional artists and musicians. In contrast to previous immigrant waves, these third-wave newcomers were "no longer sojourners," but "in America to stay."[15] "A lack of financial resources, continued political complexities, limited artistic opportunities, and skepticism after the Cultural Revolution led many artists and musicians to believe that the development of their careers and personal lives were hindered or blocked in China."[16] According to Chen, her rationale for coming to the United States was simple: China did not yet have a doctoral degree program in composition. When she became "the first woman with a Master's degree in composition" educated at the Beijing Conservatory, she "applied to Columbia to come for a DMA."[17] On a deeper note Chen, who was a wonderful student and remains intellectually engaged, was also motivated by her aspirations to expand her horizons and achieve musically as much as possible. "[I] should go to see the world: [I] can't be limited just in one place and in one culture."[18]

Speaking about several geographic moves she has experienced, such as leaving the village farm for the Beijing opera troupe, going to the Beijing Central Conservatory, and the move to New York, Chen recalled that "every time [I moved], people treated me as, 'Oh, you are coming back home....' I knew the local culture so well, and the dialect—every color. All these stories, I knew. But when I left, I left." Chen shows herself to be well aligned with attitudes of most Chinese diaspora members who came to the United States during the same period as she did. She was moving to her new home but would always be linked with China. "Absolutely, China is my homeland—my mind, my traditions, my cultural roots. And for the inspiration with all the cultural background, yes. But I don't make my home there."

Reflecting further on the significance of coming to New York, Chen spoke intensely, thoughtfully, and expansively, noting especially that learning about US culture helped her appreciate and cherish more strongly her native Chinese heritage.

> I thought that after I came to the States I could step up to another level, ... particularly when I learned Western history.... I could tell the meaning of humanity, the meaning through the history. It's cultures—it's not an individual person [that reveal the meaning of humanity].... [Then] I would treasure the age-old Chinese culture more passionately. Even in my master's degree program, I started to learn a lot of Chinese philosophy and aesthetics, [but] I still didn't compare [them] with outside cultures ... systematically. ... I think that [comparison] is helpful for me to understand human beings more than before.... I appreciate so much the new cultures, and I soaked up all this kind of nutrition. That is most important for new creation.... When you compare, then you know what's yours.

Although the United States has been Chen's home for more than thirty years (and she readily admitted to us that she feels more comfortable now in

Missouri than in China), her comments on her musical inspiration repeatedly emphasize China as her spiritual center. Among the more public and explicit reflections of this attitude are Chen's program notes for the three movements of Symphony No. 3 (2004) with its revealing subtitle, "My Musical Journey to America." In these notes, which are particularly telling about how Chen positions herself vis-à-vis diaspora, China, and Chinese culture, she pays tribute to her current home, while "only in the world of dreams" can she imagine losing a firm grasp on the rich Chinese heritage. Chen sees at least part of her undertaking as extolling the beauty of her birth heritage—preserving it, reinterpreting it, clothing it in new garments, and presenting it to transnational audiences.

SYMPHONY NO. 3, PREFACE TO SCORE

I. The Dragon Culture.
In ancient totems, in its humanized forms, in folk traditions, the dragon has long been a symbol of power and spirit in Chinese culture. I come from that culture, with its thousands of years of history. **I treasure that heritage tremendously, and want to share it with more people in the world.**

II. The Melting Pot.
I have been working in a multicultural environment in the United States for almost two decades, composing music which is **expected to be a hybrid of Eastern and Western cultures. I want my music to express the lifeblood of the new world in sound and to act as a bridge**, uniting people towards a better future in the new century.

III. Dreaming.
Only in the world of dreams can I forget that I am far away from my homeland.
[emphasis added by the authors]

The first two cities in the United States where Chen lived, New York and San Francisco, each had vibrant and sizeable communities of Chinese immigrants, including significant Chinese diasporic arts and music. During those early years in the United States and ongoing, the emigrant Chinese community provided a strong support base for her emotionally and financially, leading to artistic collaborations and commissions. For example, collaboration with the Music From China ensemble was important to Chen beginning shortly after arriving in New York, and their relationship continues to the present day as demonstrated by their thirty-fifth anniversary concert in the fall of 2019, featuring works written for them by Chen and Zhou Long. Chen credits Chou Wen-chung—beyond his important role as composition teacher—with providing broader artistic and cultural insights about China and the United States and with offering her (and other students) encouragement and support through attendance at performances and recommending specific composition projects. Chen recalls that Chou's wife even assisted her by providing some dresses before a professional trip.[19] Whereas most musicians rely on networking and connections with people for career development, Chen's interaction with the US and global Chinese diaspora has provided notable professional opportunities.[20]

Chen has also developed enduring relationships with non-Chinese performers and performing organizations, for example, Chanticleer and conductor JoAnn Falletta. Just as the circulation of musical ideas between China and the West was multidirectional for Chen, the mentoring and support she has experienced continues through her work with, and devotion to, students not only at UMKC, but also in her many residencies throughout the United States and in China.

Chen's ties to China have grown stronger as she travels there more often and connects meaningfully with students and colleagues in Chinese universities. In her musical creations the use of folk material has become more prevalent now than in earlier pieces and is even more identifiable to those sharing her diasporic experiences. One of many examples occurs in her trio "Tunes from My Home," as noted in Chapter 4: her quotation of Cantonese melodies in that work not only satisfied her own memories of her youth, but also aimed to make pianist Xun Pan "feel at home." Chen's attraction to Chinese musical culture (both folk music and Chinese opera) not only provides inspiration for her melodic and rhythmic expression but also speaks to the Chinese American community, helping them connect with their cultural heritage. Significantly, her use of material from widely separated regions of China—ranging from Mongolia in the north to Guangdong in the south and as far west as Tibet—recognizes the diversity of Chinese culture; and her mixtures of regional expressions within a single work, or sometimes even within a single melody, supports the political aim of drawing the country's numerous minority cultures into a harmonious dialogue. This aim of Chen's can perhaps be seen most directly in her settings of folk songs, such as the pieces she wrote for the Aptos Middle School and Chanticleer (see Chapter 6). Through her efforts, the Chinese children discovered their own heritage; their parents and grandparents looked on with pride and nostalgia; and the non-Chinese children developed an appreciation for the diversity of their own environment in San Francisco, and perhaps even more broadly in the United States.

In addition to arrangements of folk songs or quoted folk materials, Chen draws general inspiration from wide-ranging Chinese gestures, including music, calligraphy, painting, literature, and history, but she has avoided delving explicitly into any controversial political events from the Cultural Revolution or more recent decades—issues that have been addressed by several of her contemporaries, for example, Bright Sheng's *H'un (Lacerations): In Memoriam 1966–1976* (1988) and his opera *Madame Mao* (2002–3); Liu Sola's chamber opera *Fantasy of the Red Queen* (2008), also "loosely based"[21] on the life of Mao's wife; and Tan Dun's *Orchestral Theater III: Red Forecast* (1996) and his *Symphony 1997: Heaven Earth Mankind*, composed for the ceremony at the reunification of Hong Kong with China in July 1997.[22] None of Chen's music has been censored by the Chinese government while a few works by her Columbia classmates Sheng and Tan, among others, have been. Chen's abstention from contentious elements of her heritage in her compositions might suggest she has pursued a safer path; however, we think the evidence supports a more nuanced conclusion, and we offer an alternative assessment below. To substantiate this evaluation, we examine the Chinese contexts and reception surrounding some censored compositions by Tan and Sheng in comparison with Chen's work.

Chen Qigang, another member of the class of '78, described Tan and the reactions to his pioneering orchestral work, *Li Sao* (1979–80): Tan "was a rather rebellious and non-conformist pupil," and his symphonic work, which aroused days of polemical discussion among Conservatory faculty, "made a very modern impression on us."[23] In the end, Tan received an incentive prize. During the early 1980s many of his student colleagues, including Chen Yi, were soon composing similarly adventurous, modern works. In 1983, a spotlight was again on Tan as the first Chinese-trained composer awarded a prize at an international competition. When he returned from Dresden where he had collected the second prize for *Feng ya song* (Ballad-Hymn-Ode), a string quartet influenced by Bartók and using a Western twelve-tone row to generate motivic material, he was praised by the Chinese press, "but eventually, his success turned against him."[24] During 1983 Communist Party hardliners waged a campaign against "spiritual pollution" that led to a six-month ban of public performances and broadcasts of Tan's music in China. The Ministry of Culture criticized his music for "inclination towards Western taste," "lack of ideological content," and being "incomprehensible."[25] About fourteen years later and just before the US premiere of his opera *Marco Polo*, Tan recounted his own assessment: "I was denounced as a running dog of capitalism. Because of my boundary-less thinking, my music made people nervous. They didn't know how to appreciate it, and they encouraged young people to think of it as poison."[26] During 1984 the political climate thawed and opportunities blossomed; 1985–86 offered unprecedented artistic freedom; 1987 brought another swing back to government hardliners and more harsh criticism of young composers, but Tan along with Chen Yi and other musicians had come to New York in 1986 to study at Columbia.

We suggest at least two factors were likely contributors to Tan being the target for censorship in 1983 while other students, such as Chen, were not: compositionally, his work at that point was bolder and more visible than that of the other students; and behaviorally, he was rebellious and individualistic—characteristics not favored in China. Tan's *Symphony 1997* and *The First Emperor* (2006), both of which can be interpreted as critical of China,[27] might have precipitated censorship, but did not.[28]

In the case of Bright Sheng's *Madame Mao*, censorship certainly occurred but perhaps did not come as a surprise. The opera is still unmentioned in the Chinese press as well as unperformed in China because Mao's wife or Jiang Qing "remains she-who-must-not-be-named in the Chinese media."[29] According to Ken Smith, Asian cultural critic for the *Financial Times*, "Sheng was widely assumed to have been blacklisted from China performances for several seasons after Santa Fe [Opera] had announced the commission."[30]

Sheng's more recent opera, *Dream of the Red Chamber* (2016) with English libretto by David Henry Hwang and the composer, fared much better in China, receiving support from China's foreign ministry and Chinese financial backing for two performances each in Beijing, Changsha, and Wuhan, which drew capacity audiences. Still, the prominent National Centre for the Performing Arts in Beijing withdrew from negotiations, based primarily on the fact that the opera is in English, which they considered unattractive to Chinese audiences and financially risky. Sheng described his opera, coproduced by the San Francisco Opera and the Hong Kong Arts Festival, as "a cultural olive branch to make a gesture to China, and China accepted this olive branch."[31]

Censorship in China appears to be opaque and capricious—certainly hinging primarily on political considerations rather than any assessment or analysis of the music.[32] Both Chen and Tan have maintained strong ties with official music institutions in China and returned frequently. Since the late 1980s Tan has spent substantial time working in China and found considerable success there. When Chen made her first return for professional reasons in 1995, she received a warm welcome and acknowledgment of her success in the United States. Sheng has spent less time in China, returning for the first time in 1996 only after a fourteen-year absence to compose a cello concerto commissioned by Yo-Yo Ma. China has a long history of self-censorship[33] so possibly Chen has unconsciously engaged in this activity. More likely, despite deeply emotional expressions of grief in works such as Symphony No. 2 and *Ning*, Chen's focus on affirming life rather than making a critical appraisal of events has led her to positive texts and less controversial topics.

Syncretism, Exoticism, Intersectionality

In exploring the complex cross-cultural influences and the merging of Chinese and Western musics during the Cultural Revolution in the model works (yangbanxi)[34] and then later with the emergence of *xinchao* (new wave) composers beginning in the 1980s, scholars disagree about the nature of musical syncretisms and their cultural meanings. Concerning the complexity of this neo-Orientalism, John Corbett writes: "An Asian composer in the West uses techniques devised by a Western composer inspired by Asian philosophy [for example, John Cage]—the work is played for an Asian audience which hears it as an artifact of the bizarre West. Orientalism is reflected back-and-forth like a musicultural *mise-en-abyme*."[35]

At least as recently as the late twentieth century, official Chinese views of music during the Cultural Revolution were that of a cultural wasteland—"ten years of stagnation"[36] and a period with "no music."[37] Hong Kong musicologist Liu Ching-chih [Liu Jingzhi], although claiming his geopolitical location gives him a more balanced understanding of the yangbanxi than is possible for scholars on the mainland or in Taiwan, has repeatedly posited an extremely negative view of the model works, not only as they existed during the Cultural Revolution, but also in terms of any postrevolutionary influence. According to Liu the "emergence and subsequent decline [of the yangbanxi] show it is impossible for works of art that ... are written under coercion to stand the test of time.... The *yangbanxi* also had a very bad psychological effect on people."[38] He describes them as "just some of the grotesque products spawned by the Cultural Revolution."[39] Liu claims that changes imposed on traditional Beijing opera as it was transformed into the yangbanxi led, among other negative results, to audience dissatisfaction. "With no good singing to listen to and no exciting fights or acrobatics to watch, it was understandable that the *yangbanxi* did not attract audiences."[40] Many Western sinologists counter Liu's assessment with convincing evidence to demonstrate not only the broad appeal of the yangbanxi but also the high quality of their professional performances.[41] For example, Bell Yung states that the yangbanxi "were expected ... to meet the highest artistic standards" and "are exceptional works of art."[42] Chen, also concurring with the majority of scholars on the popularity of the model works, claimed "everyone learned to sing or play or perform"[43] the revolutionary operas, and recent renewed interest in these works confirms her evaluation of them. Drawing on her experience leading the Guangzhou troupe, Chen further addressed the quality of performances and the music itself: "We would have to make self-criticism after a performance if we made a mistake. We enjoyed every perfect performance every night as a performer. Technically it's refined, in high quality. The music is fantastic."[44]

Given the shattering brutality and trauma of the Cultural Revolution, an attempt to minimize the value and role of the model works is not surprising. Barbara Mittler, along with other China specialists, advances a new appraisal of the nature and musical significance of the model works. In an effort to create music that is both Chinese and modern, "the model works are manifestations of a hybrid taste which calls for the transformation of Chinese tradition according to Western standards, a taste which for a century has led to the creation of a Chinese music of Western imprint."[45] In a similar vein, the essays in *Listening to China's Cultural Revolution: Music, Politics, and Cultural Continuities* articulate the centrality of yangbanxi and revolutionary songs as "the backbone of the revolutionary culture ... when everyone listened to the same music and sang the same set of arias"[46] in every facet of their lives. Although some music of the Cultural Revolution may seem "clichéd and monotonous" today, "these works continue to be powerful in providing people with a sense of emotional anchorage"; "[continue] to matter in classical and popular music culture today"; and have "made a lasting impact on many Chinese musicians, however much they wanted to reject the Cultural Revolution."[47]

The hybrid orchestra of the yangbanxi is one of their enduring influences on new wave composers. The yangbanxi instrumentation maintained careful balance among the Chinese and Western instruments with the smaller number of Chinese instruments still taking the lead.[48] For xinchao composers, such as Chen, the "use of Chinese instruments—especially percussion—adds a remarkable timbre, sense of motion, rhythm, and energy. Their treatment of the timbre and articulations of Western instruments also involves extremely creative bending and sculpting of the sonority to resonate with and embody the feel of Chinese instruments or vocal styles."[49] For almost eight years, Chen led the orchestra for the opera troupe in Guangzhou, an experience that "deeply affected her musical thinking."[50] Chen's *Chinese Myths Cantata* (see Chapter 6) is an especially germane example of all these musical and dramatic features, which she absorbed through that encounter.

Composers, music journalists, and scholars frequently attach a negative connotation to exoticism—often with good reason, but by the twenty-first century an acknowledgment of borrowing may not need to have a deleterious inference.[51] However, evaluation of music by Chen and other new wave composers in the United States often creates limitations for full acceptance in either China or the United States. The blurred boundaries discussed earlier seem to be a liability in this regard: in China the music is at times "deemed too individualistic and not national enough"[52] while in the United States music by Chinese new wave composers has been homogenized by many critics, as if presenting no individuality, marginalized, and "treated as novelties rather than a part of the contemporary-music mainstream."[53] Unfortunately, Samson Young is probably correct when he concludes that elements of colonialism persist in the evaluations of compositions by xinchao composers.[54]

In his discussion of "Transcultural Composing," that is, twentieth-century works written for Western audiences that "blend, interweave, or merge musical elements that the composer (and audience) would recognize as being 'our own' with those of the distant Other culture,"[55] Ralph Locke acknowledges many compositions "that offer little or no concrete evidence of larger cultural assumptions: pieces that follow more or less exclusively the principle of Transcultural Composing. To what degree such pieces might also convey an exoticist attitude is, as [Annegret] Fauser wisely concludes, 'still open for debate.'"[56] Perhaps we need new terminology to address the interweaving of two or more musical styles that emanate from distinct musical cultures—differentiated either by national borders or by discrete cultural entities—that do not rely on imperialism, hegemony, or exploitation and thus do not warrant the label *exoticism*. Perhaps consideration of how and what the various compositional elements signify—for various audiences as well as for the composer—would offer a more constructive approach. Mittler suggests that, in general, composers of new Chinese music are not "as well-trained and as knowledgeable in the Chinese musical tradition as they are in the Western musical tradition," and for many, "the Chinese musical tradition might be more of an Other to them than the foreign compositional tradition."[57] For Chen, her background in both musical cultures—particularly her extensive work as a performer and leader in the Guangzhou opera company—seems to position her differently. However, in the reception of Chen's music, differing knowledge of the referents definitely affects audience perception. In China, especially among traditional musicians, contemporary Western elements are Other while in the United States, European American audiences may hear Chen's Chinese references as exotic. For Chen, both musics are integral parts of her reality.

Cultural theorist Stuart Hall described the concept of cultural identity as "a matter of 'becoming' as well as of 'being.' ... Cultural identities come from somewhere, have histories. But ... they undergo constant transformation. Far from being eternally fixed ..., they are subject to the continuous 'play' of history, culture and power. . . . Identities are the names we give to the different ways we are positioned by, and position ourselves within, the narratives of the past."[58] Including ethnicity, in this case Chineseness, as one dimension of a person's identity can be meaningful or useful to an individual. Further, embracing multiple identities appears to be not only a likely occurrence but also essential in representing twenty-first-century reality.[59] Allen Chun argues that ethnicity, culture, and identity are "analytically quite distinct" and that the concept of Chineseness is "ephemeral."[60] Chun recognizes shortcomings in the very concept of "identity."[61] Pointing out perceived flaws in almost any terminology or categorization can be easy; however, humans have a need or at least a desire to organize or classify material such as identity, ethnicity, and styles of composition, and these concepts can be useful, especially if conceived in a flexible and multifaceted manner.

Focusing on the sociocultural context and avoiding the concept of "art as autonomous and transcendent,"[62] Frederick Lau suggests that new wave composers employ Chinese traits where the "emphasis is on manipulating rhythms, timbres, and textures commonly found in Chinese music"[63] but that avoid the stereotypical sonic chinoiserie of earlier generations—what Chou Wen-chung labeled "superficial exoticism."[64] Lau seeks to create a nuanced and rich analysis by avoiding the strictures of dualistic thinking about East-West and by highlighting the reciprocal exchange of influences. He also notes that the xinchao composers are actually using their ethnicity to advance their careers while buying into the hegemonic global cultural marketplace, and that reviewers of their music promote an essentialized and racialized discourse through frequent references to their ethnicity.[65] "Packaging these artists and their work as coming from the cultural fringes has tacitly become an important element in promoting them."[66] Further, Lau notes that these Chinese American composers "make constant references to Chineseness in their music" even though "they want to be perceived and marketed as globalized transnational composers. . . . They have knowingly or involuntarily capitalized on the Orientalist discourse for personal gain, privileging the categories that they seek to transcend."[67]

Lau views the use of Chinese elements by various xinchao composers in transactional or market-driven terms, noting that they monetize their Chineseness. In contrast, Alicia Hunt Ciccone presents a political case that Chen's use of Chinese folk materials reinscribes Maoist ideology. Ciccone argues that Chen's interest in rural folk music creates a "superficial hybridity" and risks romanticizing the Maoist dogma of "reeducating the elite through forced contact with the 'folk.'"[68] Su Zheng offers a further alternative on this topic that we find more compelling and more meaningfully reflective about Chen Yi. She writes that Chen and other new wave composers "left behind them the ideological and social constraints imposed by the Chinese government and society," while "at the same time, they have become highly conscious of their own cultural heritage and individual identities in America's cultural pluralist and multiethnic society and strongly competitive new-music circles. Chinese cultural tradition has therefore become both part of their personal identity and a strategic capital for their professional advancement in America."[69]

Christian Utz seems correct in his analysis that in the post-1945 political climate in Europe and the United States, the desire "to install a supposedly ideology-free terrain of artistic development as a symbol of political liberty"[70] was understandable given the events that had just occurred with European totalitarian political systems. This environment had an impact on everything, including compositional styles, and led to contrasting approaches: on the one hand a reverence for serialism (and even total serialism) and on the other, the exploration of aleatory music (in John Cage's conception of music "where sounds are sounds and people are people").[71] Formalist, abstract, and essentialist methods of analysis became the norm. However, neither composers nor analysts can escape the politics of representation. Based on the work of German social theorist Ulrich Beck from the late 1990s,[72] Utz proposes "reflexive globalization" as a way to create new perspectives to controvert "both hegemonic European aesthetic discourses as well as cultural essentialist and neonationalist models outside the West."[73] Rather than any one specific analytical approach for music by Chen Yi and other new wave composers, a more revealing strategy seems to be an investigation that is multipronged, marshaling technical details in a close reading to elucidate ways in which the music constructs meaning.

In seeking a framework that addresses the complexities of the various issues raised in this chapter, the concept "transnational intersectionality" comes to mind. The term was coined by Sheila Grabe and Nicole M. Else-Quest in 2012 as a more inclusive and global iteration of "intersectionality" (sometimes called intersectional feminism), conceived in 1989 by Kimberlé Crenshaw to broaden feminist theory and antiracist discussions around the oppression of Black women and to make these debates more responsive to lived experience.[74] Initially an obscure academic term, "intersectionality" has become a leading concept in "national conversations about racial justice [and] identity politics, . . .—and over the years has helped shape legal discussions."[75] This evolving terminology acknowledges scholars' growing appreciation of multiple and intersecting identities. Rather than try to force a direct parallel between the original usage of "transnational intersectionality" in feminist theory and how the concept is employed here, we propose instead a kinship that is useful as a means to broaden the discussion of the music by xinchao composers. Transnational intersectionality suggests that many simultaneous avenues are needed for analyzing, evaluating, and understanding the multifaceted music of Chen Yi in tandem with current global realities.

Like Chen, (virtually) all of the new wave composers utilize elements of both Chinese and Western musics, seeking to craft a distinctive compositional voice and a plural identity. In Zheng's assessment, the lives and compositions of Chen and other xinchao composers enact "persistent efforts toward deghettoization and de-exoticization."[76] The nature of exoticism has changed dramatically from the nineteenth century to the late twentieth and early twenty-first century, shifting from Orientalist borrowings by European composers in furtherance of the aims of alterity to an attitude of greater respect for diversity and a postmodern appreciation of heterogeneity. Further, not every musical borrowing can or should be labeled exoticism. The scholar's responsibility in formulating any assessment of the music of Chen and her compatriots is ultimately less about identifying particular stylistic traits that can be labeled as "borrowed" than considering what the music signifies for the composer, culture and people of origin, and audiences.

Women, Gender, Bias

When asked about whether women and men were treated differently in her experience in China before moving to New York, Chen maintained that she "grew up in new China, where women and men were equal." Despite Chen's perception of equal treatment based on gender, the opportunities for women appear to have been more limited than those for men. For example, although both Chen's mother and father were from the same medical school class, her mother was the only woman in that class. Each was a well-respected physician and honored as an outstanding doctor in Guangdong Province in the 1960s. While Chen's mother was a famous pediatrician, her father participated in hospital leadership. When Chen's class at the Beijing conservatory officially began their undergraduate study in the fall of 1978, the class numbered twenty-seven: twenty-one composition majors and six ear training majors. Chen was one of five women studying as composers along with three women studying to become ear training teachers. The class was divided into two groups by skill level for some courses, with Chen and two of the women in the ear training department in the top group. Chen has a strong conviction that the Conservatory "teachers didn't treat us differently." Yet at the same time, when Alexander Goehr held his influential residency in China in 1980, Chen was the only woman among

PHOTO 12. Taken February 10, 1981; all twenty-seven students in the Beijing Conservatory composition class of 1978. Chen Yi is in the front row, second from the left; Zhou Long, in the middle row, second from the right. Photo courtesy of Chen Yi.

the six composition students chosen to work privately with him. (Four were from Beijing and two were from Shanghai.)

By today the gender distribution is almost completely reversed. Now in some classes as many as ninety percent of students at Beijing Conservatory are women.[77] Similarly, in 1999 when Chen and her UMKC colleague, James Mobberley, presented a composition workshop sponsored by the Taiwan Symphony, thirty-three composers from different universities throughout Taiwan participated and only one composer was a man.[78] Although this dramatic change in gender distribution might seem at first glance to suggest the disappearance of systemic gender bias, in fact this situation reflects instead the more limited employment opportunities for women. Chen attributes the gender shift in composition studies to the fact that "now students have more choices, opportunities for positions, selections. For example, you can go for business [where] you make more money." Judging from the shrinking participation of men in composition programs, the more lucrative business careers appear to be far more available to men than to women, who continue to populate lower-paying music positions.

At Columbia in her class of eleven composers, Chen was the only woman; however, she insists she had "no sense of gender" there. Her sterling academic record, the strength of her compositions, and the awards she received during her years at the Beijing Conservatory provided strong support for her acceptance into the doctoral program. Perhaps the fact that Chen arrived in New York the year after her husband, Zhou Long, or that she was part of a heterosexual couple also contributed to the egalitarian atmosphere she experienced with other students and the faculty. In addition to her demonstrated talent, skill, and originality, we also believe that she was welcomed in part due to individual traits, such as her positive outlook, exceptional musicianship, upbeat and smiling personality, and willingness to support other students by performing their compositions.

"I didn't have a sense [of gender difference], really, until I worked in the Women's Philharmonic," says Chen. "I saw all women for the first time. We have a huge orchestra! Seventy people, all women including all conductors and percussion." Chen did a lot of reading about women composers from Hildegard to the present and, she says, "I learned how they were discriminated against in history.... Since then, I have supported women composers strongly." She volunteered her time to work on the database of women's compositions maintained by the Women's Philharmonic and to provide lists of works for performers and ensembles. Chen also engaged in fund-raising for the orchestra through presentations, which often included her performances on violin or piano of music by historical women composers.

Today, life-work balance is an issue for both women and men; however, on the question of children, the issue still weighs more heavily on women. In an interview of Chen and Zhou by Xie Mei for a Chinese publication about members of the '78 class, Xie raised a question about why, after twenty years of marriage, they do not have children. Zhou passed the topic to Chen, who laughed: "We are so busy; no time to cook for children! Besides, students are our children." Zhou added, "Our music compositions are also our children."[79]

As a professor, Chen shows strong devotion to all of her composition students, but she admits: "I love teaching women composers. Maybe unconsciously this became a very close relationship in [the students'] minds. Many women students get inspiration from me just being on the faculty." At UMKC composition students rotate studying with various faculty members rather than working exclusively with a single teacher; however, having a woman among the composition faculty—and one who is a prominent composer—seems to make a difference to women students. When she started at UMKC, between a dozen and twenty students were composition majors.[80] In recent years, the department has had between fifty and sixty majors, ranging from beginning undergraduates through doctoral candidates. During academic year 2017–18, six of twenty-three graduate students and four of twenty-nine undergraduates were women (26 and 14 percent, respectively).[81]

As one of few women composition teachers in US colleges and universities, Chen serves "to empower and enable future generations of aspiring female composers."[82] In 2014, women held only 15 percent of composition faculty positions in the top twenty music schools as identified by rankings from *U.S. College Rankings*. More than half of the elite schools had no woman on the composition faculty. The percentage improved slightly to 18 percent in 2015–16.[83] According to composer Jennifer Higdon (Curtis Institute), the only woman chair of composition studies in 2014: "A student should be able to believe wholeheartedly that they can reach those highest levels of compositional expression.... The presence of women composers can only help encourage those who would seek out music as a career (and as a form of expression)."[84]

Although Chen doesn't think she has encountered any gender discrimination or that her life experience is any different from a man's, facts about programming among professional orchestras point to systemic discrimination—discrimination that has almost certainly affected performances of Chen Yi's music. Ricky O'Bannon, a writer for the Baltimore Symphony (Marin Alsop, music director), gathered and analyzed data about the 2014–15 season for the twenty-one major American orchestras, selected by size and operating budget. During 2014–15 with more than 1,000 works by 286 different composers in almost 4,600 performances, works by women comprised only 1.8 percent of the total.[85] Unsurprisingly, women comprised a larger percentage of the small subset of compositions by living composers: they represented 14.8 percent of this segment, which was only a little more than 11 percent of the total works performed. Only one woman placed among the top six of most-performed living composers: Jennifer Higdon, a distant third in the rankings. Higdon was also the one woman with repeat performances by different orchestras that season: *blue cathedral* (2000). A follow-up study by O'Bannon for the 2016–17 season examined the repertoire for eighty-five American orchestras performing 3091 concerts and found similar representation for women composers: 1.3 percent of the total and 10.3 percent of the music by living composers.[86]

The 2014–15 report notes that although the percentage of women represented is still extraordinarily low, improvement has occurred over the past two decades.

However, Alsop points out "that closing gender gaps in classical music is not an inevitability just because the field has achieved a few milestones."[87] "Unless we actively try to change the landscape, I don't think it's going to change on its own. I see no empirical evidence to say that's the direction we're going. I see fits and starts, but I don't see a sustained trend."[88] Alsop acknowledges that subjectivity in the evaluation of art is a complicating factor but calls for more opportunities for young women composers to succeed or fail.

The situation for programming works by women composers in Europe appears to be similar or even less favorable. In a study that examined the repertoire of major symphony orchestras and major international festivals in nine Western European countries and two Eastern European countries for the period 1998–2002, Patricia Adkins Chiti reports that "the figures for [women's] inclusion in top level programming are far lower than anyone could have imagined. Most countries in the survey gave less than 1 percent of their programming resources to music created by women."[89] In a list of the thirty-one most widely performed women composers in the eleven countries of the study, Chen, the only Asian, is tied with twenty other women in eleventh place, each with performances in two European countries. Performances for the top two women, Sofia Gubaidulina and Kaija Saariaho, far exceeded the others.[90] Adkins Chiti reaffirmed that the percentage of women on European programs through 2014 remained at 1–2 percent.[91]

Beginning in 2017–18, some organizations in Europe and the United States instituted efforts to boost the visibility of women and change the pattern of underrepresentation. Sound and Music, the UK new music charity, announced on 2017 International Women's Day that by 2020, at least 50 percent of the composers with whom they work will identify as women.[92] Although more relevant to jazz and popular music, the UK's PRS Foundation has signed forty-five international music festivals, including the BBC Proms (only for contemporary composers),[93] the Huddersfield Contemporary Music Festival, and the Aldeburgh Festival, who pledge numerical equality in their lineups by 2022.[94] Major US organizations, especially orchestras, have been slow to program women composers; for example, for the 2017–18 season nearly half of the top thirty orchestras listed no music composed by women. The Los Angeles Philharmonic and the Chicago Sinfonietta made the best showing with ten and nine compositions by women, respectively.[95] Chen's *Ge Xu (Antiphony)* was among the LA performances, led by conductor Xian Zhang, who has performed this work across China, Europe, and the United States.[96] Although the Chicago Sinfonietta (Mei-Ann Chen, music director) has only five subscription programs, its profile is elevated as a winner of a 2016 MacArthur "genius" award and as "the city's hippest orchestra" according to the *Chicago Tribune*.[97] Among major presenters spotlighting new music, gender diversity has been stronger than in the orchestral world; for example, 43 percent of New York's Miller Theatre's *Composer Portraits* series focused on women during 2010–15. Chen was featured in a full-evening concert on December 2, 2017, as one of two women out of six composers honored during the 2017–18 season.[98]

Among the top six major composition awards, the underrepresentation of women is almost tangible as they are only 9 percent of the total recipients from inception to 2014. Of these prizes, Chen received the Charles Ives Living award in 2001 and in 2018 is still the only woman recipient (one of six). Awarded first in 1998, the Ives Living offers the largest monetary award granted exclusively to American composers and is spread over two or three years.[99] Another bright spot came in 2017 when for the first time in the seventy-four-year history of the Pulitzer Prize, all three finalists were women. Du Yun won for her opera, *Angel's Bone*. "Since 1943, only fourteen finalists for the music Pulitzer have been women, and only seven women have won."[100] Chen's orchestral work, *Si Ji* (Four Seasons), was one of these finalists in 2006.

By any measure, Chen has had an exceptionally successful career of performances, commissions, and prizes in terms of sheer numbers, prominent ensembles and performers, and prestigious venues in North America, Europe, and Asia. Consider, however, how many more performances, commissions, and prizes she might have received if institutional bias were not part of the equation. We hope this book contributes to a deeper understanding of Chen Yi's life and music and stimulates more performances of her compositions. The reward, we hope, will be a benefit not only to Chen Yi, but also to her audiences and performers. She composes, she reminds us, not only to explore the deeper recesses of her heart and mind, but also to fulfill an obligation to "give back to society." "I always think that civilization and education are my obligations to work for in society. Even when I was a farmer in the countryside in China, I wanted to educate them. I wanted to read books for them. I wanted to sing for them because, like desire, I have the passion to get education to more people." Uniting people with one another and with nature is a foremost objective in Chen Yi's drive to compose. It harks back to an ancient Chinese philosophy exemplified in the refined culture of the qin, namely to create "harmony with sky and people and earth."[101]

Glossary

Following the Mandarin Pinyin romanization for Chinese terms, we provide the term in Chinese characters. Where two versions occur, simplified Chinese (used in the People's Republic of China, Singapore, and Malaysia) is presented first, followed by traditional Chinese (used primarily in Hong Kong, Taiwan, Macao, and Chinese-speaking communities outside the mainland). Where only one version is given, the glyphs are identical in these two systems.

Baban (八板): A sixty-eight-beat folk melody of ancient origin that Chen has used in more than twenty works; see Chapter 3 for detailed description and discussion.

balungan: In Indonesian gamelan music, the underlying skeletal melody over which ornamental lines are layered.

bangu (板鼓): Beijing opera drum.

bawu (巴乌) (巴烏): Side-blown free reed pipe with finger holes, shaped like a transverse flute, but containing a metal free reed and therefore producing a sound closer to that of a clarinet.

chenci (衬词) (襯詞): Syllables (phonemes, vocables) added to folk song texts or to Chinese opera lyrics that are closely related to regional dialects or local folk music; also called padding syllables or nonsense syllables. Listeners familiar with folk songs from different regions can identify the regional origination of a folk song as soon as they hear the chenci sung. Chen generally indicates chenci in her scores with italic font.

ci (词) (詞): Major artistic literary form during the Song Dynasty (960–1279) that gave special attention to word choices and featured lines of unequal length (lines with differing numbers of characters) with set rhyme schemes and linguistic tonal patterns.

cipai (词牌) (詞牌): Standard tune and fixed patterns used for a ci.
dagu (大鼓): Large Chinese drum.
dizi (笛子): Bamboo transverse flute with six finger holes and a mouth hole. The instrument also contains an extra hole between the mouth hole and the first finger hole (called a *mo kong* [膜孔]), which is covered by a thin membrane, creating a buzz whenever the instrument is sounded.
erhu (二胡): Two-string bowed fiddle; the most common member of the huqin family; see huqin for fuller description.
fangman jiahua (放慢加花): Slowing down and adding flowers; that is, stretching out a melody line and adding ornamental notes within it.
guan, guanzi (管子): Cylindrical double reed wind instrument.
guqin (古琴): See qin below.
haofang (豪放): One of the two major styles of ci, whose expression is described as "heroic abandon" (Wang Ping).
haozi (号子) (號子): Work song, a type of folk song; features a strong rhythmic pulse to facilitate hard, heavy labor; literally "crying" or "shouting."
huqin (胡琴): Family of bowed two-stringed instruments with small round, hexagonal, or octagonal bodies; the bow hair passes between the two strings. Huqin instruments come in various sizes (pitch levels). Those used commonly by Chen Yi include the erhu (the most common huqin); the midsize, lower-pitched zhonghu; and the small, high-pitched jinghu.
irama: In Indonesian gamelan music, the rhythmic proportion between the balungan (skeletal melody) and the ornamental lines.
jing erhu (京二胡): Huqin instrument that plays an octave lower than the jinghu; similar to the erhu.
jinghu (京胡): Small erhu; a major accompaniment instrument in Beijing opera.
kouxian (口弦): Three-tongued jaw harp of the Jingpo people (景颇族).
lerong (勒绒): Double-pipe bamboo instrument of the Jingpo people, held obliquely in front of the player. One of the two bamboo pipes contains finger holes. Inserted transversely into the lower part of the other one is a small cylindrical tube that creates a reed-like sound.
liuqin (柳琴): Four-string mandolin with a pear-shaped body.
lunzhi (轮指) (輪指): Technique on the pipa consisting of a circular strumming motion.
luogu dianzi (锣鼓点子) (鑼鼓點子): Set of about a hundred classic rhythm patterns used by Beijing opera percussion ensemble; the term can apply to the entire set of patterns or to an individual pattern.
luogu jing (锣鼓经) (鑼鼓經): A device for learning Beijing opera percussion patterns (luogu dianzi) through the application of verbal syllables to represent instruments and playing techniques; literally luo (gong), gu (drum), jing (score).
lusheng (芦笙) (蘆笙): Miao instrument composed of a cluster of bamboo pipes (generally five or six in different sizes), each of which contains a free reed; the pipes are tuned in pentatonic scales and sound in tight clusters.

pipa (琵琶): Large plucked lutelike instrument with an articulated fingerboard; held vertically on the lap; has a powerful sound and a wide range of performance techniques.

qin (琴): Ancient seven-string plucked zither without frets; linked with Chinese literati and elites; strong association with refinement and sophistication; played by Confucius; treasured as an objet d'art; also called guqin.

qingli (清丽) (清麗): Used by Su Shi (a major Song dynasty figure of the literati) to identify a hybrid style of ci and applied to Li Qingzhao by Wang Ping; characterized by a simple and natural style and described as "fresh and spontaneous beauty" (Wang Ping).

qinqiang (秦腔): Chinese folk opera from Shaanxi Province.

qupai (曲牌): Generic term referring to a variety of "named" fixed tunes. Historically, qupai were texted melodies that were transformed into instrumental versions and used as interludes in operas, but the term is often used in a more general sense to designate a set melody that serves as the basis for variation. Although derived from folk music rather than opera, Baban is generally also labeled a qupai.

quyi (曲艺) (曲藝): Musical storytelling; a cross between singing and reciting, along with instrumental accompaniment.

quzi ci (曲子词) (曲子詞): Original name for ci, see above; literally "tuned poetry" or "lyrics of songs."

rag dung (拉东/筒钦/大号筒/长角号) (拉東/筒欽/大號筒/长角号): Collapsible long metal trumpet from Tibet.

ruan (阮): Four-string lute with a round body and a fretted neck.

sanxian (三弦): Three-string fretless lute with long neck and a body made from snakeskin (generally python) stretched over a resonator.

shange (山歌): Mountain song; folk song type sung outdoors, such as in a field or near a mountain.

sheng (笙): Mouth organ consisting of a group of seventeen or more vertical pipes, most with free-reeds; played by both exhaling and inhaling; produces chords or clusters; similar to its Japanese descendant, the shō.

shifan luogu (十番锣鼓) (十番鑼鼓): A type of folk percussion band, sometimes including wind instruments as well, from southern Jiangsu Province.

shuangxiao (双箫) (雙簫): Vertical flute with two pipes and finger holes on both of them.

suona (唢呐) (嗩吶): Loud double reed instrument whose mouthpiece connects to a wooden shaft with finger holes and a flared copper bell.

tuo qiang (拖腔): Holding tone, literally "to drag (the) singing tune"; an approach to composition in which the last note or syllable of a phrase is held in order to create a lingering melody with embellishments.

wanyue (婉约) (婉約): One of the two major styles of ci; meaning "delicate restraint" (Wang Ping); associated with feminine sentiment.

wenren (文人): Term for Chinese literati or scholar-painters, initiated about tenth century and peaking during the Ming Dynasty (1368–1644).

xiangjiao ruoxian (相角揉弦): Type of vibrato technique on the pipa; the left hand creates a vibrato on the "big fret corner" (xiangjiao) of the pitch without the right hand plucking the string; produces a soft buzzing sound.

xiaodiao (小调) (小調): Lyrical folk song, including love songs, songs of daily life, narrative songs, and songs popular among the people; literally "little tune."

xinchao (新潮): New wave composers, many of whom were in the first postrevolutionary graduating class at Beijing Central Conservatory or other educational institutions; their compositions were more experimental and moved away from "pentatonic romanticism" (Mittler, *Dangerous Tunes*).

xiongling (雄吟/苄令): Tibetan fipple flute.

xun (埙) (塤): Globular vessel flute.

yangbanxi (样板戏) (樣板戲): Term for the model works developed during the Cultural Revolution under the direction of Mao's wife, Jiang Qing.

yangqin (扬琴) (揚琴): Trapezoidal dulcimer with seven or more courses of metal strings, struck with slender beaters.

yin song (吟诵) (吟誦): *Reciting*, a general term used to describe reading poems or prose according to the tones of words, phrasing, and rhymes of the lines.

yueqin (月琴): Lute with a round, hollow body, short fretted neck, and four strings; used as an accompanying instrument along with jinghu and jing erhu, in Beijing opera; sometimes called the *moon lute*.

yuluge (语录歌): Revolutionary songs with texts of quotations from Mao's speeches or writings.

yun wei (韵味) (韻味): Lingering charm.

zheng (筝) (箏): Zither with twenty-one strings and movable bridges. In the traditional repertoire, one hand plucks and the other presses on the strings to create microtonal pitch changes. In modern repertoire, sometimes both hands pluck the strings.

zhonghu (中胡): Type of huqin, lower in pitch than the erhu and designed to function as the counterpart of the viola in contemporary Chinese orchestras.

zhuihu (坠胡) (墜胡): Two-string bowed fiddle. Unlike the huqin instruments, the zhuihu has a fretless fingerboard against which the strings are pressed; its sound imitates the human voice.

List of Works

Double dates separated by a slash (/) indicate original composition and revision dates.

References to related works include instrumentation only if they appear in other sections of the works list (for example, a trio version of an orchestral piece). References without instrument designations pertain to works in the same category.

Dur = duration; approximate length in minutes

mvts = number of movements (only listed if more than 1); separated by a slash (/) from overall duration

CCOM = Central Conservatory of Music, Beijing

NEA = National Endowment for the Arts

UMKC = University of Missouri, Kansas City

Large Instrumental Ensembles

WORKS FOR CHAMBER ORCHESTRA, FULL ORCHESTRA, OR WIND ENSEMBLE

Date	Title	Scoring	Dur/mvts	Commissioner	Comments, awards, cross-borrowings
1984–85	Duo Ye	Chamber orchestra	7.5	China Record Company	Orchestration of Duo Ye (pf solo, 1984; see comments there).
1982/1986	Sprout	String orchestra	7		Inspired by qin; developed from a double canon written at CCOM. Orchestration of String Quartet, mvt 2 (1982).
1986	Symphony No. 1	Orchestra	24		Last composition from Beijing period; completed at the end of her MA work.
1987	Duo Ye No. 2	Orchestra	8		Reworking & expansion of Duo Ye (1984–85). Written for first US tour of Central Philharmonic of China.
1993	Symphony No. 2	Orchestra	18	Women's Philharmonic	In memory of Chen Yi's father. Inspired by student visit to a Yao village in Guangxi Province. First use of the "Chen Yi motive."
1994	Ge Xu (Antiphony)	Orchestra	10	Women's Philharmonic, as part of Meet The Composer's New Residencies Program	Inspired by the antiphonal singing of Zhuang people at the lunar new year. Pitch materials from mountain songs & dancing tunes of Zhuang, Miao, Yi, & Bouyei nationalities. Dedicated to John Duffy.
1982/1994	Shuo	String orchestra; or string quartet or quintet	8	San Jose Chamber Orchestra	Influence of Chinese folk tunes & mountain song gestures. Orchestration of String Quartet, mvt 1 (1982). Dedicated to Wu Zuqiang.
1998	Momentum	Orchestra	13	Peabody Conservatory	Inspired by Chinese calligraphy & Beijing opera tune-types.
1999	Spring Festival	High school band	5	American Composers Forum Bandquest Project	
2002	Tu	Orchestra; wind ensemble	13	Women's Philharmonic & American Composers Orchestra with grant from the NEA	Commemorates the firefighters who died in 9/11. Wind ensemble version for the UMKC Wind Symphony.

Year	Title	Ensemble	Duration	Commissioner/Performer	Notes
2003	Caramoor's Summer	Orchestra	13	Caramoor Music Festival for Orchestra of St. Luke's	For a 25th anniversary commemorative concert of the Caramoor International Music Festival. Dedicated to Francis Richard.
2004	Symphony No. 3	Orchestra	23/3	Seattle Symphony for its centennial, with support from Wah & May Lui	"My Musical Journey to the World." Mvt 1, "Dragon Culture," inspired by Chinese set bells; mvt 2, "Melting Pot," includes hip-hop references; mvt 3, "Dreaming," variations on a 6-note theme, revised in Dragon Rhyme (2010).
2005	Si Ji	Orchestra	14	Roche, Lucerne Music Festival, & Carnegie Hall for Cleveland Orchestra	Finalist for Pulitzer Prize. Four continuous movements representing the four seasons & inspired by Chinese poetry. Dedicated to Chou Wen-chung.
2007	Suite from China West	Wind ensemble	12/4	Metropolitan Wind Symphony	Orchestration of China West Suite (pf duet, 2007; see comments there).
2008	Rhyme of Fire (original title: Olympic Fire)	Orchestra	15	British Broadcasting Corp, with support of the KT Wong Charitable Trust	Premiere at BBC Proms for Beijing Olympics. Designed as "meeting of cultures." Pitch materials from folk music of West China.
2008	Prospect Overture	Orchestra; youth orchestra	9	China National Center for the Performing Arts	Youth orchestra version entitled Overture for Orchestra. Uses beginning of Baban tune as theme.
2009	UMKC Fanfare	Wind ensemble	4	For UMKC Wind Ensemble performance at College Band Directors National Association convention	Abridged version of Prospect Overture (2008); based on beginning of Baban tune.
2009	Prelude and Fugue	Chamber orchestra	21/2	St. Paul Chamber Orchestra with funding from Music Alive Extended Residencies Award program	Orchestration & revision of material from Tunes from My Home, mvts 1–2 (trio, 2007–8) & Qi (quartet, 1997). See comments for Tunes from My Home.

Year	Title	Ensemble		Commissioner/Dedicatee	Notes
2009	Symphonie "Humen 1839"	Orchestra	20/4	Guangzhou Symphony Orchestra	With Zhou Long; mvt 1 by CY; mvt 4: joint work. First prize in 16th Chinese National Composition Competition for Symphonic Works, Chinese Ministry of Culture, 2012. Commemorates the burning of opium in Humen, Guangdong, in 1839, a protest to end the British opium trade.
2010	Dragon Rhyme	Wind ensemble	14/2	National Wind Ensemble Consortium Group	Revision & expansion of Symphony 3, mvt 3 (2004), & Symphonie Humen, mvt 4 (2009). Draws on Beijing opera influences as well as the symbolism of the dragon in Chinese folklore.
2010	Wind	Wind ensemble	11/2	Mid-American Conference Band Directors Assn	Orchestration of Feng (ww quintet, 1998; see comments there).
2010	Mount a Long Wind	Orchestra	6	CCOM	Reworked in Faith and Perseverance (2011).
2011	Jing Diao	Orchestra	4	Gund/Simonyi commission for the Seattle Symphony	For Gerard Schwarz's retirement; orchestration of Jing Marimba (solo, 2009).
2011	Fountains of KC	Orchestra	10	UMKC Conservatory & the Kansas City Symphony, with support from Kauffman Foundation	For the opening of the Kauffman Center, Kansas City. First theme evokes the city's fountains; second uses melodic style of Shaanxi Province to celebrate Kansas City's sister city Xi'an.
2011	Faith and Perseverance	Orchestra	5	Gustavus Adolphus College Symphony Orchestra	Reworking of Mount a Long Wind (2010).
2012	Blue, Blue Sky	Orchestra	10	For the Beijing Modern Music Festival's 10th anniversary	Draws on elements from Dragon Rhyme (2010), China West Suite (2 pianos, 2007), & Tunes from My Home (trio, 2007–8). Inspired by Tibetan tune "Du Mu."

| 2018 | Pearl River Overture | Orchestra | 17 | Guangzhou Symphony Orchestra | To celebrate the 40th anniversary of "China's reform and opening up." Draws on Guangzhou folk songs "Drought Thunder" & "Dragon Boat Race." Shorter version also available. |
| 2018 | Introduction, Andante and Allegro | Orchestra | 18/3 | Seattle Symphony & Los Angeles Philharmonic | Mvt 1 uses revised material from Mount a Long Wind (2010); mvts 2&3 substantial revision of Four Spirits (pf concerto, 2016), mvts 2&3; inspired by 2 sacred animals in Chinese legend. |

CONCERTOS

Date	Title	Scoring	Dur/mvts	Commissioner	Comments, awards, cross-borrowings
1983	Xian Shi	Viola & orchestra	14		First Chinese viola concerto; orchestration of trio (1982). Written for violist John Graham.
1992	Piano Concerto	Piano & orchestra	16	Brooklyn Philharmonic	DMA composition. First use of Baban (as tune, rhythm, & form). For conductor Dennis Russell Davies & pianist Gwendolyn Mok.
1995	Romance of Hsiao and Ch'in	Two violins & strings; alternate: vc, pf	3.5	Lincoln Center. For Yehudi Menuhin's 80th birthday	Incorporated into Romance and Dance. Premiere by Shlomo Mintz & Elmar Oliveira with Orchestra of St. Luke's directed by Menuhin. Inspired by timbres of xiao & qin.
1997	The Golden Flute	Flute & orchestra	18/3	Supported by NEA grant	Mvt 2 opening based on Suite (Chinese quintet, 1991). Written for James Galway. Continuous variations on opening phrase of Baban; inspired by dizi & xun timbres. Fl & pf version also published.
1997	Fiddle Suite	Huqin & orchestra; also versions for string orchestra & Chinese orchestra	16/3	Fromm Foundation	Mvts 2&3 used in Romance and Dance (1998) & Percussion Concerto (1998). Three sizes of huqin instruments used in the various movements. Mvt 2 an instrumental realization of a poem by Su Shi. Orchestral imitations of Beijing opera percussion & Chinese calligraphic images.

1998	Percussion Concerto	Percussion & orchestra	20/3	Evelyn Glennie & the Singapore Symphony Orchestra	Mvts 1&2 based on Fiddle Suite, mvts 3&2 (1997). Mvt 1: variations on a Beijing opera melody. Mvt 2: percussionist recites poem by Su Shi while playing. Mvt 3 features Beijing opera fixed percussion pattern for martial scenes.
1998	Eleanor's Gift	Cello & orchestra	15	New Heritage Music Foundation	Honoring the 50th anniversary of UN's Universal Declaration of Human Rights. Premiere by Women's Philharmonic with Paul Tobias.
1998	Romance and Dance	2 violins & strings	8/2	Stuttgart Chamber Orchestra	Mvt 1 from Romance of Hsiao and Ch'in (1995). Mvt 2 from Fiddle Suite finale (1997).
1999	Dunhuang Fantasy	Organ & wind ensemble	12	American Guild of Organists	Inspired by ancient murals in the Mogao Caves; later adapted as Septet for sax quartet, Chinese instruments, & percussion (2008) and in Concerto for Reeds (2008).
2000	Chinese Folk Dance Suite	Violin & orchestra	22/3	Koussevitzky Foundation	Mvt 2 arranged for vn & 2 percussion (Yangko, 2004). Mvt 1, "Lion Dance," inspired by Chinese festival celebrations. Mvt 2, "YangKo": orchestra members chant on phonemes. Mvt 3, "Muqam," evokes Uighur music; 7/8 meter & Middle Eastern mode. Also versions for vn&pf & sax&pf.
2001	Ba Yin	Saxophone quartet & string orchestra	20/3	Stuttgart Chamber Orchestra for the Raschèr Quartet	Inspired by Chinese village musics played on traditional instruments. Mvt. 3, "Shifan Gong and Drum," is source for mvts in Wu Yu (sextet, 2002); Ballad, Dance, and Fantasy (cello concerto, 2003); Tunes from My Home (trio, 2007–8); Ancient Chinese Beauty (recorder concerto, 2008); & From the Path of Beauty (SATB chorus, string quartet, 2008).
2003	Ballad, Dance, and Fantasy	Cello & orchestra	25/3	Orange County Pacific Symphony	Written for & premiered by Yo-Yo Ma. Evocation of Silk Road. Mvt 1, "Ballad of the Earth," inspired by music of Shaanxi Province. Mvt 2, "Dance on the Silk Road," inspired by Qiu Zi music from Xin Jiang Province & Hu Xuan dance from Mongolia. Mvt 3, "Fantasy for the Global Village," adaptation of Ba Yin finale (2001).

Year	Title	Instrumentation	Duration	Commissioner/Dedicatee	Notes
2004	Suite for Cello and Chamber Winds	Cello, woodwind quintet, trumpet, trombone, & percussion; alternate version for viola	18		Orchestration of Sound of the Five (quintet, 1998; see notes there). Written for UMKC colleagues Carter Enyeart & Sarah McKoin.
2005	Spring in Dresden	Violin & orchestra	19	Friends of Dresden Music Foundation, N.Y. Philharmonic, & Staatskapelle Dresden	Revision & expansion of Happy Rain on Spring Night (quintet, 2004; see notes there). For Mira Wang.
2006	The Ancient Beauty	Dizi, erhu, pipa, zheng, & strings	10/2	New Philadelphia Classical Symphony & Montgomery County Community College, funded by the Pew Charitable Trusts	Inspired by Chinese art: the bronze taotie of the Shang dynasty & the clay figurines of the Han dynasty. Mvt 1 related to The Golden Flute (1997). Mvt 2 adapted from Han Figurines (sextet, 2006). Expanded three-movement version for different instruments, 2010.
2006	Ode to the Earth	Ruan & orchestra	20	For Prof. Xu Yang, CCOM	Alternate version of Ballad, Dance, Fantasy, mvts 1–2 (2003).
2008	Ancient Chinese Beauty	Recorder & string orchestra	14	Michala Petri	Celebrates the non-interrupted relationship between Denmark & China. Adaptation of material from Han Figurines (sextet, 2006), The Golden Flute, mvt 2 (1997), & Ba Yin, mvt 3 (2001). Inspired by Chinese art. Calls for alto & tenor recorder.
2008	Concerto for Reeds	Oboe, sheng & chamber orchestra	14	Swiss Arts Council Pro Helvetia's Swiss Cultural Programme in China	Adapted from Dunhuang Fantasy (1999).
2010	The Ancient Beauty	Ruan ensemble, zheng, & string orchestra	12/3	For Prof. Xu Yang, CCOM	Arrangement of previous works: mvts 1–2 from The Ancient Beauty (2006), mvt 3 from At the Chinese New Year Concert, mvt 1 (string quartet, 2002).

2013	Chinese Rap	Violin & orchestra	10	Kennesaw State University	Integrates rap influences with the mixed reciting/singing style of Chinese folk musical story telling (quyi). Uses some material explored in From Old Peking Folklore (duet, 2009) & Bamboo Dance (pf, 2013), heavily reworked.
2016	Four Spirits	Piano & orchestra	26/4	University of North Carolina, Chapel Hill	Inspired by the 4 sacred animals of Chinese legend (dragon, xuanwu [turtle], tiger, phoenix), representing the east, north, west, & south regions of China. Mvts 1, 2, 4 use material from Symphony No. 3 (2004), Northern Scenes (pf, 2013), & The Golden Flute (1997). Mvts 2&3 revised for use in Introduction, Andante and Allegro (2018).
2017	Southern Scenes	Flute, pipa, & orchestra	13/2	Barlow Endowment for Music Composition	Mvt 2 partially based on Bamboo Dance with substantial revision (pf, 2013).

Solo Instrumental and Chamber Music Works

SOLO PIECES

Date	Title	Scoring	Dur	Commissioner	Comments, awards, cross-borrowings
1979/2011	Variations on "Awariguli"	Piano	10		Nine variations on Uighur folksong. Premiered by Chen Min, 1979.
1984	Duo Ye	Piano; also a version for Pipa (1995)	7		Inspired by song/dance of Dong minority; first prize in China's 4th composition competition; orchestrated in versions for chamber orchestra & full orchestra.
1985	Yu Diao	Piano	2		For students. Composed for CCOM Teaching Materials Competition.
1989	Guessing	Piano	5	Renee B. Fisher Awards Competition for pianists 14–18 years old	Based on a fragment of a Chinese antiphonal folk song. For the Fisher Piano Competition (ages 16–18).

Year	Title	Instrument	Duration	Commissioner/Venue	Notes
1991	The Points	Pipa	9	New York New Music Consort. Composed for Wu Man.	Ensemble version entitled Suite (Chinese instrument quintet, 1991). Depicts the eight brushstrokes of Chinese calligraphy.
1993	Monologue (Impressions of the True Story of Ah Q)	Clarinet	5	Inter-Artes, London	Inspired by the novella The True Story of Ah Q by Lu Xun (first published in 1921–22), a satirical, political commentary.
1993	Small Beijing Gong	Piano	1		For students. Composed for 80th birthday of Li Suxin (CY's 1st piano teacher).
1999	Ba Ban	Piano	7	Carnegie Hall (pieces for the Millennium)	Draws on some material from Piano Concerto (1992). Intermingles motives from the Baban tune, a 12-tone line, & a distinctive pentachord.
2002	Singing in the Mountain	Piano	1	Royal Schools of Music Exam Board (ABRSM)	For children.
2005	Ji-Dong-Nuo	Piano	4	Carnegie Hall, for Emanuel Ax (ballade project)	Based on a Yao folk tune depicting a singing quail.
2009	Jing Marimba	Marimba	4	ZMF New Music (Zeltsman Marimba Festival)	Motive drawn from a fragment of a Beijing opera fiddle's fixed pattern featuring a leap of a seventh. Structured on Golden Section. Orchestrated as Jing Diao (2011).
2010	Memory	Violin; alternative versions for vc, fl, or vla	4		In memory of Lin Yao-ji (1937–2009), Chen Yi's violin teacher at CCOM. Premiered at a memorial concert for him.
2013	Northern Scenes	Piano	7	May Lui, John Schumann, Portland State University Foundation, Regional Arts and Culture Council, & Oregon Arts Commission	For Susan Chan. Inspired by the mountainous landscape of northern China.
2013	Bamboo Dance	Piano	4	ABRSM	Bamboo Dance II: simpler version for young students.

2013	Shuo Chang	Guitar	6.5	Wigmore Hall for Ms. Xuefei Yang	Related to Chinese Rap (violin & orchestra, 2013).
2015	Colors of Naobo	Chinese cymbals	2		For Evelyn Glennie's birthday.
2017	In Memory of Steve	Piano	1.5	Gloria Cheng	For Steven Stucky. Pitch material in part quotes a musical birthday greeting Stucky gave to Chen Yi in 2003.
2017	Totem Poles	Organ	5	American Guild of Organists	For AGO's Biennial National Convention.
2018	Jingu Suite	Cello	12/4	Prof. Siwen Wang of the Tianjin Conservatory	Celebrates the landscape & folk culture of Tianjin. Mvt 1: "The Ning Garden." Mvt 2: "The Stilt-walking." Mvt 3: "Dance with Flying Cymbals." Mvt 4: "The Haihe River."
2019	Plum Blossom	Piano	4	The Chopin Society of Hong Kong	For the 5th Hong Kong International Piano Competition. Pitch material taken from the Cantonese children's song, "Moonlight."
2019	Bamboo Song	Piano	6	Prof. Zou Xiang (CCOM)	Variations on the opening of the Baban tune.

WORKS FOR 2–12 INSTRUMENTS

Date	Title	Scoring	Dur/mvts	Commissioner	Comments, awards, cross-borrowings
1979/2011	Fisherman's Song	Duet: pf, vn	4		
1982	String quartet	Quartet: strings	23/3		Mvt 1 used in Shuo (str orch, 1994); Mvt 2 used in Sprout (string orch, 1986).
1982	Xian Shi	Trio: vla, pf, perc	14		Arranged as a viola concerto (1983).
1987	Woodwind Quintet	Quintet: fl, ob, cl, bn, hn	9		Opening section 12-tone, but inspired by the heterophonic singing of nuns on Buddha Mountain near Shanghai; B section quotes fragment of Buddhist praying tune.

Year	Title	Instrumentation	Duration	Publisher/Commissioner	Notes
1988	Near Distance	Sextet: fl, cl, vn, vc, pf, perc	10		Written for Aspen Music Festival Composers Workshop. Subtitle: "Lost in thought about ancient culture and modern civilization." Inspired by contrast between the ancient tradition of China & modern society. Atonal but not serial. For Jacob Druckman
1988	The Tide	Septet: xun, yangqin, pipa, zheng, percussion, gaohu, erhu		Music From China; N.Y. State Council of the Arts	Unpublished.
1991	Suite	Quintet: pipa, dizi, yangqin, sanxian, erhu	14/3	Music From China	3 continuous mvts. Mvt 1 arrangement of The Points (pipa, 1991). Beginning of mvt 2 used in The Golden Flute (concerto, 1997). Unpublished.
1992	Sparkle	Octet: fl, cl, pf, vn, vc, cb, 2 perc	12	New Music Consort with funding from Mary Flagler Cary Charitable Trust	Pitch materials from Baban tune & 12-tone line. Form of A section based on Baban structure. Dedicated to Mario Davidovsky.
1993	Song in Winter	Trio or Quartet: hpschd, dizi, zheng; soprano, zheng, pf; or fl, zheng, pf, perc	8	Joyce Lindorff	Inspired by pine & bamboo images in Chinese painting; uses 12-tone line periodically as well as Baban rhythm.
1995	Qin: Tomb of the Middle Kingdom	Music for a computer game: pipa, dizi/xun			Zhou Long created electronic music from a performance for a game on CD-ROM released by Luyen Chou.
1997	Qi	Quartet: fl, vc, pf, perc	10	New Music Consort (N.Y.), San Francisco Contemporary Music Players, & Los Angeles Philharmonic Assn, with funding from Meet The Composer/Readers Digest	Inspired by Chinese paintings & dancing calligraphic lines. Qi=life force. Thematic material unites three disparate Chinese sources. Structured using the Golden Section on multiple levels. Dedicated to Chou Wen-chung. Orchestrated as the central section of Prelude & Fugue, mvt 2 (orchestra, 2009).

Year	Title	Instrumentation	Duration	Commission/Dedication	Notes
1998	Sound of the Five	Quintet: str quartet, vc Alternates: perc, str quartet; vc, chamber winds (Suite for Cello & Winds), 2004	18/4	Eastman School of Music for cellist Mimi Hwang & the Ying Quartet with funding from Henry Hwang & Far East National Bank of LA	Mvt 1 evokes the lusheng ensemble of southwest China. Mvt 2 inspired by ancient bronze set bells. Mvt 3 adapted from Romance of Hsiao and Ch'in (2 vns & orch, 1995). Mvt 4: Flower Drums in Dance. Inspired by 5 Chinese instruments: zheng, di, bells, drum, mouth organ. Orchestrated as Suite for Cello&Winds (2004).
1998	Feng	Quintet: fl, ob, cl, bn, hn	10/2	San Francisco Citywinds with Chamber Music America award	Feng=wind. Mvt 1 explores a wandering chromatic theme. Mvt 2 based on a rhythmically migrating ostinato. Orchestrated as Wind (2010); sax ens arr (2018).
1999	Song of the Great Wall (CY, arr only)	8 French horns			Arrangement of 16-measure song by Li Suxin (CY's 1st piano teacher, 1905–85).
2001	Ning	Trio: vn, vc, pipa	15	Chamber Music Society of MN, with funding from Barlow Endowment & Hoeschler Fund of the St. Paul Foundation. For Yo-Yo Ma, Wu Man, Young-Nam Kim	Commemorates the Nanjing massacre of 1937–38. The song "Jasmine Flowers" (Mo li hua) arises out of portrayal of destruction & desolation. Written for concert in St. Paul, Hùn Qiáo (Bridge of Souls), memorializing victims & survivors of war atrocities.
2001	Joy of the Reunion	Quartet: ob, vla, vc, cb	4	Chamber Music Conference & Composers Forum of the East	Arrangement of a folk tune from Inner Mongolia.
2002	At the Kansas City Chinese New Year Concert	Quartet: 2 vn, vla, vc	12/3	Hanson Inst for American Music, Eastman School of Music	In mvt 1, "The Talking Fiddle," viola imitates erhu. Mvt 2 inspired by hand-pulled noodle making in Henan Province. Mvt 3: "Blue Dragon Sword Dance." Mvt 1 used in Ancient Beauty (concerto, 2010). For the Ying Quartet; dedicated to Chou Wen-chung on his 80th birthday.
2002	Burning	Quartet: 2 vn, vla, vc	4	Elements Quartet	9/11 memorial piece; basis for . . . as like a raging fire . . . (2002).

Year	Title	Instrumentation	Duration	Commissioner/Funder	Notes
2002	... as like a raging fire ...	Quintet: fl, cl, vn, vc, pf	9	Network for New Music, with grant from Meet The Composer Commissioning/USA program	Major expansion & rescoring of Burning, memorializing 9/11 firefighters. A perpetual motion score with wandering chromatics, ostinati, & clusters.
2002	Chinese Fables	Quartet: erhu, pipa, vc, perc	13/3	Music From China with funding from Mary Flagler Cary Charitable Trust	Inspired by three Chinese legends: "The Fox Profited by the Tiger's Might"; "Master Dong-guo and the Wolf"; "The Snipe and the Clam."
2002	Wu Yu	Sextet or Septet: fl, cl, bn, vn, vc, perc; or fl, ob, cl, vn, vla, vc, cb	14/2	Boston Musica Viva	Wu Yu is an ancient Chinese ritual rain dance. A reorchestration of Ba Yin, mvts 1 & 3 (concerto, 2001; see comments there).
2004	Yangko	Trio: vn, 2 perc	5	Network for New Music Ensemble	Arrangement of Chinese Folk Dance Suite, mvt 2 (concerto, 2000; see comments there).
2004	Night Thoughts	Trio: fl, vc, pf; also versions for fl, vla, hp; vn, bar sax, pf; & vn, vc, pf	8	Virginia Arts Festival, Chamber Music Society of Lincoln Center, La Jolla SummerFest, Chamber Music Northwest, with support from Meet The Composer Commissioning/USA program	Inspired by poem of Li Bai. Extremely dramatic work containing Beijing opera references, clusters, harmonics, & other special effects. Dedicated to Heather Hitchen.
2004	Chinese Ancient Dances	Duet: cl, pf; or sop sax, pf	8/2	Virginia Arts Festival, Chamber Music Society of Lincoln Center, La Jolla SummerFest, Chamber Music Northwest	Written for David Shifrin & Andre-Michel Schub; dedicated to Mario Davidovsky. Mvt 1 inspired by images of the ancient Ge Tian Shi ethnic group dancing with oxtails & singing songs in praise of the earth. Mvt 2 inspired by Hu Xuan dance described in poem by Bai Juyi (Tang Dynasty).

Year	Title	Instrumentation	Duration	Commission/Notes	Description
2004	Happy Rain on a Spring Night	Quintet: fl, cl, vn, vc, pf	12	Music from Copland House. Funding from NYSCA Council on the Arts Composer's Commissions program.	Inspired by poem of Du Fu. Beijing opera references. Structured using the Golden Ratio on multiple levels. Form used as basis for Spring in Dresden (concerto, 2005).
2006	Three Bagatelles from China West	Duet for various combos: fl, pf; 2 fl; guanzi, sheng; cl, pf; 2 cl; cb, pf; fl, cl; fl, gtr	10/3	Meet The Composer for flutist Maya Martin	Settings of folk songs from western China. Mvt 1: a Jingpo farmer's tune & evocations of the double-pipe lerong & jaw harp kouxian. Mvt 2: two songs, "Ashima" & "Nai Guo Hou" from the Yi people. Mvt 3: lusheng ensemble of the Miao culture. Mvts 2&3 expanded into China West Suite (2007).
2006	The Han Figurines	Sextet: vn, cl, ten sax, cb, pf, perc	5	Opus 21 ensemble & Fontana Chamber Arts	Inspired by clay figurines of the Han Dynasty. Revised as Ancient Chinese Beauty, mvt 1 (concerto, 2008); basis for From the Path of Beauty, mvt 5 (chorus, str quartet, 2008). Mvt 1 recalls beginning of Chinese Myths Cantata, mvt 2 (chorus, orch, 1996).
2007	Tibetan Tunes	Trio: vn, vc, pf; also vn, cl, pf	12/2	Barlow Endowment for Music Composition at Brigham Young University	Mvt 1: variations on Tibetan tune "Du Mu." Mvt 2 uses pitch materials from Tibetan folk song "Amaliehuo." Mvt 2 related to China West Suite, mvt 3 (2007).
2007	China West Suite	Duet: 2 pf; or pf, marimba; also version for wind ens	12/4	Klavier-Festival Ruhr, Germany, for Dennis Russell Davies & Maki Namekawa	Mvt 1, "Introduction," derived from Three Bagatelles, mvt 2; uses "Ashima" tune. Mvt 2, "Meng Songs," uses inner Mongolian folk song for revolutionary leader Gada Meilin. Mvt 3, "Zang Songs," 2 interwoven melodies. Mvt 4, "Miao Dances," a major expansion of Three Bagatelles, mvt 3 (2006). Wind ensemble version as Suite from China West (2007).

Year	Title	Instrumentation	Duration	Commissioner/Venue	Notes
2007–8	Tunes from My Home	Trio: vn, vc, pf	15/3	Pennsylvania Academy of Music for the Newstead Trio	Pitch materials introduced in mvt 1 from Cantonese folk music. Mvt 2 a loose fugal form. Mvt 3 a reworking of Ba Yin, mvt 3 (concerto, 2001). Mvts 1 & 2 reworked in Prelude & Fugue (orchestra, 2009).
2008	Septet	Septet: erhu, pipa, perc, sax quartet	12	Prism Saxophone Quartet & Music From China	Adapted from Dunhuang Fantasy (concerto, 1999; see comments there).
2008	Woodwind Quintet 3	Quintet: fl, ob, cl, bn, hn	13/3	Upper New York State Humanities Corridor (Mellon grant)	Adapted from China West Suite, mvts 1, 3, 4 (2007) with mvt 1 significantly revised. Sax ens arr as Suite from China West (2018).
2008	From the Path of Beauty	Quartet: 2 vn, vla, vc	22/4	Freer Gallery of Art and Arthur M. Sackler Gallery, Smithsonian (from original for Shanghai Quartet)	Mvts extracted from a 7-mvt composition for voices & string quartet. See comments in choral section.
2009	From Old Peking Folklore	Duet: vn, pf	4	Music Teachers' Assn of California, "Friends of Today's Music"	Inspired by quyi (storytelling), with singer accompanied by a drum & small ensemble.
2012	The Soulful and the Perpetual	Duet: alto sax, pf	12/2	Jessica Heller Knopf for the World Saxophone Congress, St. Andrews, Scotland	Mvt 2, arrangement of Early Spring (chorus, 2011). Mvt 2 uses Baban structure throughout.
2014	Not Alone	Quartet: 4 saxophones	14	Prism Saxophone Quartet with Nai-Ni Chen Dance Company, with support from New Music USA Live Music for Dance Award	Inspired by poem of Li Bai, "Drinking Alone under the Moon with the Shadow."

Year	Title	Instrumentation	Duration	Commissioner/Funding	Notes
2014	Three Dances from China South	Quartet: dizi, erhu, pipa, zheng	12/3	Music From China for 30th anniversary. Support from Chamber Music America Classical Commissioning Program. Funding from Andrew W. Mellon Fdn & Chamber Music America Endowment Fund.	Mvt 1, "Lions Playing Ball," quotes a folk dance tune from the Chaozhou region of Guangdong. Mvt 2, an orchestration of part of Bamboo Dance (piano, 2013), was inspired by a harvest dance of the Li people & uses the Baban rhythm. Mvt 3 recalls the lusheng ensemble of the Dong minority in Guangxi Province. For Susan Cheng.
2015	Energetic Duo	Duet: 2 vn	2		Birthday gift for violinist Ron Blessinger.
2016–17	Nian Hua (Chinese New Year's Paintings)	Duet: 2 gtr	12/3	Beijing Guitar Duo, with funding from Chamber Music America Classical Commissioning Program & the Andrew W. Mellon Foundation.	Inspired by folk paintings in Tianjin. Mvt 1: guitars imitate pipa; based on descending wandering chromatic motive. Mvt 2: fast repeated note dissonant clusters in irregular patterns. Mvt 3 based on folk song "Xiao Guang Miao" (Strolling Temple).
2018	Happy Tune	Duet: vn, vla	2.5		Celebrates the 25th anniversary of the Great Lakes Chamber Music Festival. Revised version of Three Bagatelles, mvt 3.
2018	Feng II	Sax solo, sax quartet, pf	10/2	18th World Saxophone Congress	Reorchestration of Feng (1998).
2018	Suite from China West	Sax ens (SATBB)		18th World Saxophone Congress	Reorchestration of Woodwind Quintet 3 (2008).
2019	Fire	Chamber ensemble (12 players)	6.5	Chicago Center for Contemporary Composition	For the Grossman Ensemble at the U of Chicago. Materials related to those in Burning & … as like a raging fire …, but not an arrangement of either work.

Choral Works

Poets are given here with their most common names; alternative names as well as life dates are listed below.

Date	Title	Scoring	Language: Text author	Dur/mvts	Commissioner	Comments
1985	Three Poems from the Song Dynasty	SATB with divisi up to SSSAAATTBB; sat solos	Chinese: Li Qingzhao, Xin Qiji, Su Shi; vocables	15/3		Poem in mvt. 3 used in Percussion Concerto, mvt 2. Mvt 1 & 2 use some indeterminacy & drones.
1994	A Set of Chinese Folk Songs	Originally CtTB w/ divisi, a cap. Also published in 3 vols (reordered) for SATB, some divisi; t solo in 2 songs, s in 1	Chinese: folksongs from many provinces; some use of English translations & vocables	17/10	Chanticleer	For Chanticleer's New Residencies program of touring to middle schools; some have alternative versions with instruments (string orch or str quintet, perc; optional pf) for performance with middle school choirs & instrumentalists. 3 mvts can be performed by instrumentalists only (see Table 6.1).
1994	Arirang [아리랑]	SATB, divisi especially in TB	Korean: folk song	3	Chanticleer	Title means "rolling hills"; among most popular Korean mountain songs.
1994	Sakura, Sakura (Cherry Blossoms)	SATBB	Japanese: folk song	1	Chanticleer	Minimal text for 2 B parts (humming).
1995	Tang Poems	1. CtCtTB [SATB], divisi; t solo 2. CtCtTB [SATB], minimal divisi 3. CtCtTTB [SATTB] 4. CtTBB [SATBB], divisi; strong, dramatic soloist	Chinese: Li Bai, Li Shangyin, Bai Juyi, Chen Ziang; vocables; mvt 4 includes some English	12/4	Chanticleer (New Residencies program thru Meet The Composer), w/ support by Pew Charitable Trusts, James Irvine Foundation, John S. and James L. Knight Foundation, Aaron Copland Fund, & the NEA	Mvt 4 adapted in Meditation (voice & pf, 1999/2012). Orchestrated with identical choral parts as Tang Poems Cantata (1995).

1995	Tang Poems Cantata	See Tang Poems for voicing, chamber orch	See Tang Poems	15/4	Bradley University	Choral parts identical to Tang Poems.
1995	Written on a Rainy Night	CtCtTB [SATB], minimal divisi	Chinese: Li Shangyin	3	Chanticleer	Separate publication of Tang Poems, mvt 2.
1996	Chinese Myths Cantata	CtCtTB [SATB], divisi; orchestra, 4 Chinese traditional instruments (erhu, yangqin, pipa, zheng)	Primarily vocables; individual English & Mandarin words (mvt 1); mvt 3 uses only "o" until last section in Mandarin: anonymous poem from Han Dynasty	36/3	Chanticleer & the Women's Philharmonic. Funding from Meet The Composer New Residencies program, Creative Work Fund, & the SF Art Comm, Rockefeller Fdn, Copland Fund, & the NEA.	Based on 3 well-known Chinese myths: Pan Gu creates heaven & earth; goddess & shape-shifter Nü Wa creates humans; thwarted love story of the Weaving Maid and the Cowherd. Concluding section is a related Han Dynasty poem. Audience participation in mvt 2. Optional multimedia component: Chinese dancers, lighting design, visual projections, painted backdrops, & staging. Mvt 2 beginning used in Han Figurines (sextet, 2006). Dedicated to Louis Botto.
1997	Spring Dreams	SSAATTBB, further divisi in SAT1	Meng Haoran	5	Ithaca College, School of Music	Lower voices have extensive ostinati at various tempi & mostly unpitched, B1 imitates birds with whistling & improvisation, T2B2 melodic ostinati; S melody in Beijing opera style including occasional Sprechstimme. Adapted for solo voice in Meditation (1999).
1999	Chinese Poems	Treble chorus, each mvt different voicing, but at least à 4	Chinese: Li Po, Wang Zhihuan, & folk songs; vocables in each mvt	5/10	San Francisco Girls Chorus	For 6 ensembles of different skill levels, some quite advanced; 2 mvts for all 6, 1 for the most advanced ensemble, 1 for levels 3–4, 1 for levels 5–6.

Year	Title	Voicing	Language/Text	Mvts	Commission/Dedication	Notes
2000	KC Capriccio	SATB & wind ensemble	Phonemes only	4	UMKC Conservatory of Music for Kansas City 150th anniversary	Inspired by a folk tune Chen heard played by bagpipe outside the Nelson Gallery in Kansas City, & the wild singing sound of Asian folk choral music.
2001	Chinese Mountain Songs	Treble chorus, mostly SA with occasional divisi, mvt 5 for SSAA, female soloist	Chinese: folk songs; mvts 2 & 4 only vocables	8/5	Kitka, supported by grants from NEA & the Rockefeller Foundation	Based on folk songs from 5 regions of China; mountain songs are about love & work.
2001	Know You How Many Petals Falling?	SATB, divisi to à 8	English: Meng Haoran	4	6th World Symposium on Choral Music for the Elmer Iseler Singers	Same text as Spring Dreams (1997) but a new setting & in English.
2001	Shady Grove	SATB, divisi last chord only	English: folk song; vocables	2	For the Dale Warland Singers with gift from M. Walker Pearce & Jack Weatherford; matching funds from NEA	American folk song; use of accompanimental phonemes.
2001	To the New Millennium	1. SATB, s, mz 2. SATB, mz 3. Double SATB (divisi up to à 8 for each), s, mz	Chinese: Du Fu, Wang Wei, Cao Cao; text largely carried by soloists; chorus: mostly vocables	10/3	Miami University, Oxford, Ohio, for the Music for the Millennium Project	Ancient texts address spring & the sea as symbols of the flowering of a new century & continuing of human history.
2001	Xuan	SATB, divisi last chord only	Chinese: Laozi	4	Ithaca College School of Music; dedicated to Karol Husa on his 80th birthday	Title means "profound and ineffable"; text from Dao De Jing (6th century BCE), outlining Taoism.

2003	Landscape	SATB	Chinese: Su Shi; many vocables	3	ACFEA Tour Consultants for the Kansas City Chorale as a contribution to Chorus America	Companion piece to The West Lake.
2003	The West Lake	SSAATTBBB	Chinese: Su Shi; vocables	5	Chicago A Cappella, a 9-voice ensemble	Companion piece to Landscape.
2003	Two Chinese Folk Songs	SATB, divisi in mvt 1, very minimal in mvt 2	Chinese: Hunan & Yunnan folk songs; vocables	6/2	Singapore Youth Choir	1. A Single Bamboo Can Easily Bend; 2. A Horseherd's Mountain Song; published separately under mvt titles.
2006	Looking at the Sea	SSA(A) with divisi, especially in SS	English: Cao Cao; some vocables	5	Patricia Hennings New Music Fund for the Peninsula Women's Chorus	Uses many upward slides & clusters.
2008	From the Path of Beauty	SATB (CtCtTB), with minimal divisi, string quartet (some mvts chorus alone, some quartet alone; see comments)	Text is only vocables, taken from Chinese folksongs of diverse regions & ethnic groups	35/7	Chanticleer & the Shanghai Quartet with assistance from the Carol Franc Buck Foundation, the Fleishhacker Foundation, & Kathleen G. Henschel	Mvt 1 SATB; mvts 2&4 string quartet; mvt 3 SATB (divisi in AT) & string quartet; mvts 5–7 SATB, string quartet. Mvt 4 adapted from As in a Dream (voice & pf, 1988/94); mvt 5 draws on Han Figurines (sextet, 2006); mvt 6 adapted from Sprout (str orch, 1982/86); mvt 7 a shortened version of Ancient Chinese Beauty, mvt 3 (concerto, 2008). Traces the history of beauty in Chinese visual arts. See also listing in the chamber music section (4-mvt string quartet).
2008	The Bronze Taotie	SATB (CtCtTB), divisi in last section up to à 12, a cap	Vocables taken from Chinese folksongs	2	See From the Path of Beauty	Separate publication of From the Path of Beauty, mvt 1.

Year	Title	Voicing	Text	#	Commissioned by	Notes
2008	Two Chinese Folk Songs (with Steven Stucky)	SSAATTBB	Chinese: 2 folk songs; vocables	3/2	Cornell University Chorus & Glee Club	(1) The Flowing Stream—arr. by Chen for SSA; (2) The Sun Is Rising with Our Joy—arr. Steven Stucky for TTBB; final section (Reprise) weaves together the 2 folk songs & both ensembles. Not the same as Two Chinese Folk Songs (2003).
2010	Angel Island Passages	SSAA, string quartet, with optional multimedia projections, mvt 3	Mvts 1 & 2 vocables; mvt 3 in Cantonese, Mandarin, & English: Chen Yi	15/3	San Francisco Girls Chorus	Inspired by book Island, Poetry and History of Chinese Immigrants on Angel Island, 1910–1940 (Him Mark Lai, Genny Lim, Judy Yung); 1. 1882 (reference to Chinese Exclusion Act); 2. Longing; 3. We Are America (reference to immigrant contributions to the US with video by Felicia Lowe).
2010	Spring Rain	SATB	Chinese: Du Fu; many vocables	4	Singapore Anglo-Chinese Junior College Choir	Breathy, unpitched chanting to mimic percussive sounds.
2010	With Flowers Blooming	SSA, divisi, occasionally à 6	English: Du Fu; many vocables	4	Calvin College Women's Chorale	Ode to spring rain & flowers; ends with breathy, unpitched phonemes imitating percussion; the same poem (Happy Rain) formed the inspiration for an instrumental quintet (2004).
2011	Distance Can't Keep Us Two Apart	SATB	English: Wang Bo; some vocables	5	American Choral Directors Association, Brock Memorial Commission	Created from a single motive; uses sliding tones & clusters.

Year	Title	Forces	Text	Mvts	Commissioned by	Notes
2011	Early Spring	SATB, occasional divisi & sextet (fl, cl, vn, vc, perc, pf)	English: Su Shi; vocables	9/2	University of Richmond, Dept. of Music for Schola Cantorum & eighth blackbird; support from Tucker-Boatright Fund	Mvt 2 based on Baban rhythm throughout. Arr for pf & sax as The Soulful and Perpetual (2012). Inspired by 2 paintings, Duck Playing & Wild Geese (drawn by Monk Hui Chong).
2012	I Hear the Siren's Call	SATB (CtTTB), some divisi	Vocables	2	Chanticleer	Inspired by Henri Wieniawski's Legende, Op. 17, which Chen played as a teen; programmatic musical retelling of the Greek myth with sopranos as the sirens.
2012	Let's Reach a New Height	SATB	English: Wang Zhihuan, translated by CY; vocables	3	New York Virtuoso Singers	
2013	In the Mountains	SATB, string quartet	Chinese: Su Shi; some vocables	6	St. Paul's Co-Educational College of Hong Kong	The title of the text "A Poem on Xilin Temple's Wall," refers to a Buddhist temple at the foot of Mt. Lushan in Jiangxi Province.
2015	Thinking of My Home	3 treble voices (especially for middle school, but appropriate for other ages); optional pf, triangle	English: Li Bai; a few phonemes; 2 Chinese words	2	American Composers Forum for their series ChoralQuest	
2015	The Beautiful West Lake	SATB, with or without solo voices	English: Su Shi	4	Mizzou New Music Initiative, Sinquefield Charitable Foundation	Same text as The West Lake (2003). Written for University Singers, U of Missouri (Columbia)

Vocal Solo Works

Date	Title	Scoring	Dur/mvts	Commissioner	Comments, awards, cross-borrowings
1988/ 1994/ 2010	As in a Dream	Trio: soprano, vn, vc; alternates: soprano, pipa, zheng; soprano, zheng	8/2	Invited, inspired by, & dedicated to sop, Rao Lan; Comm by Inoue Chamber Ensemble	Text: 2 poems by Li Qingzhao, female poet of Song Dynasty (sung in Chinese). Makes reference to Beijing opera style.
1999/2012	Meditation	Duet: female voice (soprano/mezzo with later versions for mezzo/alto & ten/bar), pf	6/2	Artistic Circles for Susanne Mentzer	Text: Meng Haoran & Chen Ziang (sung in Chinese). Mvt 1 adapted from Spring Dreams (1997); mvt 2 from Tang Poems, mvt 4 (1995).
2000	Bright Moonlight	Duet: voice (mezzo), pf	4	New York Festival of Song for New Century project, supported by Meet The Composer & ASCAP Foundation	Text by Chen Yi (in English) following the structure of "Picking Mulberry" by twelfth-century poet Li Qingzhao. Chen Yi translates the title as "The Palm Tree."

Poets

Bai Juyi	772–846 (Tang Dynasty)
Cao Cao	155–220 (Han Dynasty)
Chen Yi	1953–
Chen Ziang	661–702 (Tang Dynasty)
Du Fu	712–770 (Tang Dynasty)
Laozi (Lao-Tzu)	ca. 6th century BCE
Li Bai (Li Po)	701–762 (Tang Dynasty)
Li Qingzhao	1084–ca. 1151 (woman poet of the Song Dynasty)
Li Shangyin	ca. 813–858 (Tang Dynasty)
Meng Haoran	689–740 (Tang Dynasty)
Su Shi (Su Dongpo)	1037–1101 (Song Dynasty)
Wang Bo	650–676 (Tang Dynasty)
Wang Wei	701–761 (Tang Dynasty)
Wang Zhihuan	688–742 (Tang Dynasty)
Xin Qiji	1140–1207 (Song Dynasty)

Composer Websites

New Music USA Online Library, "Chen Yi," http://library.newmusicusa.org/ChenYi. Includes biography, selected chronological list of compositions (linked to program notes and basic information), list of performances (2007–12), discography, alphabetical list of published works, videography, selected radio programs, selected bibliography

Presser: In Tune with the Times since 1883, "Chen Yi," https://www.presser.com/chen-yi. Includes a summary of career highlights and a list of 300 compositions available from her publisher, Theodore Presser; some program notes; ability to search in various ways

Notes

CHAPTER 1. Introduction

1. University of Illinois Press, "Women Composers," https://www.press.uillinois.edu/books/find_books.html?type=series&search=wco.
2. Taylor, *Beyond Exoticism*, 141.
3. Chou, "Whither Chinese Composers," 509.
4. Bellman, *The Exotic in Western Music*, x.
5. For more on this topic, see Su Zheng, *Claiming Diaspora*, esp. 43–57, and Chou, "Whither Chinese Composers?" esp. 504–5.

CHAPTER 2. Biography and Framework

1. Two years later, Liu became President of the People's Republic.
2. Mangan, "A Musical Odyssey."
3. Chen Yi, application for the Herb Alpert award.
4. Kagan, "Hundred Flowers," 418. Thurston, *Enemies of the People*, 62–72, describes some specific critiques unleashed in this short open period, and the disasters they brought to critics during the succeeding Anti-Rightist Campaign.
5. Kagan "Hundred Flowers," 419.
6. Horsley, "Chen Yi."
7. Chen Yi, interview with the authors. Subsequent quotations from Chen Yi without notes are taken from interviews we conducted with her in 2015 and 2016.
8. This process had actually begun earlier at major institutions of higher education dur-

ing two waves of reorganization in the 1950s; at times, barely literate peasants were awarded faculty and administrative positions. See Thurston, *Enemies of the People*, 55–62 and 72.

9. Melvin and Cai, *Rhapsody in Red*, chapter 7.

10. Among the many sources covering the demise of the Red Guards following the establishment of Revolutionary Committees throughout the country beginning in 1967, we might cite the particularly cogent explanation in Dikötter, *Cultural Revolution*, 132–35 and esp. 165–80.

11. Kraus, *Pianos and Politics*, 154–57.

12. Thurston, *Enemies of the People*, 113–14 and 129–31.

13. Mittler, "Eight Stage Works," 386–87, and "Just Beat It," 250–53, demonstrates that prohibitions against listening to, or performing, Western classical music were not always strictly enforced and provides examples of musicians continuing to play this repertoire.

14. Dikötter, *Cultural Revolution*, 212–14.

15. Gelfand, "Composer Kept Mind on Music."

16. Piñeiro, "Interview with Chen Yi," 29.

17. On the mixture of Chinese and Western instruments in the operas of the Cultural Revolution period, see Rao, "Sonic Imaginary," esp. 219–24.

18. The model operas were later made into films. In the film of *Taking Tiger Mountain by Strategy* (https://www.youtube.com/watch?v=Gul5FvAlLpU), the parts Chen Yi sight-read appear at the following locations: 43:45–48:43 and 1:40:30–1:43:35. For a sample page of the score and a list of instruments in this opera, see Rao, "Chinese Opera Percussion," 168–70. Other excerpts from the score appear in Rao, "Sonic Imaginary"; the example on p. 228 contains a small error in m. 3 (the A in the top part should be G♯).

19. The entire troupe consisted of forty members (Piñeiro, "Interview with Chen Yi," 29).

20. Yung, "Model Opera as Model," 146.

21. Ibid., 147.

22. Dai Jiafang maps the musical changes from the 1964 modernized operas to the model operas in "A Diachronic Study."

23. Pang, *Art of Cloning*, 92.

24. Clark, *Chinese Cultural Revolution*, 13–14.

25. Almost all writings on the Cultural Revolution describe the condemnation of Wu Han's opera. For one account, see Melvin and Cai, *Rhapsody in Red*, 225–26. Wu Han was discredited and died in prison in 1969. For another perspective into the linkage between music and the Cultural Revolution, see Madeleine Thien's *Do Not Say We Have Nothing* (a line from "The Internationale"), where "music is at the centre of this ambitious saga of totalitarian China" (Baker, "At a Glance Fiction," 39). This award-winning novel, also shortlisted for the 2016 Man Booker Prize, is rooted in Chinese life and historical reality especially from the Cultural Revolution through the Tiananmen Square massacre and offers significant details and context, including about He Luting (discussed below).

26. Clark, *Chinese Cultural Revolution*, 24.

27. Kraus, *Pianos and Politics*, 135–36.

28. See Liu Ching-chih, *Critical History*, 419–21, who provides the complete instrumentation and discusses the uses of the instruments in the various scenes.

29. Kraus, "Arts Policies of the Cultural Revolution," 221.

30. Despite beatings and repeated accusations, He Luting refused to confess to antirevolutionary crimes. He was imprisoned for six years and wrote sixty-four rebuttals to the accusations against him. Through the intervention of Zhou Enlai, He Luting was finally rehabilitated and in 1979, at the age of 75, restored to his former position. Among the many sources recounting this episode is Melvin and Cai, *Rhapsody in Red*, 236–38, 273, 297.

31. Many thanks to Nancy Yunhwa Rao for clarifying the identity of Chu Lan for us.

32. Clark, *Chinese Cultural Revolution*, 10; Kraus, "Arts Policies," 240.

33. Clark, ibid., provides the most exhaustive description of the works and their evolution.

34. Kraus, "Arts Policies," 231.

35. Rao, "Sonic Imaginary," 219. See also Mittler, *A Continuous Revolution*.

36. Yung, "Model Opera as Model." See also Pang, *Art of Cloning*, 148–52.

37. Pang, *Art of Cloning*, 96.

38. Guo, "Chinese Musical Language," 58–59.

39. Huan Li Shi Zhen Xiang, "Deng Xiaoping 1977." Numbers of applicants and accepted students differ in various sources. The most recent report (Jones, "Crossing the Bridge," 6) states that the CCOM admitted 322 of the 17,000 applicants.

40. Wang, *Central Conservatory*, 124.

41. Chen Yi, interview with authors, Sept. 19, 2016.

42. Many sources give incorrect information on the number of entering and graduating students in the composition program. In addition, many sources speak of the "class of 1977" even though the program did not officially commence until 1978. (Most English sources use 1978 and most Chinese sources use 1977.) The information we present comes directly from Chen Yi (email Apr. 8, 2018) and is verified by photographs of the class at various stages of the program.

43. Wang, *Central Conservatory*, 130.

44. Zhou Long, interview with the authors, Aug. 29, 2015.

45. Jeff Hays, Facts and Details, "Oroqen," http://factsanddetails.com/china/cat5/sub88/item160.html.

46. Wiltse, Interview with Chen Yi and Zhou Long.

47. Wang, *Central Conservatory*, 127.

48. Ibid., 128.

49. The first four yangbanxi companies, established in November 1966, were the Central Philharmonic Orchestra, the First Beijing Peking Opera Company, the China Peking Opera Company, and the Ballet Dance Company (Pang, *Art of Cloning*, 95).

50. Stock, "Wu Zuqiang."

51. Jones, *Folk Music of China*, 56–66.

52. Much of the information in this paragraph comes from Schiffer, "Folgen der Kulturrevolution." This source erroneously gives the year of Goehr's visit as 1979.

53. Jones, "Crossing the Bridge," 11.

54. For Goehr's description of his development vis-à-vis serialism, see his interview with Griffiths in *New Sounds, New Personalities*, 16–18.

55. Chen Yi revised and published this piece in 2011.

56. On Chou's life and work, see Chang, *Chou Wen-Chung*, and Lai, *Music of Chou Wen-chung*.

57. Chou, "U.S.-China Arts Exchange."

58. Chou, "Whither Chinese Composers?" 503, 509.

59. Ibid., 508. Chou addresses similar issues in "Asian Esthetics and World Music."

60. Yu, "Asian Melody," 91.

61. Borger, *Force of Curiosity*, 278.

62. Xiaole Li, "Chen Yi's Multicultural Approach," 2, based on email from CY, Aug. 22, 2001.

63. Borger, *Force of Curiosity*, 278.

64. Holland, "China Orchestra"; Buendler, "Chinese Play Only Modern Works."

65. Falletta tells the same story, although the reporter cites the wrong piece. See Goldman, "Eastern Stars."

66. Most of the information in this paragraph and the next comes from Susan Cheng, interview with Miller.

67. Ibid.

68. Chen Yi, *Sound and Silence*. For details about this series of films, see Miller, *Kernis*, 52–55.

69. Reviewed in Henken, "Pairing of Eastern, Western Notions."

70. Reviewed in McLellan, "Rich Mix."

71. Edwards, "Conductor's Profile." The Meet The Composers organization is now known as New Music USA.

72. Huey, "Myths and Music," 17.

73. Support for the tour came from the International Data Group.

74. Conley, ed., *Race, Ethnicity and an American Campus*, 29–30.

75. Documents on this award courtesy of Chen Yi.

76. Anderson, "Timely 'Mao to Mozart'"; Anthony, "Duluth Orchestra." The flutist was Donna Orbovich.

77. Borger, *Force of Curiosity*, 14.

78. Unpublished copy of the talk, courtesy of the American Academy of Arts and Letters. Thanks to David Clarke for providing us with this document.

79. Li Xing, "Musical Bridge."

80. Bargreen, "Symphony Embarks."

81. For a series of essays commemorating the commission, see Rogger and Sattler, eds., *Roche Commissions*.

CHAPTER 3. Compositional Processes

1. Chen Yi, from an interview with Irene Borger, June 11, 1998, published in Borger, *Force of Curiosity*, 282.

2. Interview with the authors. As in previous chapters, subsequent quotations from Chen Yi without notes come from our interviews with her.

3. Kraus, "Arts Policies," 229.

4. Information and quotations from our interviews with Chen Yi.

5. Chen Yi, interview with the authors. On this work, see also Yeung, "Chen Yi and her Choral Music," 26–34.

6. Chen Yi, interview with the authors.

7. For a discussion of twelve-tone technique in Chinese compositions, see Zheng Ying-Lie, "Letter from China."

8. Chen Yi, email to the authors, Sept. 8, 2019.

9. Ibid.

10. For more on this topic, see Rao, "Sonic Imaginary."

11. On the eight types of oral delivery on a speech-song spectrum, see Yung, "From Speech to Song."

12. Yeung, "Chen Yi and her Choral Music," 76.

13. This piece was inspired by the extraordinary paintings in the caves at Dunhuang, located in the desert in Gansu Province in northwest China. The wall paintings are spread over more than two hundred caves and span a period of about a thousand years. Zheng Ruzhong ("Musical Instruments") has meticulously documented all of the four thousand instruments depicted. In 2008 Chen reworked the *Dunhuang Fantasy* into a Septet for saxophone quartet and Chinese instrumental trio.

14. See Rao, "Tradition of *Luogu Dianzi*," and Wichmann, *Listening to Theatre*, especially 238–41.

15. Chen knows Erno Lendvai's book on Bartók but says that it had no influence on her from a theoretical standpoint.

16. The organization has now adopted the name Silkroad; for a description of its history and activities, see https://www.silkroad.org.

17. See, for example, Thorsten, "Silk Road Nostalgia," 301 and 311–12; and Langenkamp, "Contested Imaginaries," and "Conflicting Dreams." The quotation is from Thorsten.

18. Langenkamp, "Contested Imaginaries," 253.

19. Rao, "Transformative Power," 135.

20. Borger, *Force of Curiosity*, 283.

21. Chen Yi, "I Hear the Tragic Motif."

22. Chen Yi, email to the authors, June 30, 2017.

23. Program notes to the score of Symphony No. 2.

24. Program notes to the score of *Chinese Folk Dance Suite*.

25. Rao deals with the Chinese percussion tradition in the works of contemporary composers in "Tradition of *Luogu Dianzi*."

26. See Jones, *Folk Music of China*, 261.

27. Chen Yi, personal communication.

28. Du Yaxiong, "Baban ji qi xingshi mei."

29. Chen Yi, "Piano Concerto," 17.

30. Thrasher, *Sizhu Instrumental Music*, 117; see also his "Structural Continuity."
31. Chen Yi, "Tradition and Creation," 67.
32. Thrasher, *Sizhu Instrumental Music*, 115, and "Structural Continuity," 71. For another discussion of Baban, see Xue, "Baban, a Long-Standing Form."
33. Miller, "Beneath the Hybrid Surface," 334–35, shows the implications of this alternative placement of the conjunctive phrase and cites Thrasher's writings and sources.
34. Chen Yi, email to the authors, July 26, 2018. See also Guo, "Chinese Musical Language," 113.
35. The version shown in Example 3.16 is taken from Chen Yi's dissertation. The published score contains some errors, and performers should amend it to correspond to the rendition shown in our example.
36. Chen Yi, "Piano Concerto," 12–13.
37. For brief but clear explanations of irama, see Sorrell, *Guide to the Gamelan*, 65–66, and Perlman, *Unplayed Melodies*, 84–86.
38. For a detailed study of Chen's use of Baban, see Miller, "Beneath the Hybrid Surface."
39. Chen Yi, email to the authors, June 29, 2017.
40. Howat, *Debussy in Proportion*. Another work that shows similar, though not as extensive, proportional relationships is the second movement of Chen's *Feng*. Lin ("Analysis and Comparison," pp. 60–61, drawing on Melfi, "An Investigation") identifies proportional relationships on three structural levels, each approximating the Golden Section ratio (1.618). The overall form of the movement is ABA'B'A" where ABA' is 108 mm. and B'A" is 69 mm. The strict GS would result in 109.4 and 67.6. At the midlevel the structural relationship is similar: AB = 68 mm., A' = 40 mm.; the strict GS would be 67.6 and 41.8. At the shortest phrase level, A = 40 mm., B = 28 mm.; the strict GS would be 41.8 and 25.8.

CHAPTER 4. Solo and Chamber Music Works

1. The first movement of this piece is based on *The Golden Flute* concerto, movement 2. Chen revised the piece in 2010 for ruan ensemble and string orchestra, adding a third movement.
2. Miller, "Lou Harrison and the Aesthetics of Revision."
3. Miller and Lieberman, *Composing a World*, 232.
4. Lau, "Fusion or Fission," 26.
5. Of the many analyses of this piece, Chen prefers the one by Tang ("Tradition Is Alive"), which comes from an in-person session. Among the others are Antokoletz, *History of Twentieth-Century Music*, 467–70; Lee, "Chinese Musical Influences"; Songwen Li, "East Meets West"; Mittler, *Dangerous Tunes*, 368–70; and Xiaole Li, "Chen Yi's Piano Music."
6. Notes from the score.
7. For a discussion of Chen Yi's three woodwind quintets, see Yuh-Pey Lin, "An Analysis." Lin points out that in the first quintet, Chen at times adopts the Chinese practice of "note borrowing (using some notes to replace the original(s)," 17.
8. Oteri, "He Said, She Said." The quotations that follow are from interviews with the authors.

9. The text of the tune is "Namo Amitābha." Namo means "veneration." Collins English dictionary identifies Amitābha as "a Bodhisattva who presides over a Pure Land in the west of the universe."

10. Wu Man, interview with Edwards, Feb. 19, 2016.

11. Information about the origin of *The Points* comes from our interview with Chen Yi on Sept. 19, 2016, and email to the authors, Sept. 28, 2019.

12. Wu Man, interview with Edwards.

13. Wu Man, "The Points." For another discussion of this piece, see Lai, "Old Wine in New Bottles." Lai's description is almost entirely based on Chen Yi's own writing about *The Points* in her article "Tradition and Creation."

14. Wu Man, interview with Edwards.

15. See the article "Eight Principles of Yong" in Wikipedia; Wiltse, interview with Chen Yi and Zhou Long; Meadows, *Innovation through Fusion*, 409; and Shin et al., "Sensory Calligraphy Learning System." In the last reference, the authors analyze the pressure the calligrapher expends on the various strokes, one of the features Chen used in devising her musical score.

16. Wiltse, interview with Chen Yi and Zhou Long.

17. Chen Yi, interview with the authors.

18. Notes to the score.

19. Notes to score and Chen Yi, "Tradition and Creation."

20. Minnesota Public Radio, "Hún Qiáo: Bridge of Souls," September 2001 http://music.minnesota.publicradio.org/features/0109_hun_qiao/.

21. Wu Man, interview with Edwards.

22. On Linda Hoeschler and the Minnesota Commissioning Club, see Miller, *Kernis*, 89, 126–27.

23. This concert was repeated (with a different cellist) at the 2005 Pacific Rim Festival at the University of California, Santa Cruz. For a history of this festival, see University of California Santa Cruz, "UC Santa Cruz's Pacific Rim Music Festival: A History," https://pacificrim.sites.ucsc.edu/files/2017/12/Pacific-Rim_article-miller-1az86pp.pdf.

24. Wiltse, interview with Chen.

25. Chen, "My Musical Journey."

26. Ibid.

27. In 1994 Chen had arranged "Mo li hua" for chorus as part of her *Set of Chinese Folk Songs*.

28. Translation from Wikipedia, "Mo li hua."

29. Kozinn, "At a Cultural Crossroads." Puccini used a quite different version of "Mo li hua" in *Turandot*.

30. For a description and sketch, see the online encyclopedia *Baidu Baike*, http://baike.baidu.com/item/勒绒.

31. For an excellent demonstration, see video by Tran Quang Hai, "Chinese Kou Xian Jew's Harp by Tran Quang Hai," posted to YouTube Feb. 17, 2009, https://www.youtube.com/watch?v=xs7qn1j11nI.

32. Chen Yi, interview with the authors.

33. Notes to the score.

34. For a discussion and transcription of the three tunes, see Wu, "Fusion," 12–13 and 20–23.

CHAPTER 5. **Works for Large Instrumental Ensembles**

1. This piece is discussed in Guo, "Chinese Musical Language," 144–66; Wang, "Chang chu zi ji de sheng yin," 10; and Radice, *Concert Music*, 280–81.

2. For the full melodies of the themes shown in a and d, see Guo, "Chinese Musical Language," 146 and 148. We show the first melody transposed up a step from the version in Guo's thesis in order to present it at the same pitch that Chen uses in *Ge Xu*.

3. For an extended discussion of *Momentum*, see Jiang Liu, "An Analysis."

4. Chen Yi, email to the authors, Apr. 12, 2020.

5. See also Reese, "Chen Yi," 27–31.

6. On Glennie's explanation of her hearing loss, see her "Hearing Essay." For a discussion of the Percussion Concerto, see Hsieh, "Influence of Eastern and Western Music."

7. Borger, *Force of Curiosity*, 289.

8. Rye, "Poetic Sound of the Orient."

9. For an inspired performance of folk music from Turpan, Xinjiang Province, with excellent images and demonstrations of the long-necked bowed and plucked string instruments, see Dominic Swire's video "Folk Music from Turpan, Xinjiang," posted to YouTube Nov. 29, 2013, https://www.youtube.com/watch?v=ag4rqFJ1Ijk.

10. The poems are given in notes to the score. The work is discussed in *Roche Commissions* and is the subject of dissertations by Jung and Stulman.

11. Fleming, "Roche Commissions Principle," 7.

12. Steve Smith, "Post-Minimalist Inspirations."

13. Email to the authors, Apr. 16, 2019.

14. Bertholf, "A Local Composer."

15. Notes to the score.

16. From the program notes to the piece.

17. The tune is "Baoleng Diao," but as usual Chen draws materials from the source without using it literally. *Diao* means tune or melody. *Bao* and *leng* are padding syllables without any specific meaning. Chen Yi writes that "*leng* is just a lively syllable which is easy to repeat" (email, Apr. 12, 2020).

CHAPTER 6. **Choral and Solo Vocal Works**

1. As in previous chapters, quotations from Chen Yi without notes come from interviews with the authors in 2015 and 2016.

2. Melvin and Cai, *Rhapsody in Red*, 126.

3. Chen Yi, *Sound and Silence*, DVD video.

4. Murray, who taught for twenty-eight years at Aptos Middle School in San Francisco, was named a Distinguished Teacher (1990) by President George H. W. Bush and

received Chamber Music America's Award of Excellence (1993). Golden Gate Philharmonic, "Joan Murray: Founder and Executive Director Emerita," https://ggph.org/faculty-joan-murray/.

5. Chen Yi, email to the authors, Jan. 24, 2018.

6. See Rao, "The Tradition of *Luogu Dianzi*," esp. 525–26, for analysis addressing the signification of Chen's use of *luogu dianzi* in "Riding on a Mule." See also Law, "The a cappella Choral Music of Chen Yi," 43–44; she provides a useful overview of the a cappella works, a detailed analysis of *The West Lake*, and many practical charts and guides for non-Chinese speakers.

7. Han, "Folk Songs of the Han Chinese," passim, who is primarily following the ethnomusicological work of Jiang (Shanghai National Conservatory), *Hanzu Minge Gailun*.

8. The number of recognized minority nationalities has increased since their official establishment in 1953 and stands at fifty-five as of 2006 (Benite, "Minority Nationalities in China").

9. Chen Yi, email to the authors, Oct. 29, 2017.

10. *Naked oats* refers to a so-called hulless wheat-like grain, that is, the hull would thresh off easily when the naked oats were harvested, and the resulting grain could be more easily used for feeding people than farm animals. Naked oats are sometimes also called (Chinese) buckwheat (*Avena chinensis*), which is a different grain from the buckwheat (*Fagopyrum esculentum*) grown in the United States.

11. Chen Yi, email to the authors, Jan. 24, 2018.

12. Score error (not shown): alto mm. 32–33 should read "Ge beng" (not "Si beng").

13. Han, "Folk Songs," 119, using Jiang, *Hanze Minge Gailun*, 128–29.

14. Edwards, "Women on the Podium," 227–29. Falletta was the top US woman conductor.

15. Because zhuihu and its performers are very difficult to find, Chen used an alto *zhonghu*, a midrange erhu, pitched a fifth lower, for the premiere and subsequent performances.

16. Zacher, "Far from any Cliché of Porcelain and Jade."

17. Dance and visual projections are optional and have so far been included in only two performances beyond the premiere: the 2004 performance in Manchester, England, which included visual projections with the BBC Philharmonic, BBC Singers, Gu Feng Ensemble, and conductor Jason Lai with Bi Ma Dance (2 dancers); and the 2012 performance in Kansas City, which included visual projections but no dancers.

18. Chen, quoted in Johnson, Interview on BBC.

19. Preface to score.

20. Johnson, Interview on BBC.

21. Shaw, "Discourses of Identity," 65. See her analysis of all three movements of *Chinese Myths Cantata*, 62–87.

22. Hear Chen Yi demonstrate this concept in the BBC interview with Stephen Johnson, beginning at 30:40. Discovering Music, "Chen Yi: *Chinese Myths Cantata*," BBC Radio 3, http://www.bbc.co.uk/programmes/p0202rh4.

23. Preface to the score.

24. Moh-Wei Chen, "Myths from Afar," 37.

25. See especially Beauvoir, *The Second Sex*; Irigaray, *Speculum of the Other Woman*; Irigaray, *This Sex Which Is Not One*.

26. Gross, "Irigaray and Sexual Difference," 65.

27. Ibid.

28. Ibid., 68.

29. Irigaray, *This Sex Which Is Not One*, 154.

30. Ibid., 155.

31. Ibid.

32. Some contrabassoons are capable of producing a low A. Highest possible notes for winds are not absolutely limited by instrument construction; we are using the current professional upper practical limit.

33. See Zhang Boyu, *Mathematical Rhythmic Structure of Chinese Percussion Music*.

34. We find some similarity between Chen Yi's approach here and Anton Webern's treatment of 12-tone concepts in Zwei Lieder, op. 19 (1925–26). Both works include much pitch repetition and minimal row transposition—traits not consistent with full-fledged dodecaphonic composition.

35. Chen Yi, 1993 Annual Report of the John S. and James L. Knight Foundation (1994).

36. Wu Man: Pipa Virtuoso, "Biography (English)," Aug. 2019, http://www.wumanpipa.org/about/bio-en.html.

37. Wu Man, interview with Edwards.

38. Daines, "Finding Her Way."

39. Chen, quoted in Paul, "Composer Chen Yi Melds Eastern Sounds with Western Ways."

40. Woei, "Guest Editor's Introduction," 3–19; Ames, Review of *The Path of Beauty*, 77; Laker, "Celebrating CC People."

41. Chen Yi, email to the authors, Dec. 7, 2017.

42. See Li Zehou, *The Path of Beauty*, especially the following pages of beautiful color illustrations that relate to specific movements of Chen's composition: I (48–51), II (174–77), and V (112).

43. Publisher's description of Li Zehou, *The Path of Beauty*. https://www.amazon.com/Path-Beauty-Chinese-Aesthetics-Paperbacks/dp/019586526X.

44. Li Zehou, *The Path of Beauty*, 261.

45. Ibid., 36.

46. One exception occurs in m. 20, where the voices are separated by a perfect fifth.

47. Li Zehou, *The Path of Beauty*, 174–75.

48. See reproduction in ibid., 112, or the National Museum of China, Beijing website. http://en.chnmuseum.cn/collections_577/collection_highlights_608/201911/t20191121_172563.html.

49. For the western notation version of "Jieshi Diao You Lan" that Chen studied, see Baidu Tieba, http://tieba.baidu.com/p/3896884793; for the score in cipher system, see http://www.yinyuezj.com/guqin/pu/6782.html; for the Chinese introduction to the

history of the score, see the online encyclopedia *Baidu Baike*, https://baike.baidu.com/item/碣石调幽兰/1639749?fr=aladdin.

50. Honggang Li, interview with Edwards.

51. In the published score, Chen has shortened the movement as conceived in *Ba Yin*; however, some performances and recordings use the longer version that coincides with the length of *Ba Yin*. Chanticleer did not request a shortened version; however, Chen thinks that the shorter version would be easier for ensembles to perform and believes that this change, which basically omits two variations, does not disrupt the overall structure of the piece (Chen Yi, email to the authors, Dec. 8, 2017).

52. Tyrrell, "In Good Company."

53. Honggang Li, interview with Edwards.

54. Preface to the score.

55. Kosman, "Chen Yi Woos with a Seductive and Distinctive 'Beauty.'"

56. These dates are the most commonly given by scholars; however, occasionally the birthdate is given as 1083 or even 1081. The date of death is less certain with *ca.* 1141, 1149, and 1155 also suggested.

57. Wang Ping, "Solitary Boat," 127.

58. Wong Man, trans., *Poems from China*.

59. Chen Yi, interview with the authors. Chen also noted that Li's *baimiao* style—a term most often associated with certain spare approaches in Chinese painting but equally applicable to Li's poetry due to her simple and straightforward approach to style and technique—was an inspiration for her own compositions (email to the authors, Oct. 20, 2019).

60. Wang Jiaosheng, *The Complete Ci-poems of Li Qingzhao*, vii. See also Wang Ping, "Solitary Boat" for an analysis that positions Li's ci as *qingli* or "a middle station between *wanyue* and *haofang*" poetic styles (pp. 152, 128–29), that is, between styles of "delicate restraint" and "heroic abandon."

61. Hsin Yi Lin, "Musical Settings of Selected Poetry," 21.

62. Rao Lan is a cousin of musicologist Nancy Rao, who has published several articles about Chen Yi.

63. CRI, CD804.

64. Egan, *The Burden*, 335–39.

65. The quoted phrases are from Li's ci as translated by Egan, 337.

66. Egan, *The Burden*, 232.

67. Wang Ping, "Solitary Boat," 135.

68. Egan, *The Burden*, 235.

69. Dahmer, "West-östliches Saitenspiel," 25. Translation by Edwards.

70. Su Zheng, *Claiming Diaspora*, 262, quoting Chen Yi, personal interview, Jan. 27, 1993.

71. Songwen Li, "East Meets West," 25–26, quoting from correspondence with Chen Yi, Jan. 1, 2001. Li has (apparently) added in parentheses words not in Chen's original communication. We have omitted only those parenthetical comments.

72. Due to a technical problem, all X marks are missing in versions 2 and 3. Comparing

the manuscript with the published score of version 1 for violin and cello, the publication includes most of the X marks, but they are missing in movement I, mm. 10–11 and movement II, mm. 22 and 43.

73. Chen Yi, email to the authors, Dec. 14, 2015.
74. Keller, "Boom Times for the Art Song."
75. This ci is sometimes titled with the tune name (*cipai*) "Picking Mulberry Seeds (an enlarged version)" or with the subtitle "The Banana (*ba jiao*) Tree."
76. Wen Zhang, "Infusion of Eastern and Western Music Styles," 37.
77. Chen Yi, email to the authors, Sept. 30, 2017.
78. Ibid.

CHAPTER 7. Issues

1. Chen Yi, application for the Herb Alpert award.
2. Radice, "Chou Wen-chung: A Biographical Essay," 37, indicates that after the premiere Chou "apparently" wanted this final sentence omitted; however, it continued to appear in publications of the score and recording, and it now appears on Chou's website as the closing of the program note: https://chouwenchung.org/composition/and-the-fallen-petals/.
3. Preface to score. In an earlier choral work, "Spring Dreams" (1997), Chen also set this same poetic text but in Chinese and with entirely different music, which was subsequently adapted as the first movement of *Meditation* (1999/2012) for solo voice.
4. De Jong, Review of *Diaspora and Transnationalism*, 562.
5. Decker and Winchock, eds., *Borderlands and Liminal Subjects*.
6. Gupta and Ferguson, "Beyond 'Culture,'" 18.
7. Decker and Winchock, eds., *Borderlands and Liminal Subjects*, 5.
8. Ibid., 12.
9. Ibid., 15.
10. Bhabha, *Location of Culture*, specific quotes on 52–56, 5, 13, and 309.
11. Zheng, *Claiming Diaspora*, 23. Historical information about Chinese immigration primarily follows Zheng; see also Waldinger and Tseng, "Divergent Diasporas"; and "Chinese Immigration and the Transcontinental Railroad."
12. Zheng, *Claiming Diaspora*, 45.
13. Ibid., 101.
14. Ibid., 108.
15. Ibid., 111.
16. Ibid., 114.
17. As in other chapters, quotations from our interviews with Chen Yi in 2015–16 will not be annotated.
18. Chen in personal interview with Su Zheng, Jan. 27, 1993, as quoted in Zheng, *Claiming Diaspora*, 255.
19. Chen Yi, Zhou Long, and Mark A. Radice, "Radice in Conversation," 258–59, 261, 263.

20. See Zheng, *Claiming Diaspora*, 255–56 for details.

21. Ken Smith, "Fantasy of the Red Queen," 13.

22. See Mittler, "Against National Style," 16–18, 20–23; Lau, "Fusion or Fission," 31–33; Yu Siu Wah, "Two Practices Confused in One Composition," 57–71.

23. Kouwenhoven, "Composer Tan Dun," 5, quoting from his interview with Chen Qigang, Nov. 3, 1989, in Paris.

24. Ibid., 9; see also Mittler, *Dangerous Tunes*, 120–25; Chang, "Tan Dun's String Quartet;" Zheng, *Claiming Diaspora*, 258–59 (compares the approach to twelve-tone row use by Chen and Tan).

25. Kouwenhoven, 9 (citing Sheng, "Ting Tan Dun," 7–9).

26. Cameron, "A Marco Polo Going Backward at Full Tilt."

27. See Yu Siu Wah, "Two Practices," 57–71; Ross, "Stone Opera"; Blackburn, "In Search of Third Space," 171–77.

28. Buruma, "Of Musical Import," reports Tan Dun telling him in the fall of 2007 that he had permission for a performance of *The First Emperor* on the Great Wall for the Beijing Olympics, but now "the Chinese government may not let it happen after all." Such changes in concert scheduling are not uncommon in China.

29. Ken Smith, "Classical Music and Media in China 4."

30. Ibid.

31. Clover, "Chinese Opera Beset by Intrigues"; see also Moody, "Dream of the Red Chamber."

32. See Miyoshi, "An Epic Life Sings."

33. Ross, "Symphony of Millions," 88.

34. See especially Mittler, *A Continuous Revolution*.

35. Corbett, "Experimental Oriental," 180.

36. Mittler, *Dangerous Tunes*, 13, n. 25; 98; 98, n.299; 295, where the phrase is called conventional "post-Maoist jargon."

37. Mittler, "Cultural Revolution Model Works," 54, citing violinist-composer Du Mingxin.

38. Liu Ching-chih, *A Critical History*, 438.

39. Ibid., 457.

40. Liu, *A Critical History*, 436. See Mittler, who refutes Liu's claim about acrobats, with this account: "The elaborate and impressive array of moves and jumps to be found in the repertoire of traditional operatic acrobatics is drawn on in its entirety in the revolutionary operas" (Mittler, "Cultural Revolution Model Works," 70).

41. Mittler, "Cultural Revolution Model Works," 55, passim; Clark, Pang, and Tsai, eds., *Listening to China's Cultural Revolution*; Rao, "Sonic Imaginary," 231.

42. Yung, "Model Opera as Model," 162, 163.

43. Chen, email to Rao, July 15, 2015, quoted in "Sonic Imaginary," 231.

44. Ibid.

45. Mittler, "Cultural Revolution Model Works," 73.

46. Clark, Pang, and Tsai, "Introduction" in *Listening*, 2.

47. Ibid., 2, 7.

48. Rao, "Sonic Imaginary," 222–24.

49. Ibid., 232–33.

50. Ibid., 227.

51. Among the many recent writings on exoticism, see especially (in chronological order), Bellman, *The Exotic*; Corbett, "Experimental Oriental"; Lau, "Fusion or Fission"; Everett, "'Mirrors' of West and 'Mirrors' of East"; Taylor, *Beyond Exoticism*; Locke, *Musical Exoticism*; Utz, "Erfundene Traditionen"; Utz and Lau, "Introduction. Voice, Identities, and Reflexive Globalization"; and Sheppard, "Exoticism."

52. Melvin and Cai, *Rhapsody in Red*, 333.

53. Oestreich, "New Contingent."

54. Young, "Reconsidering Cultural Politics," 616; see also Young, "Reading Contemporary Chinese Music," 28.

55. Locke, *Musical Exoticism*, 228.

56. Ibid., 244; Fauser, *Musical Encounters*, 206.

57. Mittler, "Against National Style," 23.

58. Hall, "Cultural Identity and Diaspora," 225.

59. Chun, "Fuck Chineseness," 126, 136; see also Tan Sooi Beng and Rao, "Introduction," 4–7, 11–12; Utz, "Erfundene Traditionen," esp. 58.

60. Chun, "Fuck Chineseness," 125; 129.

61. Ibid., 134–38.

62. Lau, "Fusion or Fission," 24.

63. Ibid., 27.

64. Chou, "Asian Concepts," 213.

65. Lau, "Fusion or Fission," 24–25; see also Young, "Reconsidering Cultural Politics," 614.

66. Lau, "Fusion or Fission," 37.

67. Ibid., 38.

68. Ciccone, "The Class of 1978," 74.

69. Zheng, *Claiming Diaspora*, 150.

70. Utz, "Erfundene Traditionen und multiple Identitäten," 53; "ein vermeintlich ideologiefreies Terrain künstlerischer Entfaltung als Symbol politischer Freiheit zu installieren" (translation by Edwards).

71. Cage, *Empty Words*, 179.

72. See Beck, "What Is Globalization?" interview by Zolo; Beck, *Die Erfindung des Politischen: Zu einer Theorie reflexiver Modernisierung*.

73. Utz, "Erfundene Traditionen und multiple Identitäten," 58; "sowohl hegemoniale europäische Ästhetikdiskurse als auch kulturessenzialistische und neonationalistische Modelle außerhalb des Westens betreffen" (translation by Edwards).

74. Grabe and Else-Quest, "The Role of Transnational Feminism," esp. 159; Crenshaw, "Demarginalizing the Intersection," esp. 139–40.

75. Crenshaw, "Kimberlé Crenshaw on Intersectionality."

76. Su Zheng, *Claiming Diaspora*, 115.

77. Chen Yi, interview with the authors, Sept. 21, 2016; email with authors, Apr. 8, 2018.

78. Chen Yi, interview with the authors, Sept. 21, 2016.

79. Xie, "Chen Yi and Zhou Long." Chen made similar comments in a dialogue with Rae Yuan, "Science and Music," 174–75.

80. Chen Yi and Rae Yuan, "Science and Music," 169; email with authors, Apr. 8, 2018.

81. Chen Yi, email with authors, Apr. 8, 2018.

82. Ambrose, "Her Music."

83. "U.S. College Rankings," https://web.archive.org/web/20190914062532/http://www.uscollegeranking.org/music/2014-best-americas-top-music-schools-and-colleges-ranking.html and https://web.archive.org/web/20190914062532/http://www.uscollegeranking.org/music/2014-best-americas-top-music-schools-and-colleges-ranking.html; Ambrose, "Her Music," presents data about US presenters of new music and major composition prizes; Meddaugh, "Female Composers."

84. Higdon email quoted in Ambrose, "Her Music."

85. O'Bannon, "The 2014–15 Orchestra Season." Data for gala concerts, touring, pops and family concerts, and chamber series are excluded. O'Bannon's subsequent analysis presents numbers that vary modestly from those cited in this paragraph: twenty-two orchestras (Nashville Symphony Orchestra was added) and 14.3 percent of works performed by living composers were by women.

86. O'Bannon, "The Data behind the 2016–17 Orchestra Season."

87. O'Bannon, "The 2014–15 Orchestra Season."

88. Alsop quoted in O'Bannon, "The 2014–15 Orchestra Season."

89. Adkins Chiti, "Secret Agendas," 334.

90. Ibid., 356.

91. Adkins Chiti, "Women in Music Uniting Strategies for Talent," 104; Adkins Chiti, "European Key Changes for Women," 19.

92. Eastburn, "We Need More Women Composers"; see also the detailed update one year later, Sound and Music, "Projects: International Womens Day 2018," http://www.soundandmusic.org/projects/international-womens-day-2018, and "Projects: Gender and Composition: Reviewing the Data," http://www.soundandmusic.org/projects/gender-and-composition-reviewing-data.

93. Although laudable, this goal will be a challenge since as recently as 2017, only 7.5 percent of the living composers featured at the Proms were women (Kingsley, "Female Composers and Conductors").

94. Beaumont-Thomas, "Proms among Music Festivals Pledging 50/50 Gender Split."

95. Lauritzen, "2017–18 Women Represented."

96. Harrison Parrott, "Xian Zhang Returns to Los Angeles Philharmonic," Jan. 12, 2017, https://www.harrisonparrott.com/news/2017-02-13/xian-zhang-returns-to-los-angeles-philharmonic; Swed, "Review. An L.A. Phil Reminder."

97. Von Rhein, "Local Sounds, Local Venues."

98. Ambrose, "Her Music"; Cooper, "Six Composers Are Ready"; Walls, "Brazen Virtuosity."

99. Ambrose, "Her Music"; American Academy of Arts and Letters, "Awards," https://artsandletters.org/awards/; New Music USA, "American Academy of Arts and Letters Announces 2018 Music Awards," https://nmbx.newmusicusa.org/social-news/american-academy-of-arts-letters-announces-2018-music-awards/.

100. Robin, "What Du Yun's Pulitzer Win Means for Women." Ellen Taaffe Zwilich was the first woman in 1983 (Edwards, "North America since 1920," 331).

101. Quoting Chen Yi, interview with authors, Sept. 21, 2016.

References

This list includes works cited in the notes as well as a few additional important sources. It by no means represents all of the material we have consulted in the preparation of this book.

Adkins Chiti, Patricia. "European Key Changes for Women in Music and the Performing Arts." In *European Key Changes for Women*, edited by Fondazione Adkins Chiti: Donne in Musica, 9–24. Brussels: European Parliament, 2014. https://issuu.com/donnemusica/docs/european-key-changes-for-women-in-m.
———. "Secret Agendas in Orchestral Programming." In *Culture-gates: Exposing Professional "Gate-keeping" Processes in Music and New Media Arts*, edited by Fondazione Donne in Musica, et al., 325–60. Bonn: ARCult Media, 2003.
———. "Women in Music Uniting Strategies for Talent: Working to Change the Landscape [for] Women in Music." In *The Cultural Component of Citizenship: An Inventory of Challenges*, 100–112. Brussels: European House for Culture, 2012. http://houseforculture.eu/upload/Docs%20ACP./ACPtheculturalcomponent ofcitizenshiponlinecopy.pdf#page=101.
Ambrose, Alex. "Her Music: Today's Emerging Female Composer." *Q2 Music* [NY Public Radio], Aug. 20, 2014. https://www.wqxr.org/story/her-music-emerging-female-composer-today/.
American Academy of Arts and Letters. "Composer Chen Yi Receives Prestigious Charles Ives Award." Press release, Dec. 20, 2000.
Ames, Roger T. Review of *The Path of Beauty: A Study of Chinese Aesthetics*, by Li Zehou. *Journal of Aesthetics and Art Criticism* 55, no. 1 (winter 1997): 77–79.

Anderson, Dennis. "Timely 'Mao to Mozart' Celebrates Human Spirit." *Duluth News Tribune*, Nov. 10, 1997.

"Answering the 'What Is American?' Question." [*Chamber Music*], Jan./Feb. 2009, 12–14. http://www.chamber-music.org/pdf/AmMaJ.pdf.

Anthony, Michael. "Duluth Orchestra Plays Novel Program with New Conductor." *Minneapolis Star Tribune*, Nov. 10, 1997.

Antokoletz, Elliott. *A History of Twentieth-Century Music in a Theoretic-Analytical Context*. New York: Routledge, 2014. First published London: Routledge, 2012.

Arlin, Mary I., and Mark A. Radice, eds. *Polycultural Synthesis in the Music of Chou Wen-chung*. London: Routledge, 2018.

Baker, Phil. "At a Glance Fiction." *Sunday Times* (London), July 31, 2016, 39. https://search.proquest.com/docview/1807744843.

Bargreen, Melinda. "Symphony Embarks on Energized 'Journey.'" *Seattle Times*, Mar. 20, 2004.

Bauböck, Rainer, and Thomas Faist, eds. *Diaspora and Transnationalism: Concepts, Theories and Methods*. Amsterdam: Amsterdam University Press, 2010.

Beaumont-Thomas, Ben. "Proms among Music Festivals Pledging 50/50 Gender Split in Lineups." *Guardian* Feb. 26, 2018. https://www.theguardian.com/music/2018/feb/26/proms-music-festivals-gender-pledge.

Beauvoir, Simone de. *The Second Sex*. Translated and edited by H. M. Parshley. New York: Alfred A. Knopf, 1971. Originally published as *Le Deuxième Sexe*. 2 vols. ([Paris]: Gallimard, 1949).

Beck, Ulrich. *Die Erfindung des Politischen: Zu einer Theorie reflexiver Modernisierung*. Frankfurt: Suhrkamp, 1993. Translated by Mark Ritter as *The Reinvention of Politics: Rethinking Modernity in the Global Social Order*. Cambridge, UK: Polity Press, 2005.

———. "What Is Globalization? Some Radical Questions." Interview by Danilo Zolo. *Jura Gentium: Rivista di filosofia del diritto internazionale e della politica globale* 1, no. 1 (2005). http://www.juragentium.org/topics/wlgo/en/beck.htm. Originally published in *Reset*, 1999, 5.

Bellman, Jonathan, ed. *The Exotic in Western Music*. Boston: Northeastern University Press, 1998.

Benite, Zvi Ben-Dor. "Minorities—Minority Nationalities in China." In *Oxford Encyclopedia of the Modern World*, edited by Peter N. Stearns. 8 vols. Oxford: Oxford University Press, 2008; online ed., 2008. https://www.oxfordreference.com/view/10.1093/acref/9780195176322.001.0001/acref-9780195176322-e-1031.

Bertholf, Amanda. "A Local Composer from a World Away." *Perspectives* (UMKC magazine), spring 2011.

Bhabha, Homi K. *The Location of Culture*. Rev. ed. London: Routledge, 2004. First published 1994.

Blackburn, Tong Cheng. "In Search of Third Space: Composing the Transcultural Experience in the Operas of Bright Sheng, Tan Dun, and Zhou Long." PhD diss., Indiana University, 2015.

Borger, Irene, ed. *The Force of Curiosity*. Santa Monica: Calarts, 1999.

Born, Georgina, and David Hesmondhalgh, eds. *Western Music and Its Others*. Berkeley: University of California Press, 2000.

Buendler, David. "Chinese Play Only Modern Works." *Pasadena Star-News*, Oct. 7, 1987.

Buruma, Ian. "Of Musical Import." *New York Times Magazine*, May 4, 2008, MM46.

Cage, John. *Empty Words: Writings '73–'78*. Middletown, CT: Wesleyan University Press, 1979.

Cameron, Lindsley. "A Marco Polo Going Backward at Full Tilt." *New York Times*, Nov. 2, 1997, AE38. https://www.nytimes.com/1997/11/02/arts/a-marco-polo-going-backward-at-full-tilt.html. [Author later published under the name Lindsey Miyoshi.]

Chang, Peter. "Tan Dun's String Quartet 'Feng-Ya-Song': Some Ideological Issues." *Asian Music* 22, no. 2 (spring–summer, 1991): 127–58. https://www.jstor.org/stable/834310.

Chang, Peter M. *Chou Wen-Chung: The Life and Work of a Contemporary Chinese-Born American Composer*. Lanham, MD: Scarecrow Press, 2006.

Chen, Moh-Wei. "*Myths from Afar: Chinese Myths Cantata* by Chen Yi." DMA thesis, University of Southern California, 1997.

Chen Yi. Application for the Herb Alpert Award, 1996. Personal files of Chen Yi.

———. "I Hear the Tragic Motif in My Symphony Again and Again." *John S. and James L. Knight Foundation 1993 Annual Report*. Personal files of Chen Yi.

———. "My Musical Journey to the World." Keynote presentation at the ISME 29th World Conference, Aug. 2, 2010. Personal files of Chen Yi.

———. "Piano Concerto." DMA diss., Columbia University, 1993.

———. *Sound and Silence*. Twenty episodes produced by Polish Television and Katherine Adamov Films in association with I.S.C.M, 1989. Host, Zygmunt Krauze; guest, Chen Yi; special guest, John Cage; commentary, Rolf Liebermann; music performed by Muzyka Centrum Krakow. DVD video, sound, color, 26 minutes. University of California Santa Cruz, Special Collections, DVD9193.

———. *Sparkle*. CRI, CD804, 1999, compact disc.

———. "Tradition and Creation." *Current Musicology* 67–68 (1999): 59–72.

Chen Yi and Rae Yuan. "Science and Music: An East-Western Dialogue." In *Roche Commissions: Chen Yi*, edited by Basil Rogger and Mark Sattler, 141–75. [Basel, Switzerland]: Roche, 2005.

Chen Yi, Zhou Long, and Mark A. Radice. "Radice in Conversation about Chou Wen-chung." In *Polycultural Synthesis in the Music of Chou Wen-chung*, edited by Mary I. Arlin and Mark A. Radice, 255–67. London: Routledge, 2018.

"Chinese Immigration and the Transcontinental Railroad." https://www.uscitizenship.info/Chinese-immigration-and-the-Transcontinental-railroad/.

Chou Wen-chung. "Asian Concepts and Twentieth-Century Western Composers." *Musical Quarterly* 57, no. 2 (Apr. 1971): 211–29.

———. "Asian Esthetics and World Music." *Ear Magazine East* 7, no. 3–4 (Apr.–Oct. 1982): 3; a longer version of this article is in *New Music in the Orient: Essays on Composition in*

Asia since World War II, edited by Harrison Ryker, 177–87. Buren, Netherlands: Fritz Knuf Publishers, 1991.

———. "U.S.-China Arts Exchange: A Practice in Search of a Philosophy." In *Music in the Dialogue of Cultures: Traditional Music and Cultural Policy*, edited by Max Peter Baumann, 144–64. Wilhelmshaven: Florian Noetzel Verlag, 1991.

———. "Whither Chinese Composers?" *Contemporary Music Review* 26, nos. 5–6 (Oct./Dec. 2007): 501–10.

Chun, Allen. "Fuck Chineseness: On the Ambiguities of Ethnicity as Culture as Identity." *boundary 2* 23, no. 2 (summer 1996): 111–38. http://www.jstor.org/stable/303809.

Ciccone, Alicia Hunt. "The Class of 1978: New Waves in Music and the Chinese Diaspora." Senior thesis, Amherst College, 2011.

Clark, Paul. *The Chinese Cultural Revolution: A History*. Cambridge: Cambridge University Press, 2008.

Clark, Paul, Laikwan Pang, and Tsan-Huang Tsai, eds. *Listening to China's Cultural Revolution: Music, Politics, and Cultural Continuities*. Basingstoke, Hampshire, UK: Palgrave Macmillan, 2016.

Clover, Charles. "Chinese Opera Beset by Intrigues Old and New." *Financial Times* (London), Sept. 15, 2017. https://www.ft.com/content/2efd7106-997a-11e7-a652-cde3f882dd7b.

Conley, Timothy K., ed. *Race, Ethnicity and an American Campus: A Report and Recommendations*. Peoria, IL: Office for Teaching Excellence and Faculty Development, Bradley University, 1995.

Cooper, Michael. "Six Composers Are Ready for Their Miller Theater Portraits." *New York Times*, May 10, 2017, C3. https://www.nytimes.com/2017/05/09/arts/music six-composers-are-ready-for-their-miller-theater-portraits.html.

Corbett, John. "Experimental Oriental: New Music and Other Others." In *Western Music and Its Others*, edited by Georgina Born and David Hesmondhalgh, 163–86. Berkeley: University of California Press, 2000.

Crenshaw, Kimberlé. "Demarginalizing the Intersection of Race and Sex: A Black Feminist Critique of Antidiscrimination Doctrine, Feminist Theory and Antiracist Politics." *University of Chicago Legal Forum* 1 (1989): 139–67. http://chicagounbound.uchicago.edu/uclf/vol1989/iss1/8.

———. "Kimberlé Crenshaw on Intersectionality, More Than Two Decades Later." [with unnamed interviewer] June 8, 2017. https://www.law.columbia.edu/pt-br/news/2017/06/kimberle-crenshaw-intersectionality.

Dahmer, Manfred. "West-östliches Saitenspiel." *Frankfurter Allgemeine*, July 12, 1989, no. 158, 25.

Dai Jiafang. "A Diachronic Study of *Jingju Yangbanxi* Model Peking Opera Music." Translated by Lau Sze Wing. In *Listening to China's Cultural Revolution: Music, Politics, and Cultural Continuities*, edited by Paul Clark, et al., 11–35. Basingstoke, Hampshire, UK: Palgrave Macmillan, 2016.

Daines, Matthew. "Finding Her Way to the Top of Two Worlds." *New York Times*, June 9, 1996, E32.

Decker, Jessica Elbert, and Dylan Winchock, eds. *Borderlands and Liminal Subjects: Transgressing the Limits in Philosophy and Literature*. Cham, Switzerland: Palgrave Macmillan, 2017.

De Jong, Gordon F. Review of *Diaspora and Transnationalism: Concepts, Theories and Methods*, edited by Rainer Bauböck and Thomas Faist. *Contemporary Sociology* 40, no. 5 (Sept. 2011): 562–63.

Dikötter, Frank. *The Cultural Revolution: A People's History, 1962–1976*. New York: Bloomsbury Press, 2016.

Du Yaxiong. "Baban ji qi xingshi mei." *Chinese Music* 2 (June 1984): 4–6. Translated by Sun Hai as "The Form of Baban: A Study in Aesthetics." *Journal of Music in China* 1 (Oct. 1999): 95–100.

Eastburn, Susanna. "We Need More Women Composers—and It's Not about Tokenism, It's about Talent." *Guardian*, Mar. 6, 2017. https://www.theguardian.com/music/2017/mar/06/sound-and-music-susanna-eastburn-we-need-more-women-composers-talent-not-tokenism; see also the detailed update one year later, http://www.soundandmusic.org/projects/international-womens-day-2018 and http://www.soundandmusic.org/projects/gender-and-composition-reviewing-data.

Edwards, J. Michele. "Chen Yi: Trauma, Myths, and Representation." In *The Routledge Handbook on Women's Work in Music*, edited by Rhiannon Mathias. London: Routledge, forthcoming 2021.

———. "Conductor's Profile: Congratulations to JoAnn Falletta!" *International Alliance for Women in Music Journal* 4, no. 3 (fall 1998): 16–17.

———. "North America since 1920." In *Women and Music: A History*, edited by Karin Pendle, 314–85. 2d ed. Bloomington: Indiana University Press, 2001. 1st ed. 1991.

———. "Women on the Podium." In *The Cambridge Companion to Conducting*, edited by José Antonio Bowen, 220–36. Cambridge: Cambridge University Press, 2003.

Egan, Ronald. *The Burden of Female Talent: The Poet Li Qingzhao and Her History in China*. Cambridge, MA: Harvard University Asia Center, 2013.

Everett, Yayoi Uno. "'Mirrors' of West and 'Mirrors' of East." In *Diasporas and Interculturalism in Asian Performing Arts: Translating Traditions*, edited by Hae-kyung Um, 176–203. London: RoutledgeCurzon, 2005.

Fauser, Annegret. *Musical Encounters at the 1889 Paris World's Fair*. Rochester: University of Rochester Press, 2005.

Fleming, Shirley. "The Roche Commissions Principle." In *Roche Commissions: Chen Yi*, edited by Basil Rogger and Mark Sattler, 6–11. [Basel, Switzerland]: Roche, 2005.

Gelfand, Janelle. "Composer Kept Mind on Music: Chen Yi Was Forced to Practice Secretly." *Cincinnati Enquirer*, Apr. 14, 2002.

Glennie, Evelyn. "Hearing Essay." https://web.archive.org/web/20110410092415/http://www.evelyn.co.uk/Evelyn_old/live/hearing_essay.htm.

Goldman, Mary Kunz. "Eastern Stars: Buffalo Philharmonic Turns to China for Timeless Sounds." *Buffalo News*, Nov. 18, 2005, G22.

Grabe, Shelly, and Nicole M. Else-Quest. "The Role of Transnational Feminism in Psychology: Complementary Visions." *Psychology of Women Quarterly* 36, no. 2 (2012): 158–61.

Griffiths, Paul. *New Sounds, New Personalities: British Composers of the 1980s in Conversation*. London: Faber, 1985.

Gross, Elizabeth. "Irigaray and Sexual Difference." *Australian Feminist Studies* 1, no. 2 (autumn 1986): 63–77.

Guo Xin. "Chinese Musical Language Interpreted by Western Idioms: Fusion Process in the Instrumental Works by Chen Yi." PhD diss., Florida State University, 2002.

Gupta, Akhil, and James Ferguson. "Beyond 'Culture': Space, Identity, and the Politics of Difference." *Cultural Anthropology* 7, no. 1 (1992): 6–23.

Hall, Stuart. "Cultural Identity and Diaspora." In *Identity: Community, Culture, Difference*, edited by Jonathan Rutherford, 222–37. London: Lawrence & Wishart, 1990. https://muse.jhu.edu/book/34784 (eBook). First published with minor differences in *Framework: The Journal of Cinema and Media*, no. 36 (1989): 68–81. https://www.jstor.org/stable/44111666.

Han Kuo-huang. "Folk Songs of the Han Chinese: Characteristics and Classifications." *Asian Music* 20, no. 2 (spring–summer 1989): 107–28.

Henken, John. "Pairing of Eastern, Western Notions." *Los Angeles Times*, Feb. 22, 1993.

Holland, Bernard. "China Orchestra." *New York Times*, Oct. 13, 1987, C17.

Horsley, Paul. "Woman of Two Worlds: UMKC's Chen Yi Survived China's Cultural Revolution to Become a World-Famous Classical Composer: Chen Yi: 'The Personification of Artistic Effervescence.'" *Kansas City Star*, Mar. 18, 2001.

Howat, Roy. *Debussy in Proportion: A Musical Analysis*. Cambridge: Cambridge University Press, 1983.

Hsieh, Hsien-Fang. "The Influence of Eastern and Western Music in Chen Yi's 'Percussion Concerto.'" DMA doctoral essay, University of Miami, 2016.

Huan Li Shi Zhen Xiang. "Hái lìsh ī zhēn mào: Deng Xiaoping, 1977, nián pīshì zhīchí zhōngyāng yīnyuè xuéyuàn kuòzhāo shìjiàn zhēnxiàng" (Recalling the Real History: Deng Xiao Ping in 1977, Supporting the truth about the expansion of the Central Conservatory of Music). Boxun.com, Sept. 14, 2007. http://www.peacehall.com/cgi-bin/news/gb_display/print_version.cgi?art=/gb/z_special/2007/09&link=200709140503.shtm.

Huey, Mamie. "Myths and Music." *Asian Week* 17, no. 43 (June 21–27, 1996): 17.

Irigaray, Luce. *Speculum of the Other Woman*. Translated by Gillian C. Gill. Ithaca, NY: Cornell University Press, 1985. Originally published as *Speculum de l'autre femme*. (Paris: Les Éditions de Minuit, 1974).

———. *This Sex Which Is Not One*. Translated by Catherine Porter with Carolyn Burke. Ithaca, NY: Cornell University Press, 1985. Originally published as *Ce Sexe qui n'en est pas un*. (Paris: Les Éditions de Minuit, 1977).

Jiang Mingdun. *Hanzu Minge Gailun* [An Introduction to Han Folk Songs]. Shanghai: Shanghai wen yi chu ban she, 1982.

Johnson, Stephen. Interview with Chen Yi on BBC. Discovering Music, Mar. 6, 2004 (rebroadcast on May 30, 2014), 58 min. http://www.bbc.co.uk/programmes/p0202rh4.

Jones, Stephen M. "Crossing the Bridge—The Story of the Class of '78 and the Emergence of New Music in China." *World New Music Magazine* 28 (2018): 4–15.

---. *Folk Music of China: Living Instrumental Traditions.* Oxford: Clarendon Press, 1995.
"July: Recording Chen Yi." Chanticleer's Blog, July 24, 2010. http://www.chanticleer.org/blog/july-recording-chen-yi?rq=Chen%20.
Jung, Jae Eun. "Four Seasons: A Study of Chen Yi's *Si Ji*." DMA thesis, University of Illinois, 2010.
Kagan, Alan L. "Music and the Hundred Flowers Movement." *Musical Quarterly* 49, no. 4 (Oct. 1963): 417–30.
Keller, Joanna. "Boom Times for the Art Song: A Hyperhistory of Poetry and Music." *NewMusicBox*, Feb. 1, 2002. http://www.newmusicbox.org/articles/Boom-Times-for-the-Art-Song-A-HyperHistory-of-Poetry-and-Music/.
Kelly, Jennifer. *In Her Own Words: Conversations with Composers in the United States.* Urbana: University of Illinois Press, 2013.
Kingsley, Jenny. "Female Composers and Conductors—Scoring for Gender Equality." *Artistic Miscellany*, Aug. 9, 2017. http://artisticmiscellany.com/2017/08/09/female-composers-and-conductors-the-balancing-act-is-missing/.
Kosman, Joshua. "Chen Yi Woos with a Seductive and Distinctive 'Beauty.'" *San Francisco Chronicle*, Mar. 18, 2008, E-8.
Kouwenhoven, Frank. "Composer Tan Dun: The Ritual Fire Dancer of Mainland China's New Music." *China Information* 6, no. 3 (winter 1991–92): 1–24.
Kozinn, Allan. "At a Cultural Crossroads: Yo-Yo Ma Becomes a Spice Trader." *New York Times*, May 9, 2002.
Kraus, Richard. "Arts Policies of the Cultural Revolution: The Rise and Fall of Culture Minister Yu Huiyong." In *New Perspectives on the Cultural Revolution*, edited by William A. Joseph, Christine P. W. Wong, and David Zweig, 219–41. Cambridge, MA: Council on East Asian Studies, Harvard University, 1991.
---. *Pianos and Politics in China: Middle-Class Ambitions and the Struggle over Western Music.* New York: Oxford University Press, 1989.
Lai, Eric. *The Music of Chou Wen-chung.* Farnham, England: Ashgate, 2009.
---. "Old Wine in New Bottles: The Use of Traditional Material in New Chinese Music." *ACMR Reports: Journal of the Association for Chinese Music Research* 12 (1999): 1–22.
Laker, Laurie. "Celebrating CC People: Professor Emerita Jane Cauvel," *Colorado College Bulletin* (winter 2017). https://sites.coloradocollege.edu/bulletin/celebrating-cc-people-professor-emerita-jane-cauvel/.
Langenkamp, Harm. "Conflicting Dreams of Global Harmony in US-PRC Silk Road Diplomacy." In *Music and Diplomacy from the Early Modern Era to the Present*, edited by Rebekah Ahrendt, Mark Ferranguto, and Damien Mahiet, 83–100. New York: Palgrave Macmillan, 2014.
---. "Contested Imaginaries of Collective Harmony: The Poetics and Politics of 'Silk Road' Nostalgia in China and the West." In *China and the West: Music, Representation, and Reception*, edited by Hon-Lun Yang and Michael Saffle, 163–85. Ann Arbor: University of Michigan Press, 2017.
Lau, Frederick. "Fusion or Fission: The Paradox and Politics of Contemporary Chinese

Avant-Garde Music." In *Locating East Asia in Western Art Music*, edited by Yayoi Everett and Frederick Lau, 22–39. Middletown: Wesleyan University Press, 2004.

Lauritzen, Brian [music journalist working for Classical KUSC public radio in Los Angeles]. "2017–18 Women Represented in United States Orchestras." https://twitter.com/BrianKUSC. Aug. 22, 2017.

Law, Po Kwan. "The a cappella Choral Music of Chen Yi: 1985–2010." DMA diss., University of Illinois at Urbana-Champaign, 2013.

Lee, Wendy Wan-Ki. "Chinese Musical Influences, Western Structural Techniques: The Compositional Design of Chen Yi's *Duo Ye*." *Society of Composers Journal* 1, no. 1, 2009. http://ns1.societyofcomposers.org/publicatons/isci 1/Lee.pdf.

Lendvai, Erno. *Béla Bartók: An Analysis of His Music*. London: Kahn and Averill, 1971.

Li, Songwen. "East Meets West: Nationalistic Elements in Selected Piano Solo Works of Chen Yi." DMA thesis, University of North Texas, 2001.

Li, Xiaole. "Chen Yi's Multicultural Approach in Ba Ban for Piano Solo." *Resonance*, spring 2005. http://resonanceinterdisciplinaryjournal.org/2005/Spring/Xiaole/index.html.

———. "Chen Yi's Piano Music: Chinese Aesthetics and Western Models." PhD diss., University of Hawaii, 2003.

Li Xing. "Musical Bridge United Cultures." *China Daily*, Mar. 2, 2001.

Li Zehou. *The Path of Beauty: A Study of Chinese Aesthetics*. Translated by Gong Lizeng. Beijing: Morning Glory Publishers, 1988. First published in Chinese as *Mei di li cheng* (1981 with two revised and supplemented editions during the next five years). [This translation draws on all 3 Chinese editions and adds material for Western readers, especially illustrations, which are often in color.]

Lin, Hsin Yi. "Musical Settings of Selected Poetry of Li Qing-Zhao by Four Twentieth[-]Century Composers." DMA thesis, University of Illinois at Urbana-Champaign, 2011.

Lin, Yuh-Pey. "An Analysis and Comparison of the Three Woodwind Quintets by Chen Yi." DMA diss., University of Washington, 2010.

Liu Ching-chih. *A Critical History of New Music in China*. Rev. ed. Translated by Caroline Mason. Hong Kong: Chinese University Press, 2010. Originally published as *Zhongguo xin yinyueshi lun* [On the history of New Music in China]. Taipei, Taiwan: Shaowen, 1998.

———. "'Wenge' shiqi de xin yinyue, 1966–1976" [New Music during the Cultural Revolution]. In *Zhongguo xinyinyueshi lunji* [Collected essays on the history of New Music in China, 1946–76], edited by Liu Jingzhi, 113–210. Hong Kong: Centre for Asian Studies, 1990.

Liu, Jiang. "An Analysis of Chen Yi's Orchestral Work Momentum." DMA diss., University of Nebraska, 2005.

Locke, Ralph. *Musical Exoticism, Images and Reflections*. Cambridge: Cambridge University Press, 2009.

Mangan, Timothy. "A Musical Odyssey: China's Cultural Revolution Forever Changed the Life and Work of Composer Chen Yi." *Orange County Register*, Feb. 29, 2004.

McLellan, Joseph. "The Rich Mix of Women's Philharmonic." *Washington Post*, Jan. 13, 1992.

Meadows, CJ. *Innovation through Fusion: Combining Innovative Ideas to Create High Impact*

Solutions. Berlin: Walter de Gruyter, 2020, specifically Chapter 34: Forbidden Music of the Cultural Revolution, 400–414. https://books.google.com/books?id=823cDwAAQBAJ &printsec=copyright&source=gbs pub info r#v=onepage&1&f=false.

Meddaugh, Tara. "Female Composers: Vastly Under-represented." *GarageSpin* (blog), Sept. 24, 2015. http://www.garagespin.com/female-composers-vastly-represented/.

Melfi, Cheryl Ann. "An Investigation of Selected Works by Chen Yi." DMA diss., University of Arizona, 2005.

Melvin, Sheila, and Jindong Cai. *Rhapsody in Red: How Classical Music Became Chinese*. New York: Algora Publishing, 2004.

Miller, Leta E. *Aaron Jay Kernis*. Urbana: University of Illinois Press, 2014.

———. "Beneath the Hybrid Surface: Baban as a Tool for Self-Definition in the Music of Chen Yi." *American Music* 37, no. 3 (fall 2019): 328–55.

———. "Lou Harrison and the Aesthetics of Revision, Alteration, and Self-Borrowing." *Twentieth-Century Music* 2, no. 1 (Mar. 2005): 1–29.

———. "UC Santa Cruz's Pacific Rim Music Festival: A History." https://pacificrim.sites.ucsc.edu/files/2017/12/Pacific-Rim_article-miller-1az86pp.pdf.

Miller, Leta E., and Fredric Lieberman. *Composing a World: Lou Harrison, Musical Wayfarer*. Urbana and Chicago: University of Illinois Press, 2004.

Mittler, Barbara. "Against National Style—Individualism and Internationalism in New Chinese Music (revisiting Lam Bun-Ching and others)." In *Proceedings of the Symposium at the 2003 Chinese Composers' Festival*, edited by Daniel Law and Chan Ming Chi, 2–26. Hong Kong: Hong Kong Composers' Guild, 2004.

———. *A Continuous Revolution: Making Sense of Cultural Revolution Culture*. Cambridge, MA: Harvard University Asia Center, 2012.

———. "Cultural Revolution Model Works and the Politics of Modernization in China: An Analysis of 'Taking Tiger Mountain by Strategy.'" *The World of Music* 45, no. 2 (2003): 53–81. http://www.jstor.org/stable/41700060.

———. *Dangerous Tunes: The Politics of Chinese Music in Hong Kong, Taiwan, and the People's Republic of China Since 1949*. Wiesbaden: Harrassowitz, 1997.

———. "'Eight Stage Works for 800 Million People': The Great Proletarian Cultural Revolution in Music—A View from Revolutionary Opera." *Opera Quarterly* 26, nos. 2–3 (spring–summer 2010): 377–401.

———. "Just Beat It! Popular Legacies of Cultural Revolution Music." In *Listening to China's Cultural Revolution: Music, Politics, and Cultural Continuities*, edited by Paul Clark, Laikwan Pang, and Tsan-huang Tsai, 239–68. Basingstoke, Hampshire, UK: Palgrave Macmillan, 2016.

———. "Popular Propaganda? Art and Culture in Revolutionary China." *Proceedings of the American Philosophical Society* 152, no. 4, Dec. 2008: 466–89.

Miyoshi, Lindsey. "An Epic Life Sings." *Opera News* 78, no. 12 (June 2014). https://www.operanews.com/Opera_News_Magazine/2014/6/Features/An_Epic_Life_Sings.html.

Moody, Andrew. "Dream of the Red Chamber Heads Out on European Tour." *The Telegraph. China Watch—Culture*, Dec. 21, 2017. https://www.telegraph.co.uk/china-watch/culture/dream-of-the-red-chamber-european-tour/. Originally published by *China Daily*.

O'Bannon, Ricky. "The 2014–15 Orchestra Season by the Numbers." http://www.bsomusic.org/stories/the-2014-15-orchestra-season-by-the-numbers.aspx.

———. "The Data behind the 2016–17 Orchestra Season." https://www.bsomusic.org/stories/the-data-behind-the-2016-2017-orchestra-season/.

Oestreich, James R. "A New Contingent of American Composers." *New York Times*, Apr. 1, 2001, AR1, 30.

Oteri, Frank J. "He Said, She Said: Zhou Long and Chen Yi." *NewMusicBox*, Aug. 1, 2006. https://nmbx.newmusicusa.org/he-said-she-said-zhou-long-and-chen-yi/.

Pang Laikwan. *The Art of Cloning: Creative Production during China's Cultural Revolution*. London: Verso, 2017.

Paul, Steve. "Composer Chen Yi Melds Eastern Sounds with Western Ways." *Kansas City Star*, Jan. 10, 2009.

Perlman, Marc. *Unplayed Melodies: Javanese Gamelan and the Genesis of Music Theory*. Berkeley: University of California Press, 2004.

Piñeiro, John de Clef. "An Interview with Chen Yi." *New Music Connoisseur* 9, no. 4 (fall, 2001): 27–31.

Radice, Mark A. "Chou Wen-chung: A Biographical Essay." In *Polycultural Synthesis in the Music of Chou Wen-chung*, edited by Mary I. Arlin and Mark A. Radice, 17–85. London: Routledge, 2018.

———. *Concert Music of the Twentieth Century: Its Personalities, Institutions, and Techniques*. Upper Saddle River, NJ: Prentice Hall, 2003.

Rao, Nancy Yunhwa. "Chinese Opera Percussion from Model Opera to Tan Dun." In *China and the West: Music, Representation, and Reception*, edited by Hon-Lun Yang and Michael Saffle, 163–85. Ann Arbor: University of Michigan Press, 2017.

———. "Sonic Imaginary after the Cultural Revolution." In *Listening to China's Cultural Revolution: Music, Politics, and Cultural Continuities*, edited by Paul Clark, Laikwan Pang, and Tsan-huang Tsai, 213–38. Basingstoke, Hampshire, UK: Palgrave Macmillan, 2016

———. "The Tradition of *Luogu Dianzi* (Percussion Classics) and Its Signification in Contemporary Music." *Contemporary Music Review* 26, no. 5/6 (Oct.–Dec. 2007): 511–27.

———. "The Transformative Power of Musical Gestures: Cultural Translation in Chen Yi's Symphony No. 2." In *Analytical Essays on Music by Women Composers: Concert Music, 1960–2000*, edited by Laurel Parsons and Brenda Ravenscroft, 127–52. New York: Oxford University Press, 2016.

Reese, Heinz-Dieter. "Chen Yi—A Portrait." In *Roche Commissions: Chen Yi*, edited by Basil Rogger and Mark Sattler, 12–31. [Basel, Switzerland]: Roche, 2005.

Robin, William. "What Du Yun's Pulitzer Win Means for Women in Classical Music." *New Yorker* (Apr. 13, 2017). http://www.newyorker.com/culture/culture-desk/what-du-yuns-pulitzer-win-means-for-women-in-classical-music.

Rogger, Basil, and Mark Sattler, eds. *Roche Commissions: Chen Yi*. [Basel, Switzerland]: Roche, 2005.

Ross, Alex. "Stone Opera. Tan Dun's 'The First Emperor.'" *New Yorker* (Jan. 8, 2007) (print), Dec. 31, 2006 (online). https://www.newyorker.com/magazine/2007/01/08/stone-opera.

———. "Symphony of Millions. Taking Stock of the Chinese Music Boom." *New Yorker* (July 7, 2008): 84–91. http://www.newyorker.com/arts/critics/atlarge/2008/07/07/080707crat_atlarge_ross.

Rye, Matthew. "Poetic Sound of the Orient Lifts Glennie above Gimmicks." *Daily Telegraph*, Aug. 20, 2003.

Schiffer, Brigitte. "Die Folgen der Kulturrevolution: Interview mit Alexander Goehr über seine Lehrtätigkeit in China" [The consequences of the Cultural Revolution: Interview with Alexander Goehr about his teaching in China]. *Neue Zeitschrift für Musik* 142, no. 2 (1981): 155–57.

Shaw, Chih-Suei. "Discourses of Identity in Contemporary East Asian Music: Chen Yi, Unsuk Chin and Karen Tanaka." PhD diss., University of Oxford, 2016.

Sheng Lu. "Ting Tan Dun de xianyue sichongzou Feng-Ya-Song" [Listening to Tan Dun's *Feng-Ya-Song* for string quartet]. *Renmin yinyue*, no. 7 (1984): 7–9.

Sheppard, W. Anthony. "Exoticism." In *The Oxford Handbook of Opera*, edited by Helen M. Greenwald. New York: Oxford University Press, 2014 (print), 2015 (online). DOI: 10.1093/oxfordhb/9780195335538.013.036.

Shin, Jungpil, Toshiki Okuyama, and Keunsoo Yun. "Sensory Calligraphy Learning System using Yongzi-Bafa" (Paper presented at the 8th International Forum on Strategic Technology, 2013). *Journal of Next Generation Information Technology* 4, no. 6 (Aug. 2013). http://www.globalcis.org/jnit/ppl/JNIT197PPL.

Smith, Ken. "Classical Music and Media in China 4." *Musical America Blogs*, Aug. 11, 2008. http://www.musicalamerica.com/mablogs/?p=389.

———. "Fantasy of the Red Queen." *Financial Times* (London), Nov. 12, 2008, 13. ProQuest.

Smith, Steve. "Post-Minimalist Inspirations, from Bells to Subway Noise." *New York Times*, May 1, 2007.

Sorrell, Neil. *A Guide to the Gamelan*. London: Faber and Faber, 1990.

Stock, Jonathan P. "Wu Zuqiang." *New Grove Dictionary of Music and Musicians*, 2nd ed., 2001.

Stulman, Timothy. "A Cultural Analysis of Chen Yi's Si Ji (Four Seasons) for Orchestra." DMA thesis, Bowling Green State University, 2010.

Swed, Mark. "Review. An L.A. Phil Reminder That but a Mile, and Fate, Separate Disney Hall from Skid Row." *Los Angeles Times*, Dec. 12, 2017. http://www.latimes.com/entertainment/arts/la-et-cm-laphil-xian-zhang-review-20171211-story.html.

Tang Jianping. "Tradition Is Alive: A Study of the Chamber Music Compositions *Duo Ye* and *Sparkle* by Chen Yi." Translated by Yang Ruhuai. *Journal of Music in China* 1 (1999): 133–145.

Tan Sooi Beng and Nancy Yunhwa Rao. "Introduction—Emergent Sinosoundscapes: Musical Pasts, Transnationalism and Multiple Identities." *Ethnomusicology Forum* 25, no. 1 (2016): 4–13. DOI: 10.1080/17411912.2016.1151812.

Taylor, Timothy D. *Beyond Exoticism: Western Music and the World*. Durham, NC: Duke University Press, 2007.

Thien, Madeleine. *Do Not Say We Have Nothing: A Novel*. New York: W. W. Norton, 2016.

Thorsten, Marie. "Silk Road Nostalgia and Imagined Global Community." *Comparative American Studies* 3, no. 3 (2005): 301–17.

Thrasher, Alan R. *Qupai in Chinese Music: Melodic Models in Form and Practice*. New York: Routledge, 2016.

———. *Sizhu Instrumental Music of South China: Ethos, Theory, and Practice*. Leiden: Brill, 2008.

———. "Structural Continuity in Chinese Sizhu: The 'Baban Model.'" *Asian Music* 20, no. 2 (spring/summer 1989): 67–106.

Thurston, Anne F. *Enemies of the People*. New York: Knopf, 1987.

Tyrrell, Sarah. "In Good Company: Chen Yi, Chanticleer and the Shanghai Quartet." *KC Metropolis*, Jan. 21, 2009. www.presentmagazine.com/full_content.php?article_id=1805&full=yes&pbr=1.

Utz, Christian. "Erfundene Traditionen und multiple Identitäten: Tendenzen reflexiver Globalisierung in der neuen Kunstmusik" [Invented traditions and multiple identities: tendencies of reflexive globalization in new art music]. *Österreichische Musikzeitschrift* 68, no. 4 (2013): 51–60.

Utz, Christian, and Frederick Lau. "Introduction. Voice, Identities, and Reflexive Globalization in Contemporary Music Practices." In *Vocal Music and Contemporary Identities: Unlimited Voices in East Asia and the West*, edited by Christian Utz and Frederick Lau, 1–22. New York: Routledge, 2013.

Von Rhein, John. "Local Sounds, Local Venues: Top Fall Picks." *Chicago Tribune*, Sept. 13, 2013, 5.5. ProQuest.

Waldinger, Roger, and Yenfen Tseng. "Divergent Diasporas: The Chinese Communities of New York and Los Angeles Compared." In "La diaspora Chinoise en occident," edited by Michelle Guillon and Emmanuel Ma Mung. Special issue, *Revue européenne des migrations internationales* 8, no. 3 (1992): 91–115. https://doi.org/10.3406/remi.1992.1339.

Walls, Seth Colter. "Brazen Virtuosity: The Week's 8 Best Classical Music Moments on YouTube." *New York Times*, Dec. 8, 2017, segment titled "An Alumna's Work," including video of concert and interview with composer. https://www.nytimes.com/2017/12/08/arts/music/brazen-virtuosity-the-weeks-8-best-classical-music-moments-on-youtube.html?src=twr&_r=0; also https://youtu.be/YjdJ_soKXso.

Wang Cizhao, ed. *Zhong yang jin yue xue yuan zuo qu 77 ji (Central Conservatory of Music Composition Program 77)*.

Wang Jiaosheng. *The Complete Ci-poems of Li Qingzhao: A New English Translation*. Sino-Platonic Papers, no. 13, edited by Victor H. Mair. Philadelphia: Department of East Asian Languages and Civilizations, University of Pennsylvania, 1989. http://sino-platonic.org/.

Wang Ping. "A Solitary Boat in the Autumn Chill: Chinese Ci-Poetry and Literati Painting." *Literature and Aesthetics: The Journal of the Sydney Society of Literature and Aesthetics* 20, no. 2 (Dec. 2010): 123–53.

Wang Xiao-xi. "Chang chu zi ji de sheng yin" [Singing Your Own Voice: Characteristics of Chen Yi's Work]. Unpublished translation by Yunxiang Gao. *People's Music* (Sept. 2006): 9–15.

Watkins, Glenn. "Beyond Orientalism?" In *On Bunker's Hill: Essays in Honor of J. Bunker Clark*, edited by William A. Everett, 299–308. Sterling Heights, MI: Harmonie Park Press, 2007.

Wichmann, Elizabeth. *Listening to Theatre: The Aural Dimension of Beijing Opera*. Honolulu: University of Hawaii Press, 1991.

Wiltse, Russ. Interview with Chen Yi and Zhou Long, Sept. 1, 2001. Oral History of American Music, Yale University.

Woei Lien Chong. "Guest Editor's Introduction: History as the Realization of Beauty: Li Zehou's Aesthetic Marxism." *Contemporary Chinese Thought* 31, no. 2 (winter 1999–2000): 3–19.

Wong Man, trans. *Poems from China*. Hong Kong: Creation Books; London: Hirschfeld Brothers, [1950].

Wu Man. "The Points: Story of a Pipa Solo." *Music from China Newsletter* 1, no. 4 (winter 1991): 1, 4–6.

Wu Xuelai. "The Fusion of Cantonese Music with Western Composition Techniques in *Tunes from My Home*: Trio for Violin, Cello, and Piano by Chen Yi." DMA research paper, Arizona State University, 2017.

Xie Mei. "Chen Yi and Zhou Long." In *Beijing Shi: Zhong yang yin yue xue yuan zuo qu 77 ji* [Central Conservatory of Music 77]. Unpublished translation by Yunxiang Gao. Edited by Wang Cizhao, Xie Mei, and Chen Zhiyin, 116–87. Beijing: Zhong yang yin yue xue yuan Chu ban she [Music Press of Central Conservatory], 2007.

———. "Chen Yi: Zou xiang shi jie de hua ren nv zuo qu jia" [Chen Yi: outstanding Chinese-American female composer]. Unpublished translation by Yunxiang Gao. *Music Life*, Mar. 2008, 7–11.

Xue Jinyan. "*Baban*, a Long-Standing Form in Chinese Traditional Music." Translated by Sun Hai. *Journal of Music in China* 1 (1999): 77–94. Original Chinese version, "Yi zhong yuan-yuan-liu-chang de minzu qushi." *Music Study* 4 (1984): 64–80.

Yeung, Hin-Kei. "Chen Yi and her Choral Music: A Study of the Composer's Ideal of Fusing Chinese Music and Modern Western Choral Traditions." DMA thesis, University of North Texas, 2006.

Young, Kar Fai Samson. "Reading Contemporary Chinese Music: Reconsidering Identity and Cultural Politics in Analysis." PhD diss., Princeton University, 2013.

Young, Samson. "Reconsidering Cultural Politics in the Analysis of Contemporary Chinese Music: The Case of *Ghost Opera*." *Contemporary Music Review* 26, nos. 5/6 (Oct./Dec. 2007): 605–18.

Yung, Bell. "From Speech to Song." *Music from China Newsletter* 2, no. 4 (winter, 1992): 2.

———. "Model Opera as Model: From *Shajiabang* to *Sagabong*." In *Popular Chinese Literature and Performing Arts in the People's Republic of China, 1949–1979*, edited by Bonnie S. McDougall, 144–64. Berkeley: University of California Press, 1984.

References

Yu Siu Wah. "Two Practices Confused in One Composition. Tan Dun's *Symphony 1997: Heaven, Earth, Man*." In *Locating East Asia in Western Art Music*, edited by Yayoi Everett and Frederick Lau, 57–71. Middletown, CT: Wesleyan University Press, 2004.

Yu Yi'qian. "Biao yan yi shu" [Asian Melody Marches to US Institutions of High Standing]. Unpublished translation by Yunxiang Gao. *Performance Art* 43 (May, 1996): 90–93.

Zacher, Peter. "Far from Any Cliché of Porcelain and Jade: Impressive Concert of Dresden Sinfoniker." *Dresdner Neueste Nachrichten*, May 27, 2002.

Zhang Boyu. *Mathematical Rhythmic Structure of Chinese Percussion Music: An Analytical Study of Shifan Lougu Collections*. Turku, Finland: Turun Yliopisto Kirjas [Turku University Library], 1997; closely based on his PhD diss., University of Turku, 1997.

Zhang, Wen. "An Infusion of Eastern and Western Music Styles into Art Song: Introducing Two Sets of Art Song for Mezzo-Soprano by Chen Yi." DMA thesis, University of Nevada, Las Vegas, 2012. https://digitalscholarship.unlv.edu/thesesdissertations/1791/. E-book, Saarbrücken: Lambert Academic Publishing, 2015.

Zheng, Su. *Claiming Diaspora: Music, Transnationalism, and Cultural Politics in Asian/Chinese America*. Oxford: Oxford University Press, 2010.

Zheng Ruzhong. "Musical Instruments in the Wall Paintings of Dunhuang." *Chime* 7 (1993): 4–56. https://www.chimemusic.net/back-issues.

Zheng Ying-Lie. "Letter from China: The Use of Twelve-Tone Technique in Chinese Musical Composition." *Musical Quarterly* 74, no. 3 (1990): 473–88.

Zhou Xiao-ying and Cheng Xing-wang. "Chen Yi shi nei yue Ba Ban su cai yun yong te xing ji shen mei qing xiang tan suo" [The Characteristics of Chen Yi's Chamber Music: Baban and Research in Aesthetic Aspects]. Unpublished translation by Yunxiang Gao. *People's Music*, Sept. 2006.

Interviews

Cheng, Susan. Telephone interview by Leta Miller, Nov. 22, 2016.
Chen Yi. Seventeen interviews by Miller and Edwards, Kansas City, MO, Aug. 2015 and Sept. 2016. Quotations from these interviews in the text are not cited in endnotes.
Wu Man and Honggang Li. Interview by J. Michele Edwards, St. Paul, MN, Feb. 19, 2016.
Zhou Long. Interview by Miller and Edwards, Kansas City, MO, Aug. 29, 2015.

Index

Page references in *italics* refer to illustrations; those in **bold** refer to major discussions

Adkins Chiti, Patricia, 177
Adsit, Glen, 115
Aldeburgh Festival: programming of women composers, 177
Alpert, Herb and Lani, 38–39
Alpert Award (CalArts), 37, **38–39**, 159
Alsop, Marin, 34, 176; on gender discrimination, 177
American Academy of Arts and Letters: awards, 37, **40**; membership, 43. *See also* Charles Ives Living award
American Academy of Arts and Sciences, 41
Ancient Beauty, The (Chinese instrument and strings): self-quotation in, 77
Ancient Chinese Beauty (recorder concerto), **113–15**; "The Ancient Totems," 114; Chinese markers of, 114; compositional process of, 114; opening, *115*; pentatonic modal system of, 114; premiere of, 113; self-quotation in, 77, 113, 114; "Shifan Gong and Drum" in, 113, 114, 115; visual arts references, 113, 114; wandering chromatic line, 114

Anti-Rightist Campaign (China, 1957–59), 207n4; Chen family during, 10, 13
Applebaum, Terry, 39
Aptos Creative Arts Program: Chen Yi's work with, 35, 36; Middle School, 127, 165, 214n4
"Arirang" (choral work), 125
art: effect of totalitarianism on, 172; sociocultural context of, 171
art, Chinese: Han ceramics, 113, 114, 147; painting, 217n59; social role of, 47
As in a Dream (violin, cello, and voice; alt. pipa, zheng, voice; or zheng, voice), 35, 147, **150–55**; Beijing opera recitation in, 151; boating excursion in, 151–52; Chen Yi's performance of, 125; cipai tune in, 150; Li Qingzhao's texts in, 150, 152; motives A and B, 153, *154*; opening introduction, *154*; original manuscript version, *153*; ostinato, 153, *154*, 155; pipa in, 155; Rao and, 151; second movement, 154; text narrative of, 154–55; twelve pitch classes, 154, 155, 216n34; wanyue in, 152, 217n60; X mark notations, 152, 217n72; zheng in, 155
. . . as like a raging fire . . . (chamber ensemble), 91, 122, 160

"Ashima" (Yi folk song), 63, 92, 93
At the Kansas City Chinese New Year Concert (string quartet): folk song of, 118, 214n17; reuse of, 118
"Awariguli" variations, 29–30, 78, 210n55; ostinato of, 50

Ba Ban (piano work), 71
Ba Yin (saxophone quartet): percussion of, 63–64, *65–66*; reuse of, 77, 217n51; "Shifan Gong and Drum" movement, 77, 78, 97, 107, 111, 113, 114, 115, 149; shifan luogu structure of, **63–64**, 77, 78, 97, 116; "Shui long yin" in, 73; wandering chromatic motive of, 64
Baban (folk tune), *48*; in Chen Yi's compositions, 52, **66–74**, *68*, 78, 101, 123, 211n28; in *Chinese Myths Cantata*, 72, 134; in *Chinese Rap*, 120, *121*; conjunctive phrase of, *68*, 212n33; Fibonacci sequence in, 67; in *Fiddle Suite*, 106, *106*; in *Four Spirits*, 122; in *From the Path of Beauty*, 146; in *The Golden Flute*, 71, 111; Golden Section of, 67; I Ching and, 67; lineage of, 66; motives of, 67; in *Percussion Concerto*, 107, *108*; phrase structure of, *68*; in Piano Concerto of 1992, 66, 67, **68–70**; in *Qi*, 52, 87–88; rhythmic pattern of, 67, 72, 72, 85, 87, 99; in *Si Ji*, 71, 72, 111, *112*; in *Song in Winter*, 72, *72*, 85; in *The Soulful and the Perpetual*, 73, *73*, 99; in *Sparkle*, 71–72, 111; symbolism of, 67; in *Three Dances from China South*, 99, *100*
Bach, J. S., 23; self-borrowing by, 78
Ballad, Dance, and Fantasy (cello and orchestra), **109–11**; cello symbolism in, 109; chanting in, 59, 60, 62; composition of, 89; "Fantasy," 111; folk music style of, 59, 109–10; ostinato of, 109, *110*, 116; polyrhythm in, 109; premiere of, 41; self-quotation in, 77; Shaanxi folk song in, 59, 60, 109; "Shifan Drum and Gong" in, 77, 115; Silk Road in, 59, 109; Uighur music of, 109, *110*, 111
Bamboo Dance (piano), *100*, 120; Baban in, 71; Li dance in, 99
"Baoleng Diao," 214n17

Bartók, Béla, 29, 166; folk music models of, 58, 211n15
BBC: commission by, 42; Proms, 41, 177, 221n93
Beaser, Robert, 37
Beauvoir, Simone de, 140
Beck, Ulrich, 172
Beijing City People's Congress: Chen Yi at, 30
Beijing opera. *See* opera, Beijing
Bellman, Jonathan, 2
Berio, Luciano, 35
Bernstein, Leonard, 34
Bhabha, Homi: "Third Space" concept, 161
binaries, in Western philosophy, 161
Birtwistle, Harrison: *Night's Black Bird*, 111
"Black Xuanwu in the North, The" (legend), 120
Blue, Blue Sky (orchestra): "Du Mu" in, **116–17**, *117*; glockenspiel motive, 52, 55, *55*; "Nostalgia," 116; ostinati of, 52, *54*, 57, 97, 103, 116; polyrhythms of, 97; self-quotation in, 78, 116
"Blue Dragon in the East, The" (legend), 120
border crossing: in Chen Yi's works, 2, **160–61**
borderlands, permeability of, 161
Borderlands and Liminal Subjects (essays): binaries in, 161
Botto, Louis, 35, 125, 126
Bouyei people, shuangxiao music of, 103, *104*
Bradley University: Chen Yi's residency at, 37
Bridge of Souls—A Concert of Remembrance and Reconciliation (concert), 89, 159
"Bright Moonlight" (voice and piano), 150, **155–57**; Beijing opera traits in, 156, *157*; folk material in, 157; ostinato of, 156–57; syllable count of, 156; text of, 155–56, *156*; vocal/piano interaction in, 157, *157*; Western art song influence in, 156–57; yearning in, 156
Buddhist prayer: in Symphony No. 2, 61, 62; in Woodwind Quintet, 83
Burning (string quartet), 91, 160

Cage, John: aleatory music of, 172; Asian influences on, 168
California State University, Long Beach: composition conference (1997), 37
calligraphy, 45, 67, 166; dancing lines in, 86, 113, 146; pressure of strokes in, 213n15; Zhengkai, in *The Points*, 84, 213n15
cantus firmus (medieval music), 71
Carpenter, Patricia, 31
Carroll, Lewis: *Through the Looking Glass*, 140
censorship, 166–67, 219n28
Center for US-China Arts Exchange, 32–33
Central Conservatory of Music (CCOM, Beijing): applicants to, 22, 209n39; Chen Min at, 10; Chen Yi at, 1, 2, 3, **22–30**, 50, 58, 129, 143, 163; Chen Yi's degrees from, 30; Chen Yun at, 8; composition class of 1978, 29, 166, 173, *174*; composition department, 26; curriculum of, 26; ear training, 23–24, 26, 173; facilities of, 23; folk music studies, **26–27**, 28, 48, 63, 70, 129; gender distribution at, 174; Goehr's residency at, 28–29, 173–74, 209n52; musical theater at, 28; piano shortage at, 23, 46; primary school of, 10; quyi studies at, 28; reopening of, 22–23, 25, 83; rural field trips, 28, 58, 79, 81; student body, 23, **209n42**; Tan Dun at, 166; women at, 173–74; Wu Man at, 141
Central Philharmonic Orchestra, 30, 33
Central Philharmonic Society, 25; chorale, 125
ceramics, Han, 113, *114*, 147
Chanticleer (male vocal ensemble): Chen Yi's collaboration with, **35–36, 125–26**, 127, 133, 142, 165, 217n51; *From the Path of Beauty*, 42, 149, 150; Singing in the Schools program, 35–36
chanting, in Chen Yi's compositions, 59, *60*, *62*, 79, 146
Chaozhou region (Guangdong province): folk music of, 62, 99, 157
Charles Ives Living award, **40**, 178
Chen Ernan, 7, 28; admiration of Mozart, 8, 62; Chen Yi's elegy for, 60, 62; during Cultural Revolution, 11, 12; death of, 11; 34, 60; early life of, 6; fluency in English, 7, 10; medical career of, **6–7**, 10, 11, 22, 151, 173; violin studies, 7
Chen family, **6–8**, *7*; during Anti-Rightist Campaign, 10, 13; during Cultural Revolution, **11–14**; fame of, 141–42; following Japanese invasion, 6; musical accomplishments, 7–8; Red Guards and, 12; Revolutionary Committee's raid on, 13
Chen, Mei-Ann, 177
Chen Min: at CCOM, 10; musical career of, 7, 8
Chen Qigang, 166
Chen Yi, 7, *9*, *15*, *26*; admiration of Mozart, 8, 62; at Beijing City People's Congress, 30; biculturalism of, **45–47**, 59, 161; birth of, 6; with Center for US-China Arts Exchange, 32–33; Chinese musical institution ties, 167; choral singing involvement, 124, *125*; with Chou Wen-chung, 32; chronology of activities (1999–2019), **40–44**; composer competition project (Music From China), 34; critical reception of, 2, 33, 107, 109, 170; cultural heritage of, 2, 31, 68, 134, 163, 172; during Cultural Revolution, 2, **11–16**; cultural self-awareness of, 126; empowerment of women composers, 176; forced labor by, 15–16; on gender discrimination, 1–2, 173; with Al Gore and Jiang Zemin, 38; Guangxi Province trip, 29, 59, 61, 79, 86, 99, 133; with Guangzhou Beijing Opera Troupe, 2, **16–22**, *18*, *23*, 55, 57, 94, 116, 125, 169; identity as composer, 2, 3; interviews with, 4–5, 44, 175, 215n22; on Li Qingzhao, 217n59; marriage to Zhou Long, 25, 26; on model operas, 21, 168–69; move to New York, 2, 30, 161, 163; parents, **6–8**; at Peabody Conservatory, **37–39**; prominence in US, 141–42; at Shimen, **14–16**, 17, 47; as singer, 125; successes of, 178; teaching by, 32, 36, 127; travels to China, 34, 44, 165, 167; on vocal settings, 157–58; work with immigrant parents, 36; with Wu Zuqiang, 27
—collaborations: Chanticleer, **35–36, 125–26**, 127, 133, 142, 165, 217n51; Falletta, 33, 35, 165; MFC quintet, 34, 164; Wu Man,

Index   239

Chen Yi—collaborations (*continued*) 83–84, 89, 141; Xun Pan, 94, 165; Yo-Yo Ma, 89, 109, 111; Zhou Long, 115
—compositional influences: Beijing opera, **55–58**, 127, 137, 140, 146, 152, 157; folk music, 52, **58–66**, 73; Uighur, 62, 63, 109–111, *110*
—compositional processes, 1; accumulation, 100–101; aesthetic principles of, 45–46; Chinese-Western bridge in, 46, 148; form variation and flowery variation, 48; free meter, 57; interrelationships among, 76; for large ensembles, 122–23; mapping, 134; mathematical relationships, 67, 74, 88, 101; modes, **49–50**; nature in, 85, 178; ostinato (*see* ostinati); pentatonicism (*see* pentatonicism); planning in, 45; precompositional, 51; recitation in, 55–56, 105; reorchestrations, 75; Reverse Golden Section in, 67; revision, 78; rising seventh gestures, 57; self-quotation, **76–83**; speed of, 45; structural planning, 67; stylistic blending, 62–64; Uighur influence in, 62, 63, 109–111, *110*; variation techniques, 47–48; vocables (*see* vocables [chenci]); wandering chromatics (*see* chromatic, wandering [melodic motive])
—compositions: alternative performance options in, 78; aspirations for, 159, 178; at CCOM, 29–30; chamber works, **76–83**, 192–98; Chinese gestures of, 165–66; choral music, **124–50**, 199–204; commercial, 30; cultural fusion in, 2; folk music in, 52, **58–66**, 73, 91, 171; following September 11 attacks, 159–60; instrumental works, from 1980s, **79–83**; instrumental works, from 1990s, **83–88**, **105–8**, **126–42**, **150–55**; large instrumental ensembles, 102, 122, 184–90; MIDI, 30; performances of, 177; philosophy of, 45; political themes in, 91, 159; reception of, 170; regional music in, 62–63, 91–92, 131, 165; sliding tones in, 2, 46, 57, 89, 114; solo instrumental works, 190–92; solo vocal works, **150–58**, 205; string quartets, 29, 39, 42, 76, 77, 91, 105, 115; "superficial hybridity" of, 171; from 2000s, **88–97**, **109–15**, **142–50**, **155–58**; from 2010s, **115–17**. *See also* Ba-

ban (folk tune): in Chen Yi's compositions; instruments, Chinese: in Chen Yi's compositions; *and names of specific compositions*
—education: ancient Chinese poetry, 151; at CCOM, 1, 3, 23, **25–30**, 58, 129, 143, 163; Columbia doctoral studies, 30, **31–35**, 71, 175; composition, 23, 25–26, 29–30; counterpoint, 26; dissertation, 32, 67, 70, 212n35; English language, 12–13; Eurocentric, 2–3; folk music, **26–28**, 129; in Guangzhou, 8, 10–11; harmony lessons, 22; Japanese language, 13; master's degree, 30, 163; middle schools (Guangzhou and Shimen), 11, 14, 15; piano, 8, 9; prebaroque music, 31; quyi, 28; during reeducation campaign, 14–15; study with Davidovsky, 31–32; violin, 8, *9*
—honors and awards, **36–39**; American Academy of Arts and Letters, 43; American Academy of Arts and Sciences, 41; BBC commission, 42; Charles Ives Living award, **40**, 178; Cheung Kong Scholar Visiting Professorship (CCOM), 41; Elizabeth and Michel Sorel Medal, 37; Goddard Lieberson Fellowship, 37; Guggenheim Fellowship, 36, 37; Herb Alpert Award, 37, **38–39**, 159; King Composition Prize (UT), 40; Lorena Searcy Cravens/Millsap/Missouri Endowed professorship, 39; Meet The Composer Grant, 35; Roche Commission, 41, 42, 111; Shen Xingong fellowship, 30; Society for American Music Honorary Member, 43; Stoeger Prize, 40; Tianjin Conservatory Distinguished Visiting Professor, 43
—residencies: Bradley University, 37; CalArts, 38; St. Paul Chamber Orchestra, 42; University of Toronto, 42; Women's Philharmonic, 1, 2, **35–37**, 102, 125, 133; Yaddo colony, 83
Chen Yun, 7, *15*; in Beijing opera orchestra, *18*; CCOM studies, 8, 23; during Cultural Revolution, 12, 13, 14; musical career of, 8
chenci. *See* vocables (chenci)
Cheng, Susan, 34
Cheung Kong Scholar Visiting Professorship, 41

Chicago Sinfonietta: programming of women composers, 177–78
China: censorship and self-censorship in, 166–67; cultural exchanges with, 3, 30, **31–33**, 59; disputes with USSR, 15; ethnic minorities of, 102, 129, 165, 215n8; gender discrimination in, 173–74; political climate changes in, 166–67; unification with Hong Kong, 166. *See also* Cultural Revolution; education, Chinese; folk music, Chinese; music, Chinese; People's Republic
China Conservatory of Music: traditional music studies, 66
China National Broadcasting Symphony: Zhou Long's residency with, 30
China Record Company: Chen Yi's recordings with, 30, 141–42
China West Suite (two pianos), 92, 116
Chinese Exclusion Act (US, 1882), 162
Chinese Fables (quartet), 71; instrumentation of, 46
Chinese Folk Dance Suite (violin and orchestra): Chaozhou folk tune in, 99; "Lion Dance," 62; luogu jing syllables of, 57–58, *59*; meter of, 62; minority cultures' influence in, 102; "Muqam," 62, *63*; reuse of "Awariguli," 78; Uighur music in, 111; vocables of, 58
Chinese Mountain Songs (treble chorus), **131–32**; "A Ma Lei A Ho," 131; antiphonal singing in, 132; dance in, 215n15; "Gathering in the Naked Oats," 131–32, *132*; "Mt. Wuzhi," 131, 132; pentatonic mode in, 132; perfect intervals in, 132; regional material in, 131; vocables of, 131; "When Will the Scholartree Blossom?," 132
Chinese Myths Cantata, **133–42**; audience participation in, 139; Baban rhythm in, 71, 72, 134, 140; Beijing opera influence in, 140; chaos motive of, 133, *134*; chromatic segment of, 135, *139*, *142*; commission for, 133; composition of, 125–26; creation myth in, 133, 135, 139, 140; female subjectivity in, 140; folk music influence in, 59; form of, *136–37*; Golden Section, 134, 136–37; inclusiveness metaphor of, 141; instrumentation of, 36, 46, 133, 139, 140–41; intervallic material, 133; mirroring in, 135, *138*, 140; model opera influence in, 169; Nü Wa in, 114, 133, 134–35, *138*, *139*, 139–41; "Pan Gu Creates Heaven and Earth," *134*; Pan Gu myth in, 133; premiere of, 141, 142; reuse of, 77, 114; second movement, 134–35, 140; "Song of Weaving Maid and Cowherd," 133; success of, 142; timbre of, 140–41; tritone use in, 86–87, 133, 134; twelve-tone concepts in, 141, 216n34; visual accompaniments to, 36, 133, 215n17; woodblock solo, 134, 140, *141*; yangqin in, 135, *139*; zhuihu in, 114, 135, *138*, *139*, 140, 141
Chinese Poems (treble chorus), modes of, 49, *49*, *50*
Chinese Rap (violin and orchestra), 28, **118–20**; Baban in, 120; background melody, *121*; bamboo clappers in, 118; pentatonic melody of, 120, *121*; percussion motive in, 120; quyi in, 120; self-quotation in, 120; subway music in, 118, 120; Symphony No. 3 and, 118
Chineseness, 171
Chou Wen-chung, 32, 47; *And the Fallen Petals*, 160, 218n2; arts exchange program of, **30–31**; on Chinese heritage in composition, 68; dedication of *Qi* to, 85–86; dedication of *Si Ji* to, 111; on exoticism, 171; influence of, 2, 164–65; and the New Music Consort, 83; Pacific Music Festival Composers Conference, 34; during Second Sino-Japanese War, 160; students of, 142; studies in US, 162; UMKC visit, 143; Xinghai Conservatory, 43
chromatic, wandering (melodic motive), **57**; in *Ancient Chinese Beauty*, 114; in *Ba Yin*, 64; in *Dunhuang Fantasy*, 58; in *Fiddle Suite*, 105, *106*; in *Four Spirits*, 122; in *From the Path of Beauty*, 147; in *Si Ji*, 112
Chun, Allen, 171
ci (poetic form), **150–51**, 217n60; by women singers, 150
Ciccone, Alicia Hunt, 171
cipai tune, 150
Columbia University: Chen Yi's studies at, 3, 29, 30, **31–35**, 68, 71, 81, 84, 163, 175; Chinese composers at, 142, 166, 167

Index 241

Communist Party, Chinese: takeover of, 7, 10, 162. *See also* Cultural Revolution

Composer Portraits series (Miller Theatre, New York), 178

composers, Chinese: Chen Yi's prominence among, 142; at Columbia, 167; on Cultural Revolution, 166; heritage of, 46; immigration to US, 1, 31

composers, Chinese xinchao (new wave), 2; contrasting approaches of, 172; emergence of, 168; intersectionality and, 173; marketing of, 171; plural identities of, 173; references to Chineseness, 171; use of Chinese instruments, 169; use of ethnicity, 171; use of Western music, 173

composers, women, 1, 23; awards of, 178; at BBC Proms, 177; Chen Yi's advocacy for and empowerment of, 9, 36, 176; Chen Yi's performances of, 175; CCOM 1978 class, *174*; database of, 36, 175; education of, 174–76; Ford Foundation program for, 35; opportunities for, 174–75; performances of, 176–77, 221nn85,93; Pulitzer finalists, 178; resources for, 36. *See also* women composers *for references to individuals*

composing, transcultural, 170

Conghua, Chen Yi at, 16

Corbett, John, 168

Corigliano, John, 37

Crenshaw, Kimberlé, 172

Cultural Revolution (1966–76): anti-intellectual violence during, 11–12; anti-Western musical propaganda in, 47; Chen Yi during, 2, **11–16**; Chen Yi on, 4; Chinese composers on, 166; defense activities during, 15–16; early years of, 2, 11–16; education during, 12, 14, 151; musicians following, 38; music of, **14–22**; Red Guards in, 12, 19, 24, 208n10; Revolutionary Committees, 13, 208n10; revolutionary songs of, 14, 124; social disruptions during, 12, 24; songs of, 124–25, 169; student deportations during, 14; suicides during, 11–12; viewed as cultural wasteland, 168, 219n36; Western music during, 11–12, 15, 168, 208n13. *See also* model operas (political operas)

culture, Chinese: art forms and, 143; Chen Yi's ties to, 2, 31, 68, 134, 163, 172; feudalistic, 20; male literary, 151

culture, US: Chen Yi's education in, 163; of New York, 31, 118, 126; pluralism of, 172

Dahmer, Manfred, 152

Dai Jiafang, 208n22

Daines, Matthew, 142

dance songs, 129. *See also* folk songs, Chinese

Davidovsky, Mario: Chen Yi's work with, 31–32; Composer's Conference (Wellesley), 33

Debussy, Claude: use of Golden Section, 74

diaspora, Chinese: arts and music of, 164; in Chen Yi's works, 2, 160; of New York City, 33, **161–64**

Dong people (Guangxi province): lusheng ensemble of, 99; music of, 79

"Dou Duo" (Miao tune), 92

Dragon Rhyme (wind ensemble), **115–16**, *117*, 120; Beijing opera influence in, 116; commission for, 115; ostinati of, 52, *54*, 103, 115, 116; polyrhythm of, 116; self-quotation in, 115

Dresden Frauenkirche, restoration of, 160

Du Dianqin, 7; death of, 43; during Cultural Revolution, 12–14; early life of, 6; fluency in English, 7, 10; imprisonment of, 13–14; medical career of, 10, 12, 13, 173; musical accomplishments, 7

"Du Mu" (Tibetan tune), 116, *117*

Du Yaxiong, 48, 66–67

Du Yun, *Angel's Bone*, 178

Duluth-Superior Symphony: "Mao to Mozart" concert, 38

Dunhuang caves: instrument paintings in, 211n13

Dunhuang Fantasy (organ and wind ensemble): free meter in, 57, *58*; inspiration for, 211n13; wandering chromatic of, *58*

Duo Ye (piano, later chamber orchestra), 28, 35, **79–81**, 101; Beijing opera influence in, 79; chamber orchestra version, 30, 33; chromatic pitches of, 79; mathematical concepts in, 81; ostinato of, 50, *51*, 79, *80*, 81; performance by Falletta, 33, 81; shifan luogo tradition in, 79; sources for, 133; syncretism of, 50; Tang's analysis

242   Index

of, 212n5; twelve-tone row of, 29, 81; "Ya Duo Ye" motive, 79, 81
Duo Ye No. 2 (orchestra), 35; critical reception of, 33; performances of, 35, 36, 37

ear training, at CCOM, 23–24, 26, 173
education, Chinese: during Cultural Revolution, 12, 14, 151; politicized, 10–11, 207n8; reeducation camps, 14
Edwards, J. Michele, 215n14
eight, mystical tradition of, 67
Eleanor's Gift (cello and orchestra), 39, 91; social/political issues in, 159
Elizabeth and Michel Sorel Medal, 37
Else-Quest, Nicole M., 172
En Shao, 30
exoticism, 169–70, 220n51; in Chen Yi's music, 2, 46; superficial, 171; twenty-first century, 173

Falletta, JoAnn, 210n65; collaborations with Chen Yi, 1, 33, 35, 133, 165
Farewell, My Concubine (Beijing opera), Sword Dance from, 48
Fauser, Annegret, 170
feminism: critique of Freud and Lacan, 140; female subjectivity, 140; intersectional, 172
Feng (woodwind quintet), 39; cross-borrowing in, 78; ostinato of, 52, 53, 81; proportional relationships in, 212n40
Festinger, Richard, 37
Fibonacci sequence, 67, 103. *See also* Golden Ratio; Golden Section
Fiddle Suite, **105–6**; formats of, 105; huqins in, 105, 114; instrumentation of, 39; jinghu in, 105; "The Night Deepens," 105–6; ostinato of, 105, 109, 116; qupai in, 48, 105–6; reuse of, 76, 106–7; revisions to, 76–77; wandering chromatic of, 105, *106*; "Ye Shen Chen" in, 48; zhonghu in, 105, *106*
"flowery variation" (jiahua), 47–48, 70
folk music: Bartók's models of, 58; Chen Yi's study of, 8, **26–28**
folk music, Chinese, 14–15; Bouyei, 103, *104*; categories of, 129; CCOM curriculum, 26–27, 28, 48, 63, 70; of Chaozhou, 99; in Chen Yi's compositions, 52, **58–66**, 73, 91, 171; Chen Yi's studies of, 26–28, 48; Dong, 79, 99; Hmong, 91; instrumental, 129; of Jingpo people, 91; Li, 99; pentatonicism in, 54, 55; percussion in, 63–64; preservation of, 64; principles of, 58; Qinqiang, 84; regional, 62–63, 91; re-introduction of, 26–27; Shaanxi, 59, 60, 73, 84, 109; Shanxi, 131; from Turpan, 214n9; xiongling, 54, 55; Yi people's, 63, 91, 92, 102, 103; Zhoushan Islands, 81. *See also* music, Chinese
folk songs, Chinese, **58–60**; antiphonal, 130; "Ashima," 63, 92, *93*; Chaozhou, 157; ci form in, 150; dance, 129; dialect in, 131; as educational strategy, 126; ethnic markers of, 131; Han, 129; "Jasmine Flower" ("Mo li hua"), 89, *90*, 91, 213n27, 213n29; lyrical (xiaodiao), 129, 130; Miao, 63, 91, 92, 102, 103; monophonic aspect of, 132; mountain (shange), 129, 130, 132; Shaanxi, 59, 60, 109; Shanxi, 131; vocables of, 130, 131; women singers, 150; work (haozi), 129, 130; Yao, 86; Yi, 102, 103; Zhoushan, 81; Zhuang, 87
Four Spirits (piano concerto), **120–22**, *122*; Baban in, 71, 122; cross-borrowing in, 78; legends in, 120; New York influences in, 118; ostinati of, 122; polyrhythm of, 122; self-quotation in, 120, 122; wandering chromatic line of, 122; Xuanwu in, 122
Freud, Sigmund, 140
From Old Peking Folklore (violin and piano), reuse of, 120
From the Path of Beauty (chorus and string quartet), **142–50**; "The Ancient Totems," 146; Baban motives of, 71, 146; Beijing opera style in, 146; "The Bronze Taotie," 143, 146; chenci of, 143, 147; Chinese cultural legacy in, 149; chorus of, 143, *148*; "The Clay Figurines," 147–48; commissions for, 126, 142; cross-borrowing in, 78; cross-disciplinary aspects of, 149; "The Dancing Ink," 146; harmonics of, 146; inspiration for, 142–43; modern-traditional mix in, 149; ostinato of, 147; overview of, *144–45*; performance of, 149, 150; premiere of, 149–50; published score of, 217n51; reception of, 149; "The

From the Path of Beauty (continued)
Rhymed Poems," 147; scat rendition for voices, 77, 149; "The Secluded Melody," 148–49; self-quotation in, 77, 147; "Shifan Drum and Gong" in, 149, 115; sound mass components of, 147; "spiritual" performance of, 143; *Sprout* and, 148; strings in, 146–47; timbre, 146; trichords of, 146; "The Village Band," 149, 217n51; wandering chromatic of, 147

Fu Hongjiu, 16, 17

Gang of Four, 21, 22
Ge Gan-ru, 1, 31
Ge Wu, 22
Ge Xu (*Antiphony*) for orchestra, 35, **102–4**, 114, 142, 214nn1–2; "A Xi Tiao Yue" (Dancing Tune), 103; Bouyei music in, 103, *104*; "Fei Ge" (Flying song), 103, *104*; Miao songs in, 102, 103; ostinato of, 103; performances of, 36, 177; polyrhythms in, 103; tritones in, 103; Yi songs in, 102, 103
gender discrimination: Chen Yi on, 1–2; in China, 173; in orchestras, 176, 178. *See also* composers, women
Geng Shenglian, 27
Giteck, Janice, 78
Glennie, Evelyn, 39, 41, 107; Chen Yi and, 106; hearing impairment of, 106, 214n6
globalization: aesthetic discourses of, 172; of marketplace, 171; of transnational composers, 171
Goddard Lieberson Fellowship, 37
Goehr, Alexander: CCOM residency, **28–29**, 173–74, 209n52; Chen Yi's studies with, 28, 29, 33; serialism of, 29, 210n54
Golden Flute, The (flute concerto): Baban in, 71, 111; flowery variation in, 48, *48*; polyrhythms in, 116; premiere of, 38; reuse of, 77, 78, 122, 212n1; self-quotation in, 85
Golden Ratio, Chen Yi's use of, 74. *See also* Fibonacci sequence
Golden Section (proportional relationship), 67; in Baban, 67, 72; in *Chinese Myths Cantata*, 134, 135; Debussy's use of, 74; in *Feng*, 212n40; in *Happy Rain on a Spring Night*, 74; in *Ning*, 89; in Percussion Concerto, 107, *108*; in Piano Concerto of 1992, 68; of *Qi*, 88; Reverse, 67; in *Song in Winter*, 72, *72*, 85. *See also* Fibonacci sequence
Gore, Al, 37, *38*
Grabe, Sheila, 172
Great Proletarian Cultural Revolution. *See* Cultural Revolution
Gross, Elizabeth, 140
Guangxi Province, Chen Yi's visits to, 28, 29, 44, 59, *61*, 79, 86, 99, 133
Guangzhou: Chen Yi in, 8, 10–11; during Cultural Revolution, 12; hospitals in, 6
Guangzhou Academy of Music, 8
Guangzhou Beijing Opera Troupe: Chen Yi with, 2, **16–22**, *18*, 23, 55, 57, 94, 116, 125, 133, 169, 170; new works by, 22; size of, 208n19. *See also* model operas
Gubaidulina, Sofia, 177
Guggenheim Fellowship, 36, 37
Guo Xin, 104, 214n2

Haefliger, Michael, 111
Hall, Stuart, 170–71
Han Figurines, The (sextet), 113–14; reuse of, 147; self-quotation in, 77, 114
Han Kuo-huang, 215n7
Handel, George Frideric: self-borrowing by, 78
Happy Rain on a Spring Night (quintet): linguistic tones in, 105, 152; proportional relationships of, 74, *74*; recitation style of, 55, *56*
Harrison, Lou, 78
Hartt College Wind Ensemble, 115
He Luting, 21, 208n25; imprisonment of, 209n30
Heldrich, Claire, 83
Henschel, Peter, 149
Herb Alpert Award, 37, **38–39**, 159
Higdon, Jennifer, 176
Hmong, folk music of, 63, 91
Holland, Bernard, 33
Hong Kong, 166
Howat, Roy, 74
Hu Yongyan, 32, 37–38
Huang Feili, 7
Huang Li, 8

Huddersfield Contemporary Music Festival: programming of women composers, 177
Hún Qiáo (Bridge of Souls) concert, 89, 159, 213n23
Hundred Flowers movement (1956–57), 10, 19
huqin (bowed instrument), 17; in *Fiddle Suite*, 39, 105, 114
Hwang, David Henry, 167

I Ching, 67
"I Hear the Siren's Call" (choral work), 126
identity, Chinese: Chineseness, 171; "lost," 162
identity, cultural, 170–72
ideology, Maoist: folk-elite contact in, 171
Imbrie, Andrew, 89
immigrants, Chinese, 218n11; Chen Yi's work with, 36; composers, 1, 31; "lost identity" of, 162; quotas for, 162; third wave, 3, 31, 162; to West Coast, 162
instruments, Chinese: of Beijing opera, 18–20; cave paintings of, 211n13; in Chen Yi's compositions, 46, 57, 63, 83, 89, 99; Chen Yi's playing of, 20; of *Chinese Myths Cantata*, 36; combined with Western, 16, 20, 55, 208n17; of MFC quintet, 33–34; of model operas, 17; pitched/nonpitched, 63; in *Three Bagatelles*, 63; use by xinchao composers, 169. *See also names of individual instruments*
instruments, Western: combined with Chinese, 16, 20, 55, 208n17; imitation of Chinese, 57, 86, 97, 122, 152; in model operas, 16, 20, 208n17
intellectuals, Chinese: following Communist takeover, 162
International Society of Contemporary Music (Kazimierz, Poland), 34, 127
intersectionality, transnational, 172–73
irama (gamelan music), 71, 212n37
Irigaray, Luce: *Speculum of the Other Woman*, 140

"Jasmine Flower" (Mo li hua, song): in *Ning*, 89, 90, 91; Puccini's use of, 213n29; in *Set of Chinese Folk Songs*, 213n27

Jennings, Joseph, 35, 125, 126, 127
Jiang Qing (Madame Mao): arrest, imprisonment, and death of, 22; denunciation of, 167; sponsorship of model operas, 17–18, 19–20, 25; as subject of operas, 166–67
Jiang Zemin, 37, 38
Jiangnan Sizhu music, 70–71
Ji-Dong-Nuo (piano), 122
"Jieshi Diao You Lan" (Solitary or Secluded Orchid, guqin piece), 148; cipher notation of, 216n49; western notation of, 216n49
Jin Yueling, 23
jing erhu (chordophone), 17
jinghu (chordophone), 17; in Beijing opera, 18; Chen Yi's use of, 57, 105
Jingpo people, folk music of, 63, 91
Jones, Stephen: *Folk Music of China*, 64, 73

Kagan, Alan L., 207n4
Kennesaw State University Symphony Orchestra, 118
Kim, Helen, 118
Kim, Hi Kyung, 89
King Composition Prize (UT), 40
"Know You How Many Petals Falling?" (mixed chorus), 91, 159, 160
Kosman, Joshua, 149–50
Kozinn, Allan, 91
Kraus, Richard, 20, 21

Lacan, Jacques, 140
Lan Shui, 30
Landscape (choral work), modes of, 50, 51
Lau, Frederick, 171
Lavine, Steven D., 38
Law, Po Kwan, 215n6
Lee, George, 33–34
Lemon, J. Karla, 36
Lendvai, Erno, 211n15
lerong (double-pipe instrument), 92
Li Bai, poetry of, 29, 146
Li, Honggang, 5, 149
Li Ling, 30
Li Po. *See* Li Bai
Li Qingzhao, 150; baimiao style of, 217n59; Chen Yi's admiration of, 151; ci of, 151, 217n60; dates of, 217n56; female perspec-

Index 245

Li Qingzhao (*continued*)
   tive of, 151; influence on Chen Yi, 217n59; "Picking Mulberries with Added Characters," 151, 155, 156, 218n75
Li, Songwen, 217n71
Li Suxin, 8
Li Zehou: Chen Yi and, 143; *The Path of Beauty*, 142–43, 216n42
Liang Xiaomin, 8
Liang Yulin, 8
Liebermann, Rolf, 125
Lieberson Fellowship, 37
Lin, Yuh-Pey, 212n7, 212n40
Lindorff, Joyce, 85
"Lions Playing Ball" (Chaozhou song), 157; in *Three Dances from China South*, 99
Listening to China's Cultural Revolution (essays), 169
Liu Ching-chih, 168, 209n28, 219n40
Liu Shaoqi, 8; People's Republic presidency, 207n1 (chap. 2)
Liu Sola, 23; *Fantasy of the Red Queen*, 166
location, in artistic creation, 160
Locke, Ralph: on "Transcultural Composing," 170
Lorena Searcy Cravens/Millsap/Missouri Endowed professorship, 39
Los Angeles Philharmonic: programming of women composers, 177
Luo Yinghui, 28
luogu jing (phonetic syllables): of Beijing opera, 127; Chen Yi's use of, 57–58; in *Chinese Folk Dance Suite*, 57–58, 59; in *A Set of Chinese Folk Songs*, 127, 129, 129, 130
lusheng (Miao instrument): Dong people's use of, 99; in *Three Bagatelles*, 63, 92; in *Three Dances from China South*, 99, 100
lyrical folk songs (xiaodiao), 129, 130. *See also* folk songs, Chinese

Ma, Yo-Yo, 167; *Ballad, Dance, and Fantasy*, 41, 59, 109, 111; collaboration with Chen, 89, 109, 111; in Hún Qiáo concert, 89; *Ning*, 40, 89; Silk Road Project, 59, 211n16
Maceda, José, 34
Madame Mao. *See* Jiang Qing (Madame Mao)
Mamiya, Michio, 89
Mao Zedong, 3, 10, 17, 21, 22, 24, 162; and Cultural Revolution, 10–12; "down-to-countryside" mandate, 14, 171; *Little Red Book*, 124; and model operas, 19–20; Order 626, 11; Sixteen Articles, 11, 20
Martin, Marya, 91
mathematical concepts, in Chen Yi's compositions, 67, 74, 81, 88, 101, 134. *See also* Golden Section
Meditation (voice and piano), 150, 157, 218n3
Meet The Composer Grant, 35
Melfi, Cheryl Ann, 212n40
Meng Haoran: "Know You How Many Petals Falling?," 160, 218n3
Menuhin, Yehudi, 37
Miao people, songs of, 63, 91, 92, 102, 103
Miller, Leta E., 212n33
mirroring: in *Chinese Myths Cantata*, 135, 138, 140; feminist critique of, 140
Mittler, Barbara, 208n13, 219n36, 219n40; on Chinese composers, 170; on model opera, 169
Mobberley, James, 39, 174
model operas (political operas), **16–22**, 209n49; acrobatics in, 168, 219n40; artistic standards of, 168; audience reception of, 168; in Chen Yi's compositions, 17; composition of, 20–21, 22; creative teams for, 19; critics of, 168–69; decline of, 168; films of, 208n18; influence of, 169; instrumentation for, 16, 17, 20; Jiang Qing's sponsorship of, 17–18, 19–20, 25; Mao and, 19; musical significance of, 169; performers of, 19; populist reform through, 20; psychological effect of, 168; recitation in, 55; regional speech in, 21; renewed interest in, 168; revolutionary realism of, 20; staging of, 21; vocal styles of, 20; Western instruments in, 16, 20, 169, 208n17; Wu Zuqiang's work on, 25–26. *See also* Guangzhou Beijing Opera Troupe; opera, Beijing
Momentum (orchestral piece), 39, *104*; aria style in, 55, 56; Beijing opera theme in, 103, *104*, 106; composition of, 45
mountain folk songs (shange), 129, 130, 132. *See also* folk songs, Chinese

246   Index

Mozart, Wolfgang Amadeus: Chen Yi's admiration for, 8, 62
Murai, Hajime Teri, 37
Murray, Joan, 35, 36, 127; awards of, 214–15n4 (chap. 6)
music, Chinese: Cantonese, 94, 165; in Chen family home, 8; ci form in, 150–51; of Cultural Revolution, 14–22; "flowery variation" (jiahua) in, 47–48, 70; form variation in, 48, 70–71; heterophonic, 81, 83; Jiangnan Sizhu, 70–71; modes of, 49; "note borrowing" in, 212n7; percussion in, 20, 52, 57–58, 63, 64, 65, 86, 87, 107, 127, 140, 141, 146, 149, 169, 211n25; rearrangement in, 78; rock, 23; Western imprint on, 169. *See also* folk music, Chinese; folk songs, Chinese; instruments, Chinese; model operas (political operas); opera; shifan luogu (traditional music genre)
music, Western: Chen Yi's study of, 2–3; during Cultural Revolution, 11–13, 208n13; the "exotic" in, 2; self-borrowing in, 78. *See also* instruments, Western
Music From China (MFC), Chinese instrumental quintet, 33–34, 35, 151; Chen Yi's collaboration with, 34, 84, 99, 164; composer competition, 34; Premiere Works Concerts, 34

"Nai Guo Hou" (bawu tune), 63, 92, 93
naked oats (Chinese buckwheat), 215n10
"Namo Amitābha" (Buddhist prayer), 213n9
Nanjing massacre (1937): Chen Yi's memorialization of, 40, 89, 159
National Centre for the Performing Arts (Beijing), 150, 167
National Festival of Peking Operas on Contemporary Themes (1964), 19
National Wind Ensemble Consortium, 115
Near Distance (sextet), 35; twelve-tone rows of, 51
neo-Orientalism, 168
New Music Consort, 83
New York: Chinese community of, 33, 161, 164; culture of, 31, 118, 126
Newstead Trio, Chen Yi's composition for, 94
"Ning" (character), meaning of, 89

Ning (violin, pipa, cello), **89–91**, 109; Chinese markers of, 89; Golden Section of, 89; hope in, 159, 168; instrumentation of, 46; "Jasmine Flower" in, 89, *90*, *91*; memorialization of Nanjing massacre, 89, 159; portrayal of desolation, 89, *90*, 167; premiere of, 159
Northern Scenes (piano solo), **97–99**; abstraction in, 97; declamatory melody, 97; hexachordal scales, 97, *98*, 99; retrograde melody, 97, *98*; reuse of, 122
Nü Wa (shapeshifter goddess): all-encompassing nature of, 140; in *Chinese Myths Cantata*, 114, 133, 134–35, *138*, *139*, 139–41; creation of humanity, 135, 139, 140

O'Bannon, Ricky, 176, 221n85
opera: Cantonese, 8; folk, 129; Qinqiang, 84
opera, Beijing: aria styles in, 55; in "Bright Moonlight," 156, *157*; in *Chinese Myths Cantata*, 140; in *Dragon Rhyme*, 115–16; free meter in, 57; in *From the Path of Beauty*, 146; influence in *Duo Ye*, 79; influence on Chen Yi, 48, **55–58**; instrumentation of, 18–19; in *Momentum*, 103; ostinati of, 94, 156; percussion patterns of, 57, 63, 86, 127; popularity of, 19–20, 168; recitation in, 55, 151; rhythmic patterns of, 19, 127; rising sevenths in, 57; sliding tones of, 57. *See also* model operas (political operas)
Opus 21 (ensemble), 113–14
orchestras: gender discrimination in, 176, 178; performance of women composers, 176–78
Orientalism, 168; European composers', 173; of Silk Road, 59
ostinati: of *As in a Dream*, 153, *154*, *155*; of "Awariguli" variations, 50; of *Ballad, Dance, and Fantasy*, 109, *110*, 116; of Beijing opera, 94, 156; of *Blue, Blue Sky*, 52, *54*, 57, 103, 116, *117*; of "Bright Moonlight," 156–57; in Chen Yi's compositional processes, **50–55**; of *Dragon Rhyme*, 52, *54*, 115, 116; of *Duo Ye*, 51, 79, *80*, 81, 116; of *Feng*, 52, *53*, 81; of *Fiddle Suite*, 105, 109, 116; of *Four Spirits*, 122; of *Ge Xu*, 103; of *From the Path of Beauty*, 147; of Percus-

ostinati (*continued*)
sion Concerto, 107, *108*; polyrhythmic, 52, *54*, *82*, *83*, 97, 103, 105, 109, *110*, 116, 122; of *Qi*, 51–52, *53*, 57, 87; rhythmically migrating, 53, 81, 103; of *A Set of Chinese Folk Songs*, 127, 129, *130*; of *Song in Winter*, 85; of *The Soulful and the Perpetual*, 73; of Symphony No. 3, 118; of *Tunes from My Home*, 94, 97; twelve-tone rows as, 50–51, 79, 82, 107, *108*; of Woodwind Quintet, *82*, 83; in "Yanko," 62

Pacific Music Festival Composers Conference (Sapporo, Japan): Chen Yi at, 34
Pan Gu (giant): in *Chinese Myths Cantata*, 133, *134*; creation myth of, 86
Parker, Alice, 126
Peabody Conservatory: Chen Yi at, **37–39**, 103
pentatonicism: in Chen Yi's compositional processes, 2, 46, **49–50**, 114; in Chinese folk music, 54, 55; of *Chinese Mountain Songs*, 132; of *Chinese Poems*, 50; of *Chinese Rap*, 120, 121; of *A Set of Chinese Folk Songs*, 127
People's Republic of China: establishment of, 162; Liu Shaoqi's presidency of, 207n1
Percussion Concerto, 39, 41, **106–7**; Baban rhythm in, 71, 107, *108*; conjunctive phrase of Baban in, 107, *108*; declamation in, 55, *56*, 107; Golden Section of, 107; linguistic tones in, 152; reception of, 107; self-quotation in, 77, 106–7; "Speedy Wind," 107; Su Shi poem in, *55*, 107; twelve-tone row of, 51–52, 107, *108*
Petri, Michala, 113, 114
Piano Concerto (1992), 32, **68–70**, 71, 102, 212n35; Baban in, 66, 67, **68–70**, 73, 101; concerto/Baban comparison, 69, *70*; form variation in, 48, 70, *71*; Golden Section in, 68; opening, *69*; organization of, 69–70, *70*; twelve-tone rows of, 51, 62
pipa (lute), 17; in *As in a Dream* (violin, cello, and voice), 150, 151, 155; in *Chinese Myths Cantata*, 36, 133, 139; in *Duo Ye*, 28, 81; MFC use of, 33; in *Ning*, 89; in *The Points*, **83–85**; retuning of, 84, 89; in

Three Dances from China South, 99, *100*; xiangjiao vibrato, 83–84
Poems from China (anthology), 151, 156
poetry, Chinese ancient: in Chen Yi's education, 158; Chen Yi's use of, 151; of Song Dynasty, 150, 158; of Tang Dynasty, 150, 160; women's, 151. *See also* ci (poetic form)
Points, The (pipa solo), **83–85**, *84*; calligraphy in, 84, 213n15; harmony of, 84; inspiration for, 84; origin of, 213n11; reuse of, 84–85
Poland: Chen Min and premier, 8; Chen Yi's travel to, 34, 35
political operas. *See* model operas (political operas)
polyrhythm. *See* ostinati: polyrhythmic
Prelude and Fugue (chamber orchestra work), 42, 71, 72; reuse of, 77, 116
Presser, Theodore, 125, 206
Prospect Overture: Baban in, 71; "Shui long yin" in, 73
PRS Foundation (United Kingdom), 177
Puccini, Giacomo: use of "Mo li hua," 213n29
Pulitzer Prize: *Si Ji*'s nomination for, 42, 113, 178; women finalists for, 178; Zhou Long recipient, 42. *See also* Du Yun

qi (material energy), 86
Qi (quartet), 39, **85–88**, *87*; Baban tune in, 52, 71, 87; compositional process for, 85; dedication to Chou Wen-chung, 85–86; Golden Section of, 88; ostinato of, 51–52, *53*, 57, 87; proportional relationships of, 88; reuse of, 78; tritones in, 86; Western instruments in, 86; Yao song in, 86; Zhuang folk song in, 87
qin, culture of, 178
qupai (fixed tune), Baban as, 66, 67; in *Fiddle Suite*, 48, 105–6; in Piano Concerto, 70
quyi (musical storytelling), 129; Chen Yi's study of, 28; in *Chinese Rap*, 120
quzi ci (tuned poetry), 150

Radice, Mark A., 218n2
rag dung (Tibetan trumpet), 81

Rao Lan, 217n62; dedications to, 151
Rao, Nancy, 60, 211n25, 217n62; on model opera, 21
recitation, in Chen Yi's compositions, 55–56, 105
Red Detachment of Women, The (ballet), 19, 21
Red Guards, 11; attack on Zhou family, 24; Chen family and, 12, 13; demise of, 13, 19, 208n10; interference with education, 12
"Red Phoenix in the South, The" (legend), 120
reorchestration, in Chen Yi's compositions, 75. *See also specific works*
representation, politics of, 172
Revolutionary Committees, 12, 208n10; raid on Chen family, 13
Rhymes, Busta: "Woo hah!! Got You All in Check," 118
"Riding on a Mule" (*A Set of Chinese Folk Songs*), 130; love song elements, 130; luogu dianzi in, 127, 129, 215n6; percussion patterns of, 64; phonemes of, 64
Roche Commission, 41, 42, 111
Romance and Dance (string orchestra), 39; reorchestrations of, 76
Romance for Hsaio and Ch'in (strings and two violins): alternative versions of, 76; reuse of, 76
Roosevelt, Eleanor, 39, 159
Rye, Matthew, 107

Saariaho, Kaija, 177
"Sakura, Sakura (Cherry Blossoms)," 125
San Francisco: Chinese-American community, 36, 164; Chinese Cultural Center, 36. *See also* Women's Philharmonic (San Francisco)
Schoenberg, Arnold, 29; *Sprechstimme* of, 152
self-quotation, in Chen Yi's compositions, **76–83**. *See also specific works*
September 11 attacks: Chen Yi's commissions following, 159–60
Septet: instrumentation of, 46
Set of Chinese Folk Songs, A, 125, **126–30**; "Fengyang Song," 127, 130; impetus for, 126; "Mo li hua" in, 213n27; no. 8, 78; ostinati of, 127; pentatonic melody in, 127; regional material in, 131; rhythm patterns (luogu jing) in, 127, 129, *129*, *130*; "Riding on a Mule," 64, **127**, **129**, **130**, *130*, 215n6
Shajiabang (model opera), 19, 21; instrumentation for, 20
"Shange Diao" (jingpo music), 63
Shanghai String Quartet, 42, 126, 142; performance of *From the Path of Beauty*, 150
Shaw, Chih-Suei, 134
Shen Xingong fellowship, 30
sheng (mouth organ): Chen's evocations of, 57, 97; Chen's playing of, 34; Chen's use of, 57, 63
Sheng, Bright, 1, 31, 166–67
"Shifan Gong and Drum," **63**; in *Ancient Chinese Beauty*, 113, *114*, 115; in *Ba Yin*, 77, 78, 97, 107, 111, 113, 114, 115, 149; in *A Set of Chinese Folk Songs*, 127
shifan luogu (traditional music genre): in *Ancient Chinese Beauty*, 113, 115; in *Ba Yin*, **63–64**, **65–66**, 77, 78, 97, 107, 116; in *Ballad, Dance, and Fantasy*, 111; in *Dragon Rhyme*, 116; in *Duo Ye*, 79; in *Fiddle Suite*, 105; in *From the Path of Beauty*, 149; in *Qi*, 52, 87; rhythmic patterns of, 51–52; in *Song in Winter*, 85; in *Tunes from My Home*, 97
Shimen (village): Chen Yi at, **14–16**, 17, 47
Shui Lan, 106
"Shui long yin" (Shaanxi shawm band piece): Chen Yi's use of, 73–74
Si Ji (orchestral work), 41, 42, **111–13**, 116; Baban in, 71, 72, 111, *112*; commission for, 111; dedication of, 111; final movement, *113*; performances of, 113; Pulitzer Prize nomination, 113, 178; "Spring" movement, 111; Su Shi's texts in, 111, 214n10; wandering chromatic of, *112*; Zeng Gong's texts in, 111, 214n10
Silk Road (trade routes): in *Ballad, Dance, and Fantasy*, 59, 109; Orientalism of, 59; romanticization of, 109
Silk Road Project, 59, 211n16
Singin' in the Dark (*Songs of the American Frontier*), 126
Sino-Japanese War, Second (1937–45), 10, 160

sliding tones, 46; of Beijing opera, 57; Chen Yi's use of, 2, 89, 114
Smith, Ken, 167
Society for American Music, 43
Sollberger, Harvey, 37
Song Dynasty, poetry of, 111, 150, 158
Song in Winter (trio or quartet), **85–86**; Baban's use in, 71, 72, 72, 85; Golden Section in, 72, 72; instrumentation of, 46; quartet version, 86; twelve-tone row of, 51, 85; zheng in, 155
Sorel Medal, 37
Soulful and the Perpetual, The (saxophone and piano): Baban's use in, 71, 73, 73, 99; Golden Section of, 73; ostinato of, 73
Sound and Music (UK music charity): programming of women composers, 177
Sound of the Five (cello and string quartet), 39, 42; Baban's use in, 71; reorchestration of, 76; reuse of, 77
Sparkle (CD), 151
Sparkle (octet): Baban in, 71–72, 111; twelve-tone line of, 51, 62
speech-song spectrum, oral delivery of, 211n11
"Spring Dreams" (choral work), 39, 118, 126; text of, 218n3
Spring Festival (band work): Chaozhou folk tune in, 99
Spring in Dresden (violin and orchestra): healing in, 160
Sprout (for string orchestra), 30; *From the Path of Beauty* and, 148
Stanford University Orchestra: tour of China, 36
Stern, Isaac, 38
Stoeger Prize, 40
Su Shi, 55, 56; "Prelude to Water Tune," 55, 107; texts in *Si Ji*, 111, 214n10; use in *Fiddle Suite*, 105; use in Percussion Concerto, 107
Suite (quintet of Chinese instruments): self-quotation in, 84–85
Summer Courses for Young Composers: Chen Yi's teaching at, 127
Symphonie "Humen 1839": reuse of, 115; self-quotation in, 77
Symphony No. 1, recording of, 30

Symphony No. 2, 102; "Chen Yi motive," 60, 61; commission for, 35; expression of grief in, 34, 167; folk singing in, 59–60, 61, 62, 133; performances of, 36, 40; sources for, 133; success of, 142; twelve-tone row of, 50, 60, 85
Symphony No. 3: asynchronicity in, 118; Buddhist praying tune, 61, 62; *Chinese Rap* and, **118–119**; "The Dragon Culture," 118; "Dreaming," 118, 120; "The Melting Pot," 118, 119; performances of, 41; program for, 164; reuse of, 115, 120, 122; "Shui long yin" in, 73; Silk Road influence in, 59; subway music in, 118; tribute to China, 164
syncretism, 168, 170; of *Duo Ye*, 50; of Silk Road, 59

Taiwan, Chen Yi's visit to, 34
Taking Tiger Mountain by Strategy (model opera), 19; Chen's sight-reading of, 17, 208n18; film of, 208n18
Tan Dun, 1, 31, 32, 38; at CCOM, 166; censoring of works, 166, 219n28; China's denunciation of, 166–67; individualism of, 166, 167; international recognition of, 166; references to Cultural Revolution, 166; ties to Chinese musical institutions, 167. Works: *Feng ya song*, 166; *The First Emperor*, 167, 219n28; *Li Sao*, 166; *Marco Polo*, 166; *Symphony 1997*, 167
Tang Jianping, 79, 212n5
Tang Poems (a cappella work), 36, 125; "Wild Grass" movement, 52
Tang Poems Cantata (SATB chorus, orchestra), 37
Taoism, 122; Eight Diagrams in, 67
Taylor, Tim, 2
Thien, Madeleine, 208n25
Thomas, Augusta Reed, 35
Thomas, Michael Tilson, 34
Thrasher, Alan, 67, 212n33
Three Bagatelles (flute and piano), **91–92**; alternative versions of, 91; "Ashima" in, 92, 93; Chinese instrumentation in, 63; "Dou Duo" in, 92; finale of, 92; lerong in, 92; lusheng in, 92; "Nai Guo Hou," 63, 92, 93; ostinato of, 97; regional folk music

in, 62–63, **91–93**; shange tune, 63, 93; Tibetan tunes in, 92

Three Dances from China South (dizi, erhu, pipa, zheng): Baban rhythm in, **99, *100***; Chaozhuo music in, 99; clapping motive, 99; Li dance music in, 99; "Lions Playing Ball," 99; lusheng ensemble music, 99, *100*; "Swallow Flying with Mud in its Mouth," 100; zheng in, 99, 155

Three Poems from the Song Dynasty (mixed chorus), 125; "Picking Mulberries with Added Characters," 151, 155, 218n75

Thurston, Anne, 14

Tianjin Conservatory, 43

totalitarianism, European: effect on artistic ideology, 172

"Tradewinds from China" concert (Pacific Symphony, 2004), 109

transnationalism: Chen Yi's, 2, 133, 143, 160, 164; Chinese-American, 161–62, 171, 172–73

Tu (orchestra), 91, 159

Tunes from My Home (piano trio), **94–97**; *Ba Yin* in, 97, 115; Cantonese tunes in, 94, 165; excerpts from, *95–96*; final movement, *96*, 97; folk song styles in, 94; ostinato of, 94, 97; polyrhythms of, 97; "Prancing Horses," 94, *96*; "Racing the Dragon Boat," 94, *95*; reuse of, 77, 116; "Shifan Drum and Gong" in, 115; "Summer Thunder," 94, *95*

Turpan (Xinjiang), folk music of, 214n9

twelve-tone rows: Chen Yi's study of, 29; Chen Yi's use of, 4, 33, 50–51, 75, 101; of *Chinese Myths Cantata*, 141, 216n34; of *Duo Ye*, 29, 50, 79, 81; of *Near Distance*, 51; of Percussion Concerto, 51–52, 107, *108*; of *Song in Winter*, 51, 85; of *Sparkle*, 62, 72; of Symphony No. 2, 51–52, 60–61, 62, 85; of Woodwind Quintet, 33, 50, 81, 82

Two Sets of Wind and Percussion Instruments, 30

Tyrrell, Sarah, 149

Uighur music, 30, 62, 63, 109, *110*; twelve mughams of, 111

UMKC Fanfare (wind ensemble work), 71

United Nations, Universal Declaration of Human Rights, 39, 159

University of Missouri–Kansas City (UMKC) Conservatory of Music and Dance: Chen Yi at, 39, 40, 43, 165, 175–76; Chou Wen-chung's visit to, 143; composition students at, 175–76

USSR: disputes with China, 15

Utz, Christian, 172, 220n51, 220n73

violin: Chen Yi's performances, 14–15, 16–22, *18*, 47; Chen Yi's study of, 8, *9*

vocables (chenci): in Chen Yi's compositions, 58, *59*, *60*, 62, 79, **130–32**, 143, 158; in *Chinese Myths Cantata*, 139; Dong, 79; in *From the Path of Beauty*, 143, 147, **149**

Wang Shu: Chen Yi's studies with, 143

Wang, Tienjou and Aiyan, 33

wanyue, 152, 217n60

Weaving Maid and the Cowherd (myth), 133

Webern, Anton: Zwei Lieder, 216n34

Wen Zhang, 157

wenren (philosopher-artists), 31, 47

"White Tiger in the West, The" (legend), 120

Wilson, Olly, 37, 40

Wind (wind ensemble work): orchestration of woodwind quintet, 78

Wollongong Conservatorium of Music (Australia), 30

women: at CCOM, 173–74; creativity of, 1; folk singers, 150; life-work balance of, 175

women composers: Du Yun, 178; Giteck, Janice, 78; Gubaidulina, Sofia, 177; Higdon, Jennifer, 176; Jin Yueling, 23; Liu Sola, 23, 166; Parker, Alice, 126; Saariaho, Kaija, 177; Thomas, Augusta Reed, 35; Zwilich, Ellen Taaffe, 222n100. *See also* composers, women *for general discussions*

women conductors: Alsop, Marin, 34, 176, 177; Chen, Mei-Ann, 177; Falletta, JoAnn, 1, 33, 35, 133, 165, 210n65; Lemon, J. Karla, 36

women poets, Chinese: male literary culture and, 151. *See also* Li Qingzhao

Women's Philharmonic (San Francisco): Chen Yi's residency with, 1, 2, **35–37**, 102,

Index   251

Women's Philharmonic (*continued*)
125, 133, 175; Meet The Composer New Residencies Program, 35, 39; Women Composers Resource Center, 36
Wong, Herman, 33
Wong Man, 151, 156
Woodwind Quintet, 33, 35, 78; Chinese Buddhist prayer in, **81–83**; ostinati of, 82, 83, 116; polyrhythms of, 97, 116; twelve-tone rows of, 50, 81; Zhoushan folk song in, 81
work folk songs (haozi), 129, 130. *See also* folk songs, Chinese
Wu Han: condemnation of, 208n25; *Hai Rui Dismissed from Office*, 20
Wu Man: on Chen family, 141–42; collaborations with Chen Yi, 83–84, 89
Wu Yu (mixed sextet or septet): self-quotation in, 77, 115
Wu Zuqiang, 27, 28; Chen Yi's studies with, 23, 25–26; works of, 25–26

Xian Shi (viola concerto), 30; Chaozhou folk tine in, 99
Xiao Tiqin, 14
Xie Mei, 175
xinchao (new wave) composers. *See* composers, Chinese xinchao (new wave)
Xinghai Conservatory, 43
Xinjiang, Russian attack on, 15
xiongling (Tibetan fipple flute), 54, 55
Xuanwu (Taoist god), in *Four Spirits*, 120, 122
Xun Pan, Chen Yi's collaboration with, 94, 165

Yaddo colony, 83
Yan Liangkun, 125
yangbanxi. *See* model operas (political operas)
Yao people (Guangxi Province): singing of, 59, *61*, 86, 133
Yao Wenyuan, 20
Yi people: folk music of, 63, 91, 92, 102, *103*
Young, Samson, 170
Yu Huiyong, operas of, 20–21
Yu Suxian, 26
Yu Yiqing, 31
Yuan Jingfang, 28

Yuasa, Joji, 34
yuluge (revolutionary songs), 124
Yun, Isang, 34
Yung, Bell, 21, 168

Zeng Gong: texts in *Si Ji*, 111, 214n10
Zhang Hongyi, 28
Zhang, Xian, 177
Zhangjiakou City Art Troupe: Zhou with, 24–25
Zhao Songguang, 27
zheng (zither): in *As in a Dream*, 150, 151, 155; in "Bright Moonlight," 156; in *Chinese Myths Cantata*, 36, 133; in *Four Spirits*, 122, *122*; in *Qi*, 86; retuning of, 85, 99, 155; in *Song in Winter*, 85, 155; in *Three Dances from China South*, 99, 100, 155
Zheng Rihua, 8, 14, *15*
Zheng, Su, 161, 162, 171–72, 173, 218n11
Zheng Zhong, 8, 22
Zhengkai calligraphy, 84
zhonghu: in *Fiddle Suite*, 105, *106*
Zhou Enlai, 209n30
Zhou Feng, 24
Zhou Long, 1, 5, 26; arrival in New York, 175; at CCOM, 24, 29, 83, 174; chamber works, 30; China National Broadcasting Symphony residency, 30; Columbia studies of, 30–31, 32, 175; commercial compositions, 30; compositions of, 164; during Cultural Revolution, 24–25, 25; early life of, 24; family attacked by Red Guards, 24; in Guangxi, 29; interviews with, 175; marriage to Chen Yi, 25, 26; MFC quintet compositions, 34, 164; Pulitzer Prize recipient, 42; radio work of, 125; *Symphonie "Humen 1839,"* 115; Taiwan visit, 34; at UMKC, 40, 43; with Zhangjiakou City Art Troupe, 24–25
Zhou Zutai, 24
Zhoushan Islands: folk song of, 81
Zhu Lei, 17
Zhuang people: antiphonal singing of, 102; choral folk song of, 87; Lunar New Year gathering, 102
zhuihu (erhu instrument): in *Chinese Myths Cantata*, 114, 133, 135, **138**, *139*, 139, 140, 141; rarity of, 215n15

LETA E. MILLER is a professor of music emerita at the University of California, Santa Cruz, and the author of biographies of Aaron Jay Kernis and Lou Harrison.

J. MICHELE EDWARDS, musicologist and conductor, is a professor emerita of music at Macalester College and focuses her research on women musicians, especially from the twentieth and twenty-first centuries.

WOMEN COMPOSERS

Kaija Saariaho   *Pirkko Moisala*
Marga Richter   *Sharon Mirchandani*
Hildegard of Bingen   *Honey Meconi*
Chen Yi   *Leta E. Miller and J. Michele Edwards*

The University of Illinois Press
is a founding member of the
Association of University Presses.

University of Illinois Press
1325 South Oak Street
Champaign, IL 61820-6903
www.press.uillinois.edu